ARDA RECONSTRUCTED

ARDA RECONSTRUCTED

The Creation
of the Published *Silmarillion*

Douglas Charles Kane

Lehigh
University
Press

Bethlehem: Lehigh University Press

First paperback printing and new hardcover printing 2011 by
Lehigh University Press
Co-published with The Rowman & Littlefield Publishing Group, Inc.
4501 Forbes Boulevard, Suite 200, Lanham, Maryland 20706
www.rlpgbooks.com

Estover Road, Plymouth PL6 7PY, United Kingdom

978-1-61146-056-8 (cloth: alk. paper)
978-1-61146-089-6 (pbk.: alk. paper)

Originally published by Associated University Presses
2010 Eastpark Boulevard
Cranbury, NJ 08512

Library of Congress Cataloging-in-Publication Data
Kane, Douglas Charles, 1963–
  Arda reconstructed : the creation of the published Silmarillion / Douglas
Charles Kane.
    p. cm.
  Includes bibliographical references and index.
  1. Tolkien, J. R. R. (John Ronald Reuel), 1892–1973. Silmarillion—1. Criticism,
Textual. 2. Fantasy fiction, English—Criticism, Textual. 3. Tolkien, Christopher.
4. Fiction—Editing. I. Title.
PR6039.O32S5335 2009
823'.912–dc22
                                                                    2008035909

∞™ The paper used in this publication meets the minimum requirements of American National Standard for Information Sciences—Permanence of Paper for Printed Library Materials, ANSI/NISO Z39.48-1992.

Printed in the United States of America

To Beth, With Love and Thanks

Contents

Part III: The *Akallabêth, Of the Rings of Power and the Third Age*, and the Appendices to the *Silmarillion*

Illustrations

Tables

Preface

I FIRST ENCOUNTERED *THE SILMARILLION* AS A YOUNG MAN IN THE MID-1980s. I was already a big fan of J. R. R. Tolkien's writing, having read *The Lord of the Rings* and *The Hobbit* many times over the previous decade, but I only had a vague concept of this other, more esoteric work. From the opening line of the book, "There was Eru, the One, who in Arda is called Ilúvatar . . ." I was hooked. I had never encountered a work like this before, and I am sure that I never will again. It has certainly had a greater influence on me than any other single work of literature that I have read before or since.

After devouring *The Silmarillion* I moved quickly to *The Unfinished Tales of Númenor and Middle-earth*. When Christopher Tolkien began documenting his father's work in *The History of Middle-earth* I soaked up each volume as quickly as I could find it. I found it all utterly fascinating; what a wonderful opportunity to observe the creative process of such a unique person! I became ever more astounded at the true breadth and scope of Tolkien's work and the secondary universe that he invented.

In the course of an online discussion with a group of friends, a question was raised regarding how the published *Silmarillion* actually came into being after Tolkien's death. Attempting to answer this question has led to a journey of my own that has been at different times both fascinating and frustrating. Little did I comprehend the scope of the journey that I was embarking upon; had I understood, I do not know that I would have dared to set out on it. However, once the daunting nature of the task did become apparent, I found that I could not easily turn back. Sheer momentum carried me forward through many hundreds of hours of often tedious work interspersed between my other duties and interests. I did not set out with the intention of writing a book, but as "the tale grew in the telling" it become more and more clear that it deserved a wider audience.

It is my hope that this work will be of interest to a wide range of people, from the serious Tolkien scholar to a more casual reader. It not only provides the first comprehensive portrait of the final step of the creation of *The Silmarillion*, but also documents a fascinating and unique collaboration that reaches beyond the grave.

13

Acknowledgments

THERE ARE MANY PEOPLE WHO PROVIDED INVALUABLE ASSISTANCE IN preparing this work. In particular, I would like to extend my sincerest thanks to Kristin Landon, Beth Jarvis, Van Fuller, Merlin DeTardo, Jason Fisher, Don Anger, and Bill Hicklin for their invaluable assistance, as well as to my friends and colleagues at thehalloffire.net, where this project was born. David Bratman twice reviewed my manuscripts for Lehigh University Press and provided key suggestions for revising and reorganizing the work. However, all of the judgments expressed in this book are strictly my own, and of course any remaining inaccuracies are solely my responsibility. A special thank-you as well to Professor Scott Gordon of Lehigh University Press as well as the staff of both Lehigh University Press and Associated University Presses, for their invaluable assistance throughout this process. Finally, my deepest gratitude goes to Anushka Mouriño for her extraordinary illustrations, which often seem to come directly from my own vision of Tolkien's work.

Portions of the discussion of chapter 6, "Of Fëanor and the Unchaining of Melkor," appeared in Mythlore 27.1/2 (#103/104, Fall 2008)

Source Materials and Conventions

I FOLLOW THE STANDARD PRACTICE IN WORKS ABOUT TOLKIEN'S WRITings (first adopted by Christopher Tolkien) of referring to the published text *The Silmarillion* in italics (abbreviated as "*Silm*" in citations), while referring to the body of constituent texts from which that work was created as "The Silmarillion." All citations to the published text are to the second edition of *The Silmarillion*, edited by Christopher Tolkien (Boston: Houghton Mifflin, 1999). For consistency's sake, the spellings of the names of persons, places, and things that were used in the published text of *The Silmarillion* are used throughout this text. However, a table tracing the different forms of many of these names can be found at the end of the text.

VOLUMES OF *THE HISTORY OF MIDDLE-EARTH* (*"HOME"*) CITED (WITH ABBREVIATIONS IN PARENTHESES)

I: *The Book of Lost Tales, Part One.* Edited by Christopher Tolkien. Boston: Houghton Mifflin, 1984 ("*BoLT1*").

II: *The Book of Lost Tales, Part Two.* Edited by Christopher Tolkien. Boston: Houghton Mifflin, 1984 ("*BoLT2*").

III: *The Lays of Beleriand.* Edited by Christopher Tolkien. Boston: Houghton Mifflin, 1985.

IV: *The Shaping of Middle-earth.* Edited by Christopher Tolkien. Boston: Houghton Mifflin, 1986 ("*SoMe*").

V: *The Lost Road and Other Writings.* Edited by Christopher Tolkien. Boston: Houghton Mifflin, 1987 ("*Lost Road*").

VII: The *Treason of Isengard.* Edited by Christopher Tolkien. Boston: Houghton Mifflin, 1989.

IX: *Sauron Defeated.* Edited by Christopher Tolkien. Boston: Houghton Mifflin, 1992.

X: *Morgoth's Ring.* Edited by Christopher Tolkien. Boston: Houghton Mifflin, 1993 ("*MR*").

XI: *The War of the Jewels.* Edited by Christopher Tolkien. Boston: Houghton Mifflin, 1994 ("*WotJ*").

XII: *The Peoples of Middle-earth.* Edited by Christopher Tolkien. Boston: Houghton Mifflin, 1996 (*"PoMe"*).

OTHER WORKS BY TOLKIEN USED AS SOURCE MATERIAL FOR *THE SILMARILLION* OR OTHERWISE CITED HEREIN

The Children of Húrin. Edited by Christopher Tolkien. Boston: Houghton Mifflin, 2007 (*"CoH"*).

The Letters of J. R. R. Tolkien. Edited by Humphrey Carpenter with the assistance of Christopher Tolkien. Boston: Houghton Mifflin Paperback, 2000 (*"Letters"*).

The Lord of the Rings, 50th Anniversary Edition. Boston Houghton Mifflin, 2004 (*"LOTR"*).

Unfinished Tales of Númenor and Middle-earth. Edited by Christopher Tolkien. Boston: Houghton Mifflin, 1980 (*"UT"*).

"Words, Phrases and Passages in various tongues in *The Lord of the Rings.*" Edited by Christopher Gilson. *Parma Eldalamberon: The Book of Elven-tongues* (August 2007) ("Words, Phrases and Passages").

SECONDARY WORKS CITED

Agøy, Nils Ivar. "Viewpoints, Audiences, and Lost Texts in *The Silmarillion.*" In *The Silmarillion: Thirty Years On,* edited by Allen Turner, 139–63. Zurich: Walking Tree Press, 2007.

Bratman, David. "The Literary Value of *The History of Middle-earth.*" In *Tolkien's Legendarium: Essays on "The History of Middle-earth,"* edited by Verlyn Flieger and Carl Hostetter, 69–94. Westport, CT: Greenwood Press, 2000.

Carpenter, Humphrey. *J. R. R. Tolkien. A biography.* Paperback edition, Boston: Houghton Mifflin, 2000.

Fisher, Jason. "From Mythopoeia to Mythography: Tolkien, Lönnrot, and Jerome." In *The Silmarillion: Thirty Years On,* edited by Allen Turner, 111–38. Zurich: Walking Tree Press, 2007.

Flieger, Verlyn. *Interrupted Music: The Making of Tolkien's Mythology.* Kent, OH: Kent State University Press, 2005.

———. *Splintered Light: Logos and Language in Tolkien's World.* 2nd ed. Kent, OH: Kent State University Press, 2002.

Flieger, Verlyn and Carl Hostetter, eds. *Tolkien's Legendarium: Essays on "The History of Middle-earth."* Westport, CT: Greenwood Press, 2000.

Gilson, Christopher. "Gnomish Is Sindarin." In *Tolkien's Legendarium: Essays on "The History of Middle-earth,"* edited by Verlyn Flieger and Carl Hostetter, 95–104. Westport, CT: Greenwood Press, 2000.

Hammond, Wayne G. "'A Continuing and Evolving Creation': Distractions in the Later History of Middle-earth," in *Tolkien's Legendarium: Essays on "The History of Middle-earth,"* edited by Verlyn Flieger and Carl Hostetter, 19–29. Westport, CT: Greenwood Press, 2000.

Noad, Charles E. "A Tower in Beleriand: A Talk by Guy Gavriel Kay." *Mythprint* no. 107 (April 1989): 3–4, 6. Also published in *Amon Hen* no. 91 (May 1988).

———. "On the Construction of 'The Silmarillion.'" In *Tolkien's Legendarium: Essays on "The History of Middle-earth,"* edited by Verlyn Flieger and Carl Hostetter, 31–68. Westport, CT: Greenwood Press, 2000.

Scull, Christina, and Wayne G. Hammond. *The J. R. R. Tolkien Companion and Guide, Reader's Guide.* Boston: Houghton Mifflin, 2006.

Shippey, T. A. *The Road to Middle-earth.* 3rd ed. Boston: Houghton Mifflin, 2003.

Turner, Allan, ed. *The Silmarillion: Thirty Years On.* Zurich: Walking Tree Press, 2007.

Abbreviations of Source Texts

AAm = *Annals of Aman,* published in *MR.*

CMW = "Coming of Men into the West," chapter 14 of the "later *Quenta*" (used in chapter 17), published in *WotJ.*

FM 1 = The earliest version of the story of Finwë and Míriel (used in chapter 6), published in *MR.*

FM 4 = The fourth (and last) version of the story of Finwë and Míriel (used in chapter 6), published in *MR.*

GA = *The Grey Annals,* published in *WotJ.*

L&C A = The first version of the essay *Laws and Customs among the Eldar* (used in chapter 6), published in *MR.*

LQ = The "later *Quenta*" (the post–*Lord of the Rings* work on the *Quenta Silmarillion*), published in *MR* and *WotJ.*

LQ (Conc) = The final revisions made to the conclusion of the "later *Quenta*" (used in chapter 24), published in *WotJ.*

LQ (CtD) = Chapter 13 of the "later *Quenta*," entitled "Concerning the Dwarves" (used in chapter 10), published in *WotJ.*

LQ (Later chap. 7) = The "second-phase" version of chapter 7 of the "later *Quenta*" (used in chapter 9), published in *MR.*

QN = *Quenta Noldorinwa* (the first version of the *Quenta*), published in *SoMe.*

QN 1 and *QN* 2 = Different versions of the later part of the *Quenta Noldorinwa* (used in chapters 23 and 24), published in *SoMe.*

QS = The "earlier *Quenta*" (the pre–*Lord of the Rings* work on *Quenta Silmarillion*), published in *Lost Road.*

QS(Conc) = The conclusion of the "earlier *Quenta*" (used in chapter 24), published in *Lost Road.*

QS I and QS II = Different versions of portions of "earlier *Quenta*" (used in chapter 19), published in *Lost Road.*

QS16(C) and QS16(D) = Different versions of the pre–*Lord of the Rings* work on chapter 16 of the *Quenta Silmarillion* (used in chapter 20), published in *Lost Road.*

WH = The *Wanderings of Húrin,* used in chapter 22, published in *WotJ.*

ARDA RECONSTRUCTED

Introduction:
Reconstructing Arda

ALTHOUGH J.R.R. TOLKIEN IS BEST KNOWN FOR HAVING WRITTEN *THE Lord of the Rings* (and to a lesser extent, *The Hobbit*), *The Silmarillion* is arguably his most important work. He began working on the stories that provided the basis of what would become *The Silmarillion* in 1917, while he was fighting in World War I, and he continued revising them in one context or another throughout the rest of his life, until his death in 1973. These stories originally stemmed from two main sources: his interest in inventing languages, and his desire to create a mythology for England (*Letters,* 144, 230–31). However, they eventually became the vehicle for his most profound reflections on such themes as: death and immortality, and the perils of timeless beauty; pride and hubris, and the struggle between good and evil (as symbolized by the Silmarils, the holy jewels that alone preserved the "pure" Light, yet also generated so much of the strife described in these tales); and perhaps most importantly, the tension between fate and free will. Even more than *The Lord of the Rings, The Silmarillion* reflects the melding of Tolkien's abiding Catholic faith with his deep knowledge of and respect for ancient pagan myth (and language).

Unfortunately, however, Tolkien never completed this work. He left behind a complex array of interrelated texts, none of which could be considered "finished." In addition to the *Quenta Silmarillion* (the History of the Silmarils) itself, there were also closely related texts that were written in the form of annals (short chronological records of the events of successive years, although they often extended into longer narrative passages). There were also a number of essays, commentaries, and other works that further developed what became known as Tolkien's "legendarium," including extended prose and verse versions of the three "Great Tales" that formed the core of the mythology: the tales of Beren and Lúthien, *The Fall of Gondolin,* and *The Children of Húrin.*[1] These works were left in varying states of completion. The earlier portions of the narrative underwent a significant amount of revision after *The Lord of the Rings* was published in the mid-

1950s, whereas some of the later portions were never updated after 1930, or even earlier. Moreover, toward the end of his life, Tolkien contemplated a vast reworking of many critical elements of his mythology, but he never carried through on this plan.

After Tolkien's death, it was left to his son and literary executor, Christopher Tolkien (for ease of reference, I will from here on refer to him as "Christopher," while continuing to refer to his father as "Tolkien"), to attempt to publish *The Silmarillion*. The factors described above made that a particularly daunting and difficult task.

In most of the twelve-volume work *The History of Middle-earth*, Christopher documents in amazing detail the development of the work of his father that would become *The Silmarillion* (four volumes trace the history of the creation of *The Lord of the Rings*). However, save for an occasional hint here and there, he mostly does not show the final step: his actual creation of the published work, with the assistance of Guy Gavriel Kay (who was then a graduate student but would later go on to become a successful fantasy author in his own right).

Many readers of *The Silmarillion* have developed the impression that it was essentially written by the editor from the author's notes. Christopher himself calls this "a serious misapprehension to which my words have given rise" (*BoLT1*, 6–7). Other readers make the assumption that they are basically reading what Tolkien himself wrote, with only minor editorial interference. This assumption is equally mistaken.

As Christopher states in the foreword to *The War of the Jewels* (the second of the two volumes of *The History of Middle-earth* that covers the "later Silmarillion"), "The published work is not in any way a completion, but a construction devised out of the existing materials. Those materials are now made available . . . and with them a criticism of the 'constructed' *Silmarillion* becomes possible. I shall not enter into that question . . ." (*WotJ*, x). The purpose of the present work, however, is to "enter into that question": to document the major changes, omissions, and additions that were made to Tolkien's work by Christopher (and Guy Kay) in preparing *The Silmarillion* for publication, and to trace how the disparate source materials were used to create what is in essence a composite work.

One of the most remarkable things that I have noted is how much of the published text really does come from Tolkien's own writings, with inserts that seemed initially to have been inventions of the editors often turning out to have come from some remote other portion of Tolkien's vast body of work. Indeed, as will be seen, there is only one chapter that consists mostly of editorial invention. The tapestry that was woven by Christopher Tolkien and Guy Kay from different portions of Tolkien's work is often quite mind-boggling. It is also fascinating to see how, in the final portions of the *Quenta Silmarillion,* the older material was included with remarkably little editorial change.

I have, of course, been mostly limited to comparing the published text with the texts printed in *The History of Middle-earth* (and to some extent *Unfinished Tales, The Children of Húrin,* and, in at least one instance, Tolkien's letters). It is possible, even likely, that some of the changes, omissions, and additions that I describe reflect textual material not included (for whatever reason) in those works, or some other source only available to Christopher (including, perhaps, personal conversations that he had with his father). Indeed, I provide one example of a recently published linguistic text that may have influenced Christopher's choice regarding one small but significant omission. It is also important to acknowledge that Christopher was in a unique position to interpret his father's work and intentions. From early on, they shared a close bond. Tolkien wrote in his diary about Christopher that he "had grown into 'a nervy irritable, cross-grained, self-tormenting, cheeky person. Yet there is something intensely lovable about him, to me at any rate, from the very similarity between us.'"[2] However, with so little commentary regarding many of Christopher's editorial choices, we are left with no option but to speculate as to his reasoning, based on the material available. Fortunately, the emendations made from other sources appear to be negligible and do not detract from the basic value of this work.

As Christopher stated in discussing the pre–*Lord of the Rings* version of the story of Beren and Lúthien, "I hope that it will be possible later to present the major texts from the post–*Lord of the Rings* period, on the basis of which and in relation to what has thus far been published almost every detail of the 'constructed' text will be determinable" (*Lost Road,* 302). Christopher did, of course, get the opportunity to "present the major texts from the post–*Lord of the Rings* period." It is a shame, however, that he did not further explain his own thoughts about the process of constructing the published text, as I believe that doing so would have helped illuminate this final step in the "history of Middle-earth." It is my hope, however, that the present work will shed some light on the scope of what creating that "constructed text" entailed, thus making it possible to attempt to, as Christopher puts it, "judge either it or its justification" (ibid.).

In the process of presenting this material, it would be impossible for me to fail to express my own opinion regarding how successful Christopher was in achieving this task. There is an obvious tension in the creation of *The Silmarillion* between Christopher's responsibility to accurately reflect his father's vision and his responsibility to create the most coherent and literary text possible. As Jason Fisher writes in his article in the retrospective *The Silmarillion: Thirty Years On,* "Christopher would have been faced with the challenge of gaining some measure of literary acceptance for the work his father had failed to complete, and a maximalist approach might have run counter to this goal."[3] However, I believe that in some instances he erred in leaning too far toward the latter responsibility, at the expense of the former. In his sometimes excessive (as he himself admits) search for "consistency," he cut out what I consider to be some of the most important and profound portions of the work—portions that Tolkien clearly intended to be included—so that only those who are willing to wade through the daunting, highly scholarly volumes of *The History of Middle-earth* get the opportunity to appreciate those important parts of Tolkien's vision. As Nils Ivar Agøy stated in his article in *The Silmarillion: Thirty Years On,* "the 1977 text has a far larger audience than the exceedingly complicated welter of texts in *The History of Middle-earth*. For the great majority of Tolkien readers, it is the standard, authoritative source of 'information' about the Elder Days."[4] Tom Shippey makes a similar point in his seminal work, *The Road to Middle-earth.*[5]

Perhaps my biggest complaint is that a significant number of edits tend to weaken the roles of many of the strong female characters in the tales, to great negative effect. Tolkien has sometimes been criticized for marginalizing female characters in his writings.[6] Christopher's edits unfortunately only serve to exacerbate those complaints.

One thing that I have tried to do as much as possible is to point out what material from the latest version of each part of the story was not used in the published text. Indeed, most of the major disappointment that I express relates to material that was omitted, not changed or added, with my greatest grievance probably being the removal of most of the story of Finwë and Míriel. Not only do those major omissions result in the reduction of the role of an important female character (Míriel), they also remove some of Tolkien's most profound philosophical and spiritual musings.

I cannot, however, question Christopher's basic decision to "construct a text from different sources." It seems to me that given the state in which his father's work was left, he had no other option if he was going to publish a work called *The Silmarillion*. His father had envisioned a much longer work than that ultimately produced by Christopher, one roughly equal in length to *The Lord of the Rings*. (*Letters,* 138). After Tolkien's death, his publisher, Allen & Unwin, officially stated that it was hoped Christopher would "be able to complete the two to three-volume novel."[7] In his essay "On the Construction of 'The Silmarillion'" in *Tolkien's Legendarium,* Charles Noad speculates as to what that longer work might have looked like. He proposed that it would have consisted of the *Quenta Silmarillion* itself, followed by a series of other works.[8] Such a structure would not have been feasible, however, given the state that the different works were left in.[9]

It is particularly interesting that Noad suggests that the *Annals of Aman* and the *Grey Annals* would have been left out entirely in Tolkien's final version.[10] In discussing what actually was included in the published work, Noad notes that "what was published consisted of the *Quenta Silmarillion,* filled out where necessary and finished with passages from the various *Annals* and narratives, together with the *Ainulindalë* and *Valaquenta,* supplemented with the *Akallabêth* and *Of the Rings of Power.*"[11] However, my closer analysis reveals that Christopher did more than "fill out where necessary and finish" with passages from the various annals. Indeed, as will be seen, a large percentage (probably even a majority) of the material published as the *Quenta Silmarillion* was actually taken from the *Annals of Aman* (the final version of the annals related to Valinor, the home of the Valar, or gods) or the *Grey Annals* (the final version of the annals related to Beleriand, the land in Middle-earth where the Elves and their human allies battled Morgoth, the first Dark Lord). Christopher's justification for this will be explored in the discussions of chapters 8 and 9, and an example that may have been used as precedent for this process of amalgamation will be seen in the chapter on the *Akallabêth.*

I do not attempt to trace in this book the full history of the development of the tales that would become *The Silmarillion* (although I do describe some of that history where it is helpful in understanding the choices made by Christopher in the creation of the published text). In addition to the extensive discussion of that history contained in the volumes of *The History of Middle-earth,* there are excellent summaries of the history of the material for each chapter in the entries for those individual chapters in the *Reader's Guide.* The essays by Scull, Hammond, Noad, and David Bratman in *Tolkien's Legendarium* also provide helpful insights regarding that history.

Table 1 provides a list of each text that was used as source material for the published *Silmarillion,* indicating when the text was created and which volume of *The History of Middle-earth* (or other book) the text is printed in. This should provide a convenient reference to help the reader navigate the often confusing array of disparate source materials discussed.

Arda Reconstructed is designed as a companion to *The Silmarillion,* but the reader should be able to follow along through the text without having to constantly refer back to that work. An abundance of minor edits were made to the source material in creating the published book, but to document each minor edit would serve only to drown the significant changes in insignificant ones, and obscure the patterns of stylistic changes. I have therefore structured the work in the following manner: for each chapter in *The Silmarillion* (starting with the short separate works called the *Ainulindalë* and the *Valaquenta*, continuing with the individual chapters of the *Quenta Silmarillion* itself, and concluding with the additional separate works called the *Akallabêth* and *Of the Rings of Power and the Third Age*), I begin by giving the general construction of the particular chapter from its sources. I then go on to provide descriptive and evaluative commentary on *only* the significant changes, as well as discussion of some paragraphs with really complex multiple sources. Almost all of the individual chapters also contain a table detailing the major and minor sources for each *Silmarillion* paragraph. This will assist those readers who wish to engage in the often tedious but sometimes surprisingly rewarding task of making a close, paragraph-by-paragraph comparison between the published text and the source materials, while allowing other readers to quickly move on. I also include a discussion regarding the appendices, focusing mainly on those ancillary works that Tolkien either suggested or implied should be appended to *The Silmarillion*, but were not. The final chapter discusses the patterns of general stylistic changes mentioned above (both major and minor), with a final table describing changes in names and related material.

Anyone who has read *The Silmarillion* knows that "Arda" is the word Tolkien uses to designate the world in which his mythology plays out. The title of the present work, *Arda Reconstructed,* is meant, therefore, to reflect my belief that Christopher—while using mostly his father's own words—reconstructed his father's vision for *The Silmarillion* to fit his own image of how the work should appear. I wish to make clear, however, that none of the criticisms that I make should be taken as a sign that I have anything but the deepest admiration for Christopher Tolkien, and profound gratitude to him for the tireless work that he has done to make so much of his father's incredible work accessible to the public. Needless to say, without that effort, the present work would have been impossible.

Table 1. Source Material by Date

Year(s) written	Text	Book printed in
c. 1916–19	Tuor and the Exiles of Gondolin (The Tale of the Fall of Gondolin)	The Book of Lost Tales, Part 2
c. 1917–19	The Nauglafring: The Necklace of the Dwarves	The Book of Lost Tales, Part 2
c. 1917–19	Turambar and the Foalókë	The Book of Lost Tales, Part 2
c. 1925–31	Lay of Leithian	The Lays of Beleriand
1930	Quenta Noldorinwa (QN)	The Shaping of Middle-earth
c. 1937	"Earlier Quenta" (QS)	The Lost Road
c. 1948	Ainulindalë version C	Morgoth's Ring
c. 1950–52	"Later Quenta" (LQ) (first phase)	Morgoth's Ring and The War of the Jewels
1951	Ainulindalë version D	Morgoth's Ring
c. 1951–52	Annals of Aman (AAm)	Morgoth's Ring
c. 1951–52	Grey Annals (GA)	The War of the Jewels
c. 1951–52	The Tale of Years	The War of the Jewels
c. 1951–52	Of Tuor and His Coming to Gondolin	Unfinished Tales
c. 1951–58	Narn I Chîn Húrin and related texts regarding Túrin Turambar (Narn)	Unfinished Tales, The War of the Jewels, and The Children of Húrin
c. 1958–60	"Later Quenta" (LQ) (second phase, including the Valaquenta, The Laws and Customs of the Eldar and the later versions of the story of Finwë and Míriel)	Morgoth's Ring
c. 1958	Amended Legend of Origin of Dwarves	The War of the Jewels
c. 1958–59 or later	Of the Ents and the Eagles	The War of the Jewels
c. 1959	Athrabeth Finrod Ah Andreth	Morgoth's Ring
1959–60	Quendi and Eldar	The War of the Jewels
Late 1950s	The Wanderings of Húrin (WH)	The War of the Jewels
September 20, 1963	Letter 247 to Colonel Worskett	The Letters of J. R. R. Tolkien
1968	The Shibboleth of Fëanor	The Peoples of Middle-earth
1968 or later	The Problem of Ros	The Peoples of Middle-earth
c. September 1969	Of Dwarves and Men	The Peoples of Middle-earth
c. 1970	Maeglin	The War of the Jewels

I
The *Ainulindalë* and the *Valaquenta*

Ainulindalë (The Music of the Ainur)

THE SILMARILLION BEGINS WITH THE SHORT SEPARATE WORK CALLED the *Ainulindalë* (The Music of the Ainur). This work tells of the creation of Arda by the primary creator, Ilúvatar, or Eru (the One), and the secondary creators, the Ainur (the Holy Ones), who were the offspring of his thought. Eru propounded three musical themes to the Ainur, from which come all creation. The Children of Ilúvatar, Elves and Men, come from the Third Theme and were conceived by Him alone; the Ainur had no part in their creation.[1] The *Ainulindalë* describes the initial rebellion of Melkor, the most powerful of the Ainur, and how he and some of the other mightiest of the Ainur passed into Arda and became known as the Valar, the Powers of the world. It tells of the strife between Melkor and the other Valar as they sought to make real the vision that Eru showed them of what they had created from their Music.

The final development of the *Ainulindalë* (insofar as Tolkien's work is considered) is traced in *Morgoth's Ring* (the first of the two volumes of *The History of Middle-earth* dealing with the "later Silmarillion"; the other one is *The War of the Jewels*). There are three versions of the *Ainulindalë* printed (in whole or in part) in that book, which Christopher labels (in order of creation) "Ainulindalë C*," "Ainulindalë C," and "Ainulindalë D." The first of these texts, C* (chronologically speaking, though printed last in *Morgoth's Ring*), is remarkable in that it is a "round world version," completed by 1948, before *The Lord of the Rings* itself was finished. It had long been a prime feature of Tolkien's "legendarium" that the world started out as flat, and later was "bent" so that there was no longer a "straight path" to the Blessed Realm where the Valar eventually dwelt. Much later, Tolkien expressed serious doubts regarding the viability of the "flat world" aspect of his legendarium.[2] So it is interesting that he considered a "round world" version this early in the process (he also drafted a "round world" version of the story of the fall of Númenor at around this time, as will be discussed in the chapter on the *Akallabêth*).

However, Tolkien then went back to the older "flat world" version (labeled by Christopher as "Ainulindalë B" and printed in full in *The Lost Road*) and created a new version based on that. That is version

33

C, which is given in full in *Morgoth's Ring*. He then revised version C and created "a manuscript of unusual splendour, with illuminated capitals and a beautiful script" (*MR*, 29–30). That is version D. Christopher traces the differences between C and D, until D diverges so far that he needs to give the full text. Christopher notes that "D was the last version of the *Ainulindalë*" (*MR*, 39). It is version D that Christopher used as the source material for the published text, but since much of that version follows version C exactly and is not printed separately, version C provides much of the source material with which the published text must be compared.

I do not believe that there can be any doubt that Christopher made the right decision in using the text D as the basis for the published text, rather than attempting to carry out his father's late suggestion that the "flat world" concept be abandoned. In order to take up his father's suggestion, he would have needed to either use the already superseded text C* as the basis for the published text, or try to construct a new text himself, since his father only made the brief suggestion that the change be made, but never came back and drafted a new text. Moreover, it would likely have required taking up other, related transformations to the mythology that Tolkien also suggested, but never carried out.

Tolkien had come to see the "flat earth" concept as untenable because the Númenóreans—the descendents of the "fathers of Men" who were allies of the Elves in their wars against Melkor and whom he came to conceive as the bearers of this mythology—would know that this concept was astronomically absurd. However, as Tolkien himself points out, eliminating the "flat world" concept would lead to losing "the dramatic impact of such things as the first 'incarnates' waking in a starlit world—or the coming of the High Elves to Middle-earth and unfurling their banners at the *first* rising of the Moon" (*MR*, 370).[3] Furthermore, retaining the "flat world" concept facilitates the expression of Tolkien's important themes of pride and hubris and the relations between mortal and divine, particularly in the tale of the drowning of Númenor.[4] For these reasons, I am convinced that Christopher made the right decision in not attempting to eliminate the "flat world" concept.

There are only twenty-five paragraphs in the version of the *Ainulindalë* in *The Silmarillion*. Since there are forty in version C, and more than that in version D, it is clear that quite a bit has been deleted. We shall see later, however, that not all of that material was omitted entirely from *The Silmarillion*. The source material is tracked by paragraph in table 2.

The editorial changes made to the *Ainulindalë* (other than the significant portion at the end of the work that was not used at all in the

Table 2. *Ainulindalë* Source Material by Paragraph

Paragraph no.	Paragraph headwords	*Silm* page no.	Source material
1	"There was Eru . . ."	15	§1 of version C
2	"And it came to . . ."	15	§2 of version C
3	"Then Ilúvatar said . . ."	15	§3 of version C
4	"Then the voices . . ."	15–16	§4 of version C
5	"But now Ilúvatar . . ."	16	§5 of version C
6	"Some of these . . ."	16	§6 of version C
7	"Then Ilúvatar arose . . ."	16–17	§7 of version C
8	"In the midst . . ."	17	§8 of version C
9	"Then Ilúvatar spoke . . ."	17	§9 of version C
10	"Then the Ainur. . ."	17	§10 of version C
11	"But when they . . ."	17	§§11 and 12 of version C
12	"And many other . . ."	17–18	§13 of version D
13	"Now the Children . . ."	18	§14 of version D
14	"But the other . . ."	19	§15 of version C
15	"Now to water . . ."	19	§16 of version D
16	"Then Ilúvatar spoke . . ."	19	§17 of version D
17	"Then Ulmo answered: . . ."	19	§18 of version C
18	"But even as Ulmo . . ."	19–20	§19 of version D (including footnote)
19	"Then there was . . ."	20	§20 of version D
20	"Thus it came . . ."	20	§20 of version D
21	"But when the Valar . . ."	20–21	§§22 and 23 of version D
22	"But Manwë was . . ."	21	§24 of version D
23	"Now the Valar took . . ."	21	§25 of version D
24	"And the Valar drew . . ."	21–22	§26 of version C
25	"Thus began the . . ."	22	§27 of version D, with the last sentence based on a sentence in §28

Note: Version C of the *Ainulindalë* is given in *MR*, 8–23 (with commentary following). Then the discussion of version D and the portion of the text of that version that is given in full appears in *MR*, 29–37 (again with commentary following). Unless otherwise indicated, where version C is referenced as the source, there are no differences from that passage cited in version D, and it can be presumed that the passage appeared in the same form in version D.

published version) are mostly very minor. One significant change that we see here, and again later in the *Akallabêth*, is the removal of the context of these tales, in this case as having been written by Rúmil, an Elvish loremaster and the original inventor of writing, and then

told to Ælfwine by Pengoloð (another Elvish loremaster) in Tol
Eressëa. In the original Lost Tales, Ælfwine (Elf-friend) was a Man
who had found the straight path to the Lonely Isle where the Elves
dwelt. In his foreword to the first volume *of The History of Middle-earth*
Christopher admits that it was an error that there was no "framework"
for *The Silmarillion,* but claims that "in the latest writing there is no
trace or suggestion of any 'device' or 'framework' in which it was to
be set" (*BoLT1*, 5). This is not entirely true. Although no "framework"
is described in the later version of the *Quenta Silmarillion* itself, there
are similar attributions in other "Silmarillon" texts, particularly the
annals, which we will see actually provide a larger portion of the published text than the *Quenta* itself.[5] Tolkien also makes several other
explicit statements of intent about the nature of the "framework" of
the mythology as being preserved by Men from their association with
Elves, but "blended and confused with their own Mannish myths and
cosmic ideas" (*MR*, 370). Christopher evidently concluded that the
best solution to this confusion was to eliminate any reference to the
context of all the works. Although this decision is understandable, I
believe Christopher would have better served his father's interest to
retain (and perhaps even, where necessary, further expand upon)
this "framework," and it appears from the doubts that he expressed
when he first began the process of presenting *The History of Middle-
earth* that he might agree.

We see this elimination of the context of the tale reflected most
clearly in the omission of most of the introductory words on the title
pages. The final version, D, has these words:

> *Ainulindalë*
> The Music of the Ainur
>   This was made by Rúmil of Túna in the Elder Days. It is here written as
> it was spoken in Eressëa to Ælfwine by Pengoloð the Sage. To it are added
> the further words that Pengoloð spoke at that time concerning the Valar,
> the Eldar and the Atani; of which more is said hereafter.
>
> (*MR*, 30)

The published version retains only the title:

> *Ainulindalë*
> The Music of the Ainur
>
> (*Silm*, 15)

The further introductory words in D, "First he recited to him the
Ainulindalë as Rúmil made it" (*MR*, 30), are also omitted.

The next change of any interest is in the first sentence of the fourteenth paragraph ("But the other Ainur . . ."; *Silm*, 19), where the

phrase "habitation set within the vast spaces of the World" is changed from "habitation in the halls of Aman." Christopher specifically states that D still has the phrase "habitation in the halls of Aman" (see *MR*, 30). However, he later notes that in the course of emending version D the word "Aman" was changed from referring to "the World" to referring to only the Blessed Realm, that a new term "Eä" had been created, and that it was an oversight that this new term did not replace "Aman" in this sentence (see *MR*, 37). It is interesting that Christopher nonetheless changed the language to "set within the vast spaces of the World" instead of just "in the Halls of Eä."[6]

In the next paragraph, which details the provinces of the chief male Valar—Ulmo, Manwë, and Aulë—of water, air, and Earth, respectively, there is an interesting change in the last sentence, where "is" is changed from "was" regarding Aulë's "delight and pride" in making things. Christopher notes that he made that change because the past tense "was" conflicted with an amendment that his father made to a phrase describing Aulë later in the sentence, changing it from past tense to present tense (*MR*, 30–31).

In the subsequent paragraph, in which Ilúvatar tells Ulmo that even Melkor's efforts to destroy the work of the other Valar only leads to new forms of beauty, after "Behold the snow, and the cunning work of frost!" the phrase "Behold the towers and mansions of ice" is, according to Christopher, omitted in version D "perhaps inadvertently," but is not added back into the published version. That is a shame, because it is a nice descriptive phrase. There is no clear evidence that it was omitted inadvertently, however, and the omission in the published text is certainly justifiable on the grounds that the latest version of this passage did not contain it.

Paragraph 23 ("Now the Valar took to . . ."; *Silm*, 21), which describes how the Valar clothed themselves in forms resembling the Children of Ilúvatar that they had seen in the Vision, has by far the most changes of any paragraph thus far. Two significant portions of the source material are removed altogether. The first omitted section describes Manwë, Ulmo, Aulë, Varda, Yavanna, Nienna, and Melkor as the "Seven Great Ones of the Kingdom of Arda" and includes the small but significant detail that Yavanna was Varda's sister. The second omitted passage describes how Pengoloð observed Yavanna in the likeness of a tree, and describes her beauty and majesty in that form (*MR*, 15–16). Both of these omissions are unfortunate, particularly the second one, as Tolkien's poetic prose is particularly well displayed in that passage.

Finally, the twenty-fifth paragraph, which describes the first battle of the Valar, also has fairly significant changes and omissions. These mostly relate to the removal of Pengoloð, Ælfwine, and Rúmil from the narrative, as discussed above.

Yavanna in the likeness of a tree. By Anushka Mouriño. Courtesy of the artist.

At this point, we have reached the end of the version of the *Ain-ulindalë* published in *The Silmarillion*. And yet, version C still has twelve more paragraphs, and version D has sixteen more to go! Christopher gives no explanation of why this significant portion of the work was omitted from the version in the published *Ainulindalë*. However, as we will see, much of the omitted material does reappear later in the published *Silmarillion*. The text of what was omitted can be found at *MR*, 17–22 (C) and 31–37(D).

Valaquenta (Account of the Valar)

THE *VALAQUENTA*, THE SECOND SHORT WORK THAT APPEARS BEFORE THE *Quenta Silmarillion* itself, gives additional details about the Valar, as well as lesser related spirits called the Maiar (Gandalf, Saruman, Sauron, and probably the Balrog from *The Lord of the Rings* were all Maiar). The text that became the *Valaquenta* was originally the first chapter of the *Quenta* itself, entitled "Of the Valar." The pre–*Lord of the Rings* version of this chapter can be found in *Lost Road, 204–8.* When Tolkien returned to working on the *Quenta Silmarillion* in 1951 or so he wrote a new version of this chapter, but it was still part of the *Quenta* (see *MR,* 143–47). It was when he again revised the work in the late 1950s (in what Christopher describes as the "second phase" of his father's work on the "later *Quenta*") that he broke off this first chapter into a separate work, the *Valaquenta* (see *MR,* 200).

Christopher has actually done much of my work for me here. He details many of the editorial changes that were made to the *Valaquenta* in the published version of the *Silmarillion* and makes some interesting observations about the process (*MR,* 200–205). I wish he had provided this kind of detail about the editorial process in the rest of the book.

Since Christopher did not print the final version of the *Valaquenta* (which he designated as *Vq* 2), it is not possible to do a paragraph-by-paragraph comparison. There is, therefore, no table in this chapter. Instead, I only note the important changes that he describes or that I can discern.

There is a small change in the first sentence of the fifth paragraph, which begins "With Manwë dwells Varda . . ." (*Silm,* 26); as Christopher recognizes, it has greater significance than at first glance. The word "now" is omitted from between "With Manwë" and "dwells Varda." Christopher notes that at the time the published *Silmarillion* was created, he did not see the word "now" as having any particular significance and felt that it contributed to problems of tense in the *Valaquenta* (which I will discuss at the end of this chapter), so he omitted it. He later came to realize that it did have significance in distinguishing the history of the relationship of Manwë and Varda from the

40

relationship between Aulë and Yavanna. The *Annals of Arda* originally stated that Manwë and Varda were spouses "from the beginning," but that text was then amended to "from the beginning of Arda." This was specifically in contrast to the later union of Aulë and Yavanna "in Eä" (see *MR*, 49, 69, 201). So "now" is significant and should have been retained. Similarly, in the ninth paragraph ("The spouse of Aulë is Yavanna . . ."; *Silm*, 27) the description of Yavanna being Aulë's spouse "in Arda" is removed. Christopher again notes that he was wrong to change this, since the omitted words clearly have significance. This is a minor detail, but the change is still somewhat unfortunate. The idea of Manwë and Varda being the "primeval" couple is an appealing concept and should have been retained.

Another interesting change is made in the eleventh paragraph ("Námo the elder . . ."; *Silm*, 28). Námo is one of the two Fëanturi, or masters of spirits. The younger one is Irmo. Both are more commonly referred to by names of the regions where they dwell, Mandos and Lórien. In the first sentence, which describes the location of Mandos, "westward" is changed from "northward." In his discussion of the original version of this story, the Lost Tale "The Coming of the Valar," Christopher explains:

> I changed this to "westward" in the published work (and similarly "north" to "west" on p. 52) on the basis of the statement in the same passage that Nienna's halls are "west of West, upon the borders of the world," but are near to those of Mandos. In other passages it is clear that Mandos' halls were conceived as standing on the shores of the Outer Sea. . . . The conceptions of "northward in Valinor" and "on the shores of the Outer Sea" are not however contradictory, and I regret this piece of unwarranted editorial meddling. (*BoLT1*, 82)

There is a small example of the cutting and pasting from different sources that occur throughout the book in paragraph 14 ("Greatest in strength . . ."; *Silm*, 28–29). The sentence "He came last to Arda, to aid the Valar in the first battles with Melkor" (referring to Tulkas), derives from §31 of version C of the *Ainulindalë* (see *MR*, 17), which is part of the portion that was omitted from the published version of that work.

In the following paragraph, one of the alternate names given for Oromë, "Aldaron," is added from the older versions, before the *Valaquenta* was split off into a separate work. Christopher notes that it should not have been reintroduced in the published version (*MR*, 202). In addition, after the words "for the pursuit of the evil creatures of Melkor" a sentence is omitted that states that Oromë's horn, the Valaróma, and his horse, Nahar, are no longer heard and seen in

Middle-earth after the world is changed and the Elves, whom he loved, began to wane. Christopher states that he regrets the exclusion of this sentence from the published version, and so do I. The "change of the world" and "the waning of the Elves" are important concepts in Tolkien's mythology, and this omitted sentence evokes those concepts poignantly. We will see other instances later in the text where references to these concepts are again removed.

In the eighteenth paragraph ("Chief among the Maiar . . ."; *Silm*, 30), the words "whose might in arms is surpassed by none in Arda" (describing Eönwë, the herald of Manwë) are added "in order to prepare for his leadership of the hosts of the West at the Great Battle." Christopher points out here (as has already been observed) that there is very little material describing the end of the Elder Days written after *The Lord of the Rings* (*MR*, 203).[1] This comment of Christopher's (about preparing for Eönwë's leadership in the Great Battle) is particularly interesting, because we will see in the final chapter of the *Quenta Silmarillion* and in the *Akallabêth* that Eönwë's role is actually greatly reduced by his edits.

Another unfortunate omission is made in paragraph 23 ("Of Melian much is told . . ."; *Silm*, 31.) At the end of this paragraph the following sentences regarding Olórin were omitted: "He was humble in the Land of the Blessed; and in Middle-earth he sought no renown. His triumph was in the uprising of the fallen, and his joy was in the renewal of hope." Christopher notes that this passage was wrongly omitted from *The Silmarillion* (*MR*, 203). This is another omission that I greatly regret. Olórin, of course, is Gandalf, the wizard who plays such central roles in *The Lord of the Rings* and *The Hobbit*. This excellent description of his character is a sad loss.

The *Valaquenta* ended with the following words: "Here ends *The Valaquenta*. If it has passed from the high and beautiful to darkness and ruin, that was of old the fate of Arda Marred; and if any change shall come and the Marring be amended, Manwë and Varda may know; but they have not revealed it, and it is not declared in the dooms of Mandos" (*MR*, 203–4).

In the published version, only the words "HERE ENDS THE VALAQUENTA" appear at the end of the *Valaquenta*. The rest of this text was used as the conclusion of the *Quenta Silmarillion* itself.[2]

Finally, as mentioned above, Christopher notes that there were numerous inconsistencies in tense in the text of the *Valaquenta* that he attempted to fix. He states that in preparing the published text, one of his prime concerns was "the achievement of coherence and consistency" and that a major obstacle was the lack of clarity regarding his father's conception in his later work of how the "Lore of the

Eldar" was transmitted. In hindsight, Christopher concludes that he "attached too much importance to the aim of consistency, which may be present when not evident, and was too ready to deal with 'difficulties' simply by eliminating them" (*MR*, 204–5).

I strongly agree with this latter statement. As will be seen, there are many instances where important material is sacrificed for this elusive ideal.

II
Quenta Silmarillion
(The History of the Silmarils)

Chapter 1 "Of the Beginning of Days"

THIS CHAPTER IS ONE OF THE MOST COMPLICATED TO TRACE IN THE whole book, with parts from three main sources woven together. However, before those sources are described, a little background history regarding Tolkien's work on the *Quenta Silmarillion* after *The Lord of the Rings* was completed would be helpful.

In *Morgoth's Ring*, Christopher describes two "phases" of the first part of what he calls the "later *Quenta*" (LQ), up to the chapter entitled "Of the Sun and Moon and the Hiding of Valinor" (the rest of the "later *Quenta*" is in *The War of the Jewels*). But the second phase only relates to the *Valaquenta* (as has already been seen) and material related to what would become chapters 6 through 9. So that second phase can be ignored for now.

Looking at the first-phase material (which dates to around 1950 to 1952, when *The Lord of the Rings* was completed but not yet published), we see that there is no chapter entitled "Of the Beginning of Days." Chapter 2 (which followed the chapter that was broken off to become the *Valaquenta*) is entitled "Of Valinor and the Two Trees." However, in the parallel work in annal form that covered the same time period, the *Annals of Aman* (AAm), there is a heading "Of the Beginning of Time and its Reckoning." It seems likely that the title of this first chapter was adopted from this heading. Indeed, much of this chapter seems to be based more on the *Annals* than on the *Quenta* itself.

Actually, at first blush this chapter appears to have been liberally rewritten by Christopher and/or Guy Kay, since much of it cannot be traced directly traced to either the "later *Quenta*" or the *Annals of Aman*. However, there is another source covering this period: the portion of the *Ainulindalë* that is not included in the published version of that text. That turns out to be the source for a significant portion of the chapter.

A fairly strong argument can be made in favor of this move. First of all, it is specifically stated in §29 of Tolkien's final version of the *Ainulindalë* (version D) that the work as made by Rúmil ended with the previous paragraph (the last one used as the source for the published version), and that the rest of the work consists of additional words of Pengoloð (see *MR*, 17). Thus, the version of the *Ainulindalë* printed in *The Silmarillion* could be considered to be the work written by Rúmil (even though it is not so designated), with the additional words of Pengoloð merged into the *Quenta*. Moreover, the material that was moved covers the same time period as the portions of the "later *Quenta*" and the *Annals of Aman* that were also used as source material for this chapter.

Nonetheless, I still feel some uneasiness at the idea of significant material written by Tolkien as part of the *Ainulindalë* being published as part of the *Quenta Silmarillion* in a book that is billed as including both works. It seems just a bit misleading.

It is quite fascinating the way these three sources were melded together in this chapter. The source materials are described by paragraph in table 3.

The first significant omission in this chapter is from the fourth paragraph ("Now it came to pass . . ."; *Silm*, 36). Where the source material (*AAm* §17) discusses the Maiar whom Melkor had converted to his cause, it specifically states that the chief of these was Sauron, who was a great craftsman of the household of Aulë. I presume that the editors omitted this because they felt it was redundant, since Sauron is already mentioned at the end of the *Valaquenta* (*Silm*, 31–32), but this is an important point that may have been worth retaining nonetheless.

The ninth paragraph ("Thus ended the . . ."; *Silm*, 37), which describes the ending of the "Spring of Arda" in which the Valar leave Middle-earth for the westernmost land of Aman (or Valinor), helps illustrate a central problem in the creation of *The Silmarillion*. As shown in the table, the primary source for the paragraph was *AAm* §23. The word "Ekkaia," which was part of the material inserted from the "later *Quenta*," was a late change in the final version (designated by Christopher as "LQ2") from "Vaiya," the name of the Outer Sea in the *Ambarkanta*, the important essay written in the early 1930s in which Tolkien established the physical parameters of his invented universe (see *SoMe*, 235–61). The name "Belegaer" for the Great Sea does not appear in either the *Annals of Aman* or the "later *Quenta*" and is added in here from the *Ambarkanta*.

As Christopher discusses at length, there is a fair degree of confusion as to the extent that the view of the universe established in the *Ambarkanta* was retained. Unfortunately, that confusion is exacerbated by the process that Christopher used to create *The Silmarillion*. He notes that "in the revision of 'The Silmarillion' made in 1951 the phrase in QS §12 (V.209) 'the Walls of the World fence out the Void and the Eldest Dark'—a phrase in perfect agreement of course with

Table 3. Source Material by Paragraph for Chapter 1 "Of the Beginning of Days"

Paragraph no.	Paragraph headwords	*Silm* page no.	Primary source	Secondary sources
1	"It is told among . . ."	35	§31 of version D of the *Ainulindalë*	*AAm* §13: "Arda was filled with the sound of his laughter" and "Melkor fled before his wrath and his laughter, and forsook Arda"
2	"In that time . . ."	35	§31 of version D of the *Ainulindalë*	*LQ* §11: "at the prayer of Yavanna"
3	"Then the seeds . . ."	35–36	§31 of version D of the *Ainulindalë*	
4	"Now it came to . . ."	36	*AAm* §§16 and 17	
5	"Now therefore the . . ."	36	*AAm* §18	
6	"Then Tulkas slept . . ."	36	*AAm* §19	
7	"Now Melkor began . . ."	36–37	*AAm* §§20 and 21	*Ainulindalë* version D, §32: "dyed the earth with blood"
8	"In the confusion . . ."	37	*AAm* §22	*LQ* §12: "that is called by the Elves Ekkaia" (see text) and "how wide is that sea none know but the Valar"
9	"Thus ended the . . ."	37	*AAm* §23	*LQ* §13: Final two sentences (with their order reversed) *Ambarkanta* (*SoMe*, 250, 254): "Belegaer"
10	"Behind the walls . . ."	37–38	*AAm* §23	*LQ* §13: "and there were their houses, their gardens, and their towers"

(continued)

Table 3. Continued

Paragraph no.	Paragraph headwords	*Silm* page no.	Primary source	Secondary sources
11	"And when Valinor . . ."	38	AAm §§25 and 26 (§24 was skipped)	LQ §13: "beyond the mountains" and "Valmar of many bells" LQ §14: the last sentence AAm §122 and LQ §58d: Corollairë (see text) *Quendi and Eldar* (*WotJ*, p. 399): "Máhanaxar"
12	"And as they . . ."	38	LQ §15	AAm §26: "And as they watched, upon the mound" and "the saplings grew and became fair and tall, and came to flower"
13	"The one had . . ."	38	LQ §15 and LQ §16	AAm §28: "But the light that was spilled from the Trees endured long, ere it was taken up into the airs or sank into the earth"
14	"In seven hours . . ."	38–39	LQ §17	AAm §29: the final sentence
15	"But as the ages . . ."	39	§33 of *Ainulindalë* version D	AAm §24: "Middle-earth lay in a twilight beneath the stars that Varda had wrought in the ages forgotten of her labours in Eä"

16	"From the beauty . . ."	39	§34 with §35 of Ainulindalë version D	
17	"But Manwë Súlimo . . ."	39–40	§36 of Ainulindalë version D	
18	"Manwë has no . . ."	40	§36 of Ainulindalë version D	
19	"But Ulmo was . . ."	40	§37 of Ainulindalë version D	
20	"And in that . . ."	40–41	§34 of Ainulindalë version D	AAm §31: "and his white horse Nahar shone like silver in the shadows. Then the sleeping earth trembled at the beat of his golden hooves," "quailed in Utumno" and the last sentence
21	"Now all is said . . ."	41	A paragraph in Ainulindalë version D that is not numbered because it did not appear at all in version C (see MR, pp. 35–36) (see text)	
22	"For it is said . . ."	41–42	§§38 and 39 of Ainulindalë version D	
23	"But Ilúvatar knew . . ."	42	First paragraph of §40 of Ainulindalë version D	
24	"It is one with . . ."	42	Second paragraph of §40 of Ainulindalë version D	

Note: The chapter from the "later *Quenta*" entitled "Of Valinor and the Two Trees" appears in *MR*, 152–56 (with commentary that follows), and the relevant sections are LQ §§11–17 (the § designations follow the paragraphs from the earlier version of the *Quenta*, the *Quenta Noldorinwa*, which is published in *The Lost Road*). The relevant sections in the *Annals of Aman* are AAm §§16–29 and one small insert from §31, which are printed in *MR*, 52–56 and 70. The portion of the *Ainulindalë* that is used as a source for this chapter consists of §31 of version C, and 31–40 of version D (and one unnumbered paragraph that derives from the older versions, as will be seen), which can be found in *MR*, 17–18 and 31–37.

the *Ambarkanta*—was retained" (*MR*, 63–64). That phrase, however, is *not* included in the published text, resulting in the mistaken impression that that concept from the *Ambarkanta* of the Outer Sea extending to the Wall of the World (or the Walls of the Night) was not in fact retained. This demonstrates the pitfalls of the compilation approach used by Christopher, in which much of the text of the *Quenta Silmarillion* itself was replaced with other sources.

In this case, Christopher appears to have left this phrase out because of concerns that it contradicted statements in the *Ainulindalë* regarding Eä coming into being in the void (see *MR*, 64). This is another case where something is lost because of Christopher's sometimes excessive search for consistency. I would have preferred that the statement be retained and the reader be allowed to puzzle out the inconsistencies himself or herself. Such inconsistencies would only enhance the sense that these works are old works from different sources.

Beginning with the twelfth paragraph ("And as they watched . . ."; *Silm*, 38), the next three paragraphs are the only ones in the chapter that have as their primary source the "later *Quenta*" itself. In the first sentence of the thirteenth paragraph the description of Telperion, the elder of the Two Trees, bearing white blossoms as if it were a great cherry-tree is removed, as well as the statements that the Sindar called Telperion "Galathilion" and Laurelin "Galadlóriel" (see *MR*, 155). The Sindarin names were probably omitted to avoid confusion, but I do miss the detail of Telperion bearing white blossoms like a great cherry-tree. That kind of descriptive detail is one of the qualities that makes Tolkien's writing so compelling, and is one of the distinguishing features that leads many readers to prefer *The Lord of the Rings* to *The Silmarillion*.

The rest of the chapter is taken primarily from the material moved from the *Ainulindalë*, with some inserts from the *Annals of Aman* (the equivalent chapter in the "later *Quenta*" ended with LQ §17, the source of the previous paragraph). As seen in the table, the paragraphs are not taken completely in order, and the twenty-first paragraph ("Now all is said . . ."; *Silm*, 41) comes from a paragraph in *Ainulindalë* version D that is not numbered because it did not appear at all in version C (see *MR*, 35–36). It was actually added into version D from the old version B (see *Lost Road*, 160–61) and is not greatly modified from a paragraph in the original *Music of the Ainur* (see *BoLT1*, 57), with only very minor changes (mostly related to removing the context of Pengoloð speaking to Ælfwine).

Finally, it is worth noting that in the final paragraph, the short sentence "Memory is our burden" is omitted (see *MR*, 37). That is significant, given the importance of the concept of the timelessness of the Elves becoming a prison to them. As Flieger states, Tolkien "makes a clear distinction between unending life, which he sees as bondage to the world without hope of renewal, and eternal life, which transcends death and leads to God."[1] This short omitted sentence emphasizes that distinction.

And that concludes this chapter. What a process it must have been, combining pieces of these three different works!

Chapter 2 "Of Aulë and Yavanna"

THIS CHAPTER IS COMPLETELY MANUFACTURED BY CHRISTOPHER, though using his father's own writings. There had never been an equivalent chapter in the *Quenta Silmarillion*, and it is made up almost entirely of parts of texts completely separate from the *Quenta* or the *Annals*. Moreover, the two separate parts of the chapter—one concerning the Dwarves, and the other the Ents—are largely unrelated to each other.

The first portion of it, regarding the Dwarves, comes mostly from a manuscript headed "Of Aulë and the Dwarves." This text was enclosed in a paper wrapper bearing the words *Amended Legend of Origin of Dwarves*. It is related to Chapter 13 "Concerning the Dwarves" in the "later *Quenta*" (which had previously been Chapter 10 "Of Men and Dwarves" in the "earlier *Quenta*"). Christopher mentions that "there are a number of insignificant editorial alterations in the published text" (*WotJ*, 210). The only specific one that he points out is that his father was in doubt as to whether to use "you" or "thou," and that though his father settled on "you," Christopher changed it to "thou" (see *WotJ*, 210–11).

The final paragraph of the section on the Dwarves ("Since they were . . ."; *Silm*, 44) comes from chapter 13 itself, specifically from §§2 and 3 (see *WotJ*, 203–4). There are a number of minor edits, including the insertion of the phrase "the Maker, whom they call Mahal" from *The Grey Annals*, §21 (*WotJ*, 10).

The second portion of this chapter comes from a separate document that Christopher describes in *The War of the Jewels*, Part Three, section IV: *Of the Ents and the Eagles* (see *WotJ*, 340–41). The original draft is titled "Anaxartamel." That was then expanded on in a new draft, which is what is included in the published *Silmarillion*, with minor changes, which Christopher describes. The only one worth noting is that at the end of the sixteenth paragraph ("'Yet it was in the Song' . . ."; *Silm*, 45–46), the statement that some of the trees sang to Eru in "the glitter of the Sun" is deleted because, as Christopher explains, it implies "that the Sun existed from the beginning of Arda" (*WotJ*, 341). As I stated in the discussion of the *Ainulindalë*, I agree with Christopher's decision not to try to take up his father's intention to abandon the "flat world" aspect of his mythology and the associated tale of the creation of the Sun and the Moon. Still, this edit is of particular interest, since it is one of the only examples of a text in which Tolkien actually incorporated those proposed changes.

Overall, this chapter really does push the limits of editorial intervention. Apparently, Christopher felt that it was necessary to move the story of the origins of the Dwarves to a considerably earlier place in the narrative than his father had placed it. There is a certain logic to this from a chronological point of view. However, it gives the narrative a jerky, interrupted feel, as if this chapter were inserted after the fact (which, of course, it was).

The inclusion of the portion about the Ents is even more puzzling. It appears that Christopher felt that the material on the Dwarves was too short to make a full chapter, so he added this additional, largely unrelated material. Perhaps he felt it was necessary to include some explanation of the Ents. In his commentary on this text, he cites a 1963 letter of his father in which it is stated that "some" (including Galadriel) held the opinion the Ents were the result of Yavanna beseeching Eru (through Manwë) to "give life to living things not stone" in response to His mercy to Aulë (see *WotJ*, 341 and *Letters*, 335).[1] However, there is certainly no indication whatsoever that Tolkien had any intention of including this text as part of *The Silmarillion*, any more than any number of other similar texts printed in either *The History of Middle-earth* or *Unfinished Tales*. Still, it is an interesting text, and its inclusion does bolster the length of the chapter.

Chapter 3 "Of the Coming of the Elves and the Captivity of Melkor"

THIS IS THE FIRST CHAPTER THAT ACTUALLY USES A CHAPTER NAME THAT is taken from the "later *Quenta*." The original title of chapter 3 in the "later *Quenta*" was "Of the Coming of the Elves," but Tolkien eventually did add the additional phrase "and the Captivity of Melkor." Nonetheless, this chapter is taken at least as much from the *Annals of Aman* as from the "later *Quenta*." And in some cases, the language of the two versions is so similar that it becomes difficult to tell which was the primary source text. I will show a few examples of this in the text, but it is amply demonstrated in table 4, which traces the source material paragraph by paragraph.

The first two paragraphs (*Silm*, 47) together provide a good first example of the way the primary source switches back and forth. The first paragraph describes the twilight that fell upon Middle-earth when the Valar dwelt in the bliss of the Light of the Trees in Aman, and how only Yavanna and Oromë continued to give heed to Middle-earth. The second paragraph describes Melkor building his strength in his fortress of Utumno. Both of these paragraphs blend elements from LQ §18 and *AAm* §30 (*MR*, 70 and 158, respectively). However, in the first paragraph, *AAm* §30 is the primary source, with the second and third sentences added from LQ §18. In contrast, a greater percentage of the second paragraph comes from the "later *Quenta*" (though it switches back and forth between the two sources, as shown in table 4).

There are also two edits worth noting in this second paragraph. First, a statement referring to the Balrogs as "ëalar" is eliminated, along with a footnote explaining that the word "ëalar" did not refer to an incarnate spirit, which was "fëa," and that it simply referred to "being" (see *MR*, 165). Christopher points out that while the text of the "later *Quenta*" retained the statement that the Balrogs were the "first made" of Melkor's creatures, his father noted on one of the copies that the *Valaquenta* (which describes the Balrogs as being Maiar that he corrupted to his service; *Silm*, 31) had the "true account." Presumably, Christopher felt that describing the Balrogs as having "ëalar"

Table 4. Source Material by Paragraph for Chapter 3 "Of the Coming of the Elves and the Captivity of Melkor."

Paragraph no.	Paragraph headwords	*Silm* page no.	Primary source	Secondary sources
1	"Through long ages . . ."	47	*AAm* §30	LQ §18: second and third sentences, beginning with "While the lamps . . ." and "But already . . ."
2	"But in the North . . ."	47	LQ §18	*AAm* §30: "and he slept not, but watched, and labored; and the evil things that he had perverted walked abroad, and the dark and slumbering woods were haunted by monsters and shapes of dread" and "And in Utumno he"
3	"And Melkor made . . ."	47	Footnote to LQ §12 (see *MR*, 156)	
4	"It came to pass . . ."	47–48	LQ §18a	*AAm* §32: "for they became troubled by the tidings that Yavanna and Oromë brought from the Outer Lands; and Yavanna spoke before the Valar"
5	"And Tulkas cried: . . ."	48	LQ §18a	
6	"But at the . . ."	48	LQ §18a	
7	"Then Varda went . . ."	48	Second paragraph of LQ §19	*AAm* §34: first two sentences appendix E of *The Lord of the Rings*: "Menelmacar"

(*continued*)

Table 4. Continued

Paragraph no.	Paragraph headwords	*Silm* page no.	Primary source	Secondary sources
8	"It is told that . . ."	48	AAm §37	LQ §20: first sentence and "while they dwelt yet silent by Cuiviénen" LQ §19: "Elentári" LQ §52a: "Cuiviénen" (see *MR*, 277)
9	"In the changes . . ."	48–49	AAm §38	
10	"Long they dwelt . . ."	49	AAm §39	
11	"And on a time . . ."	49	AAm §41	
12	"Thus it was that . . ."	49	Second paragraph of LQ §20	AAm §42: The first sentence and the second sentence up to "as though they were"
13	"In the beginning . . ."	49	First paragraph of LQ §20	AAm §42: "And Oromë loved the Quendi"
14	"Yet many of the . . ."	49–50	AAm §43	
15	"Thus it was that . . ."	50	AAm §44	
16	"But of those . . ."	50	AAm §45	
17	"Oromë tarried a . . ."	50	AAm §46	Third paragraph of LQ §20: "over land and sea," "Valmar," and "Then the Valar rejoiced, and yet were in doubt amid their joy"
18	"Manwë sat long . . ."	50	LQ §20	AAm §47: "Manwë sat long in thought upon Taniquetil"
19	"Then Manwë said . . ."	50–51	Fourth paragraph of LQ §20 and the beginning of LQ §21	

20	"Melkor met the . . ."	51	AAm §§48 and 49	LQ §21: "In that time the shape of Middle-earth was changed" (but with "that time" taken from AAm §49, replacing "those days") GA §6: "and it broke . . ." through "mountains about Hithlum." (two and a half sentences)
21	"But at the last . . ."	51	AAm §50	LQ §21: "that Aulë had wrought" and "and the world had peace for a long age"
22	"Nonetheless the . . ."	51	LQ §21	Footnote to LQ §12: "fortresses of Angband and Utumno" and "and Sauron they did not find"
23	"But when the . . ."	51–52	LQ §22	AAm §51: "and he was brought to the Ring of Doom. There he lay upon his face before the feet of Manwë and sued for pardon; but his prayer was denied" and "in the fastness of Mandos, whence none can escape"
24	"Then again the . . ."	52	First paragraph of LQ §23	
25	"But the Elves . . ."	52	Second paragraph of LQ §23	
26	"Then befell the . . ."	52	AAm §57	AAm §55: "ambassadors who should go to Valinor and speak for their people" AAm §56: the last sentence, beginning with "Then Oromë"

(*continued*)

Table 4. Continued

Paragraph no.	Paragraph headwords	*Silm* page no.	Primary source	Secondary sources
27	"The Eldar prepared . . ."	52–53	LQ §§24 and 25	
28	"Next came the . . ."	53	LQ §26	
29	"The greatest host . . ."	53	LQ §27	
30	"These were the . . ."	53	LQ §29	
31	"It is told . . ."	53	AAm §58	LQ §24: the first sentence up through "shod with gold"
32	"Long and slow . . ."	53–54	AAm §§59, 60 and 61	AAm §62: First two sentences, and the beginning of the third sentence through "Those were the Nandor"
33	"Then one arose . . ."	54	Second paragraph of LQ §29	*Quendi and Eldar* (*WotJ*, 418–19): "Denethor, son of Lenwë"
34	"At length the . . ."	54	AAm §63	GA §2: "Ered Luin" and "the Blue Mountains" GA §8: "Between Drengist and the Bay of Balar," "into the woods and highlands," "Oromë departed" and "and left them"
35	"And the host . . ."	54	AAm §64	GA §9: final two sentences, except "Beyond the River Gelion" and "eastern regions" (which are taken from AAm §64)

Note: Chapter 3 of the "later *Quenta*," which consists of LQ §§ 18–30, is given in *MR*, 158–65, with some additional changes given in the commentary that follows on 165–71. The relevant portion of the *Annals of Aman* is AAm §§30–64, which can be found in *MR*, 70–75, 80–83. There are also several additions from *The Grey Annals*, particularly a long one from §6, which can be found in *WotJ*, 6 and from the essay *Quendi and Eldar*.

rather than "fëa" would tend to contradict the "true account" contained in the *Valaquenta*. However, in one of the "Myths Transformed" texts Tolkien suggests that Eru would not provide "fëar" (the plural of "fëa") to Maiar who had been corrupted into Orcs or Balrogs (see *MR*, 410). This would imply that the distinction Tolkien was trying to make by describing the Balrogs as having "ëalar" rather than "fëa" would not contradict the statement in the *Valaquenta* about the origin of the Balrogs. A good argument can be made that the omitted statement referring to the Balrogs as "ëalar" might have been confusing to the reader if it had been retained, but Tolkien's discussion of the nature of the body/spirit relationship is one of his most fascinating and important philosophical concepts, and very little of it is included in the published *Silmarillion*.

The second omission from this paragraph worth noting is that a sentence is removed describing the Orcs as "mockeries and perversions of the Children of Eru" and stating that they did not appear until after the Elves awoke (see *MR*, 165). This is particularly interesting, because Christopher did nonetheless incorporate the theory of the origin of the Orcs as "perversions of the Children of Eru" later in this chapter, ignoring a note of his father to the contrary.[1]

The next paragraph ("And Melkor made . . ."; *Silm*, 47) is inserted from a different source altogether from those used so far in this chapter. This paragraph describes Melkor's second stronghold of Angband, commanded by Sauron. It is taken directly from a late, hastily scribbled footnote to LQ §12, which is part of the mostly unused previous chapter of the "later *Quenta*," "OfValinor and the Two Trees" (see *MR*, 156).

The following two paragraphs (beginning with "Thus it was that . . ."; *Silm*, 49) provide another good example of how the primary source material switches back and forth. In the first of these two paragraphs— paragraph 12, which chronicles Oromë's finding of the Elves—the primary source actually changes in the middle of a sentence from *AAm* §42 to the second paragraph of LQ §20. The next paragraph, which describes the Elves, is taken mostly from the *first* paragraph of LQ §20, with a portion of it ("And Oromë loved the Quendi") added from the one sentence in *AAm* §42 that was not used in paragraph 12. It is difficult to know what to make of such constant switching back and forth between the source texts. I think Christopher might have better served his father if he had stuck more closely to one text at a time. This is one area where it would be very helpful to have more detail from Christopher as to what guidelines—if any—he used to determine which pieces of which text he would use where. It would be helpful to know why he concluded that such complicated manipulation of the text was really necessary.

The fourteenth paragraph ("Yet many of the . . ."; *Silm*, 49–50) tells of how Melkor caused many of the Elves to fear the coming of Oromë, and comes directly from *AAm* §43, leaving the "later *Quenta*" behind for now. Next to this section Tolkien wrote a note saying, "alter this. Orcs are not Elvish" (see *MR*, 80). Nonetheless, two paragraphs later the description of the Elvish origin of the Orcs (from *AAm* §45) is included in the narrative.

The version of the origin of the Orcs contained here was actually added to this part of the *Annals* to match the new story that Tolkien developed when editing a later section (*AAm* §127), replacing the old story that the Orcs were created by Melkor out of stone (see *MR*, 78, 123).[2] Ironically, however, Tolkien himself eventually deleted the description of the Orcs being Elvish in origin in that later portion of the *Annals*, and it therefore only appears in this portion of the published text, despite Tolkien's note just two paragraphs earlier indicating that the Orcs were not "Elvish." One cannot really blame Christopher for that, however, because his father never quite figured out exactly what to do about the origin of the Orcs.[3]

There is also one nonchange worth noting in this sixteenth paragraph. In the third sentence the words "this is held true by the wise of Eressëa" are retained; this is one of the only remaining indications in *The Silmarillion* that it represents lore that had been maintained on the Lonely Isle.

With the eighteenth and nineteenth paragraphs ("Manwë sat long . . ." and "Then Manwë said . . ."; *Silm*, 50–51), the primary source turns back from the *Annals* to the "later *Quenta*." There is a notable omission in the nineteenth paragraph. It describes the reluctance of Aulë and others of the Valar to challenge Melkor (see *MR*, 161). I miss the added depth that these types of details add to the story.

Then, in the following paragraph, the main source turns back yet again to the *Annals*. This paragraph includes a curious addition from §6 of *The Grey Annals* (the final version of the *Annals of Beleriand* and the companion to the *Annals of Aman*). This insert, two and a half sentences long, describes how the shape of Middle-earth was changed in the war between the Valar and Melkor after the first appearance of the Elves. In his commentary on the *Ambarkanta* in *The Shaping of Middle-earth* (the most extensive description of the physical nature of Arda that Tolkien wrote), Christopher compares the statement in that work about the changes to Middle-earth caused by this first battle with this very passage in the published *Silmarillion*. He says that the older account does not mention the Great Gulf or the Bay of Balar that are described in the passage in the published text; it speaks "rather of the vast extension of the sea of Ringil and its joining to the

Eastern and Western Seas"), but he notes that those features were shown on the maps that were contemporaneous with the *Ambarkanta* (*SoMe*, 257–58). However, he fails to mention that this passage was taken from a different source than the *Quenta Silmarillion* itself, or even the part of the *Annals of Aman* used as the source for much of this chapter, but rather was added from a portion of *The Grey Annals* that relates to a considerably later place in the tale. This is a good example of how Christopher was careful to trace the development of his father's work leading to the published *Silmarillion*, without acknowledging his own role in shaping the final form of the published text.

Next, two very interesting sentences are omitted from the following paragraph ("But at the last the gates . . ."; *Silm*, 51), which continues from *AAm* §50. This passage describes how Melkor sends a "host of Balrogs" who assail Manwë's standard but are "withered in the wind of his wrath and slain with the lightning of his sword" (see *MR*, 75). The omission regarding the Balrogs is understandable, since the idea of a "host of Balrogs" is inconsistent with Tolkien's stated intention to reduce the number of those spirits of shadow and flame to a total of three to seven (*MR*, 80), but it is a shame to lose this rare image of Manwë's power.

Also in this paragraph there is a small but helpful addition. The words "that Aulë had wrought" regarding the chain Angainor that is used to bind Melkor is inserted from LQ §21. The idea that Aulë wrought the chain Angainor appeared in the original *Book of Lost Tales*, but then does not reappear again until this mention in LQ §21, and is not present in the text of the *Annals* that is the primary source of this paragraph. This is a small item, but as mentioned earlier, this type of detail adds depth to the story.

With the next paragraph, we return again to the "later *Quenta*" as the main text (it is dizzying how much switching back and forth there is in this chapter). This paragraph comes from the latter part of LQ §21, with a couple of small but significant additions from LQ §12, which is part of the mostly unused previous chapter of the "later *Quenta*," "Of Valinor and the Two Trees." Added is a reference to "the fortresses of Angband and Utumno," even though there is no mention of Angband in LQ §21, only Utumno. Also added is a statement the Valar did not find Sauron, Melkor's main lieutenant. These changes come from a late, hastily scribbled footnote to LQ §12 (see *MR*, 156) and are consistent with paragraph 3 (which, as discussed above, also was taken from that source).

Turning to paragraph 24 ("Then again the . . ."; *Silm*, 52) we find the first occasion where Christopher's edits appear to seriously change his father's intentions. This paragraph, which comes directly from LQ §23, describes the Valar's decision to summon the Elves to Valinor. At the end of the last sentence, after stating that many woes that afterward befell came from this summons, Christopher omits the explicit statement that those who claim that the Valar erred in making this summons, and that they were thinking of the happiness of Valinor rather than of the Earth and their own pleasure, "speak with the [tongue] of Melkor" (*MR*, 162).

Christopher's only remark about this in his commentary is that the belief that the Valar erred (but "with good intent")—as is stated in the earlier version of the *Quenta Silmarillion*—"is harshly repudiated" by this statement (*MR*, 168). That Christopher would then remove that "harsh repudiation" is quite surprising. Most readers of *The Silmarillion* do come away with the impression that the Valar erred (but with good intent) in bringing the Elves to Valinor, and it appears from this passage that that was not Tolkien's final intent. Moreover, in the "Myths Transformed" text entitled "Notes on motives in the *Silmarillion*," Tolkien explicitly states, "This appearance of selfish *fainéance* in the Valar in the mythology as told is (though I have not explained it or commented on it) I think only an 'appearance'" (*MR*, 401).

However, a recently released text reveals that, later still, Tolkien seemed to return to his previous stance that the Valar did err. In a document entitled "Words, Phrases and Passages in various tongues in *The Lord of the Rings*" (published in August 2007 in volume 17 of the linguistic journal *Parma Eldalamberon: The Book of Elven-tongues*), the entry on the root PHAN contains an explicit statement that "the invitation given to the Eldar to remove to Valinor and live unendangered by Melkor was not in fact according to the design of Eru. It arose from anxiety, and it might be said from failure in trust of Eru, from anxiety and fear of Melkor" ("Words, Phrases and Passages," 178). It is unclear exactly when this text was written, but it appears from Gilson's comments in the foreword of that work to be in the mid-1960s. In any event, it was clearly written after the first-phase work on the "later *Quenta*" (and mostly likely the "Myths Transformed" text as well), since it was definitely written after *The Lord of the Rings* was published in the mid-1950s. There is no indication as to whether Christopher was aware of the content of this text at the time that he was preparing *The Silmarillion* for publication in 1973–77. Nor does it directly contradict the statement that was omitted from the *Quenta* text. Nonetheless, this does provide a cautionary example of the limitations of comparing the published text with the texts printed in the volumes of *The History of Middle-earth*.

Two paragraphs later ("Then befell the . . ."; *Silm*, 52), the primary source switches yet again, with this paragraph coming entirely from

AAm §57. It has one particularly interesting change and a notable deletion. In referencing the three "kindreds" of the Elves (what would become the Vanyar, Noldor, and Teleri), "Elwë" is changed from "Olwë." It is very strange that here Tolkien refers to "the kindred of Olwë" when several paragraphs earlier Elwë is included among the ambassadors who went to Valinor and later became kings, and several paragraphs later, it is mentioned that the Teleri had two lords, Elwë and Olwë. I can see why the editors felt the need to make this change. Less easily explicable is that there are several sentences explaining why some of the Elves refused the summons and referring to the lies of Melkor about Oromë and Nahar (see *MR*, 81–82) that were omitted from this paragraph.

There is a change of note in the thirty-first paragraph ("It is told . . ."; *Silm*, 53), regarding the continued confusion about the geographic features of Middle-earth. The phrase "and passing northward about the Sea of Helcar they turned towards the west" is changed from "and passed by the Sea of Helkar ere they went somewhat westward" (see *MR*, 82). This in turn was an emendation by Tolkien from "went north until Helkar was passed and then northwest" (*MR*, 87). So Christopher did not quite return it to the original reading, but he moved it back in that direction.

Two paragraphs later there is another small but interesting change. In the discussion of how the Nandor became a people apart, in the statement that says their leader, Denethor, turned west, the name of his father is changed from Dân to Lenwë. Denethor's father is Dân (or Nano) in both the *Annals of Aman* and the "later *Quenta*," so where did the name "Lenwë" come from? The answer is, from the essay *Quendi and Eldar* published in *The War of the Jewels*. Christopher confirms in a footnote to that essay that Lenwë replaced the "long-standing name Dân of Denethor's father" and that the form used in the published text was taken from that essay (*WotJ*, 418–19 n. 16).

The final two paragraphs have a number of additions from *The Grey Annals* and one that goes back to an earlier section in the *Annals of Aman*. The names "Ered Luin" and "the Blue Mountains" do not appear in the *Annals of Aman* or the portion of the "later *Quenta*" published in *Morgoth's Ring*, but they do appear in the *Grey Annals*, the later sections of the "later *Quenta*," and the essay *Quendi and Eldar* (all printed in *The War of the Jewels*), with the first appearance in *GA* §2 (with the spelling "Eryd Luin"). Several other phrases in the penultimate paragraph, and most of the last two sentences of the last paragraph, are also added from *The Grey Annals* (see table 4).

And that concludes chapter 3. This is certainly one of the most convoluted chapters in the whole book.[4]

Chapter 4 "Of Thingol and Melian"

LITTLE NEED BE SAID ABOUT THIS SHORT (FOUR-PARAGRAPH) CHAPTER.
It is the first that is taken almost entirely from the equivalent chapter
in the "later *Quenta*" (with the same title and chapter number), though
there are several additions from the *Annals of Aman* (and one change
that is based on the *Annals*) and a deletion at the very beginning.
There are also some additions based on *The Grey Annals*. As there are
throughout the book, there are a multitude of small edits in this chapter, but none worth discussing at length. The source materials are
traced by paragraph in table 5.

Table 5. Source Material by Paragraph for Chapter 4 *Of Thingol and Melian*.

Paragraph no.	Paragraph headwords	*Silm* page no.	Primary source	Secondary sources
1	"Melian was a . . ."	55	second paragraph of LQ §31 (the one-sentence first paragraph was not used)	*GA* §3: "and in that time when the Quendi awoke beside the waters of Cuiviénen she departed from Valinor and came to the Hither Lands" based on "In this same time the Quendi awoke by Kuiviénen" (the idea that Melian left Valinor for Middle-earth at the time when the Quendi awoke comes from *AAm* §40)
2	"Now when their . . ."	55	First paragraph of LQ §32	*AAm* §64: "people of the Teleri rested long in East Beleriand, beyond the River Gelion" *GA* §9: "at that time many of the Noldor still lay to the westward, in those forests that were afterwards named Neldoreth and Region. Elwë, lore of the Teleri, went often through the great woods to seek out Finwë his friend in the dwellings of the Noldor"
3	"She spoke no . . ."	55	LQ §32	
4	"Thus Elwë's folk . . ."	55–56	LQ §33	*AAm* §74: "he became a king renowned and his people were all the Eldar of Beleriand; the Sindar they were named, the Grey-elves, the Elves of the Twilight, and King Greymantle was he, Elu Thingol in the tongue of that land" and the final sentence, beginning "And of the love of"

Note: Chapter 4 of the "later *Quenta*" is given in *MR*, 171–173, and the relevant sections are LQ §§31–33. The three section from the *Annals of Aman* that are used are *AAm* §§40, 64 and 74, which can be found in *MR*, 72, 83 and 86. The sections used from *The Grey Annals* are *GA* §§3 and 9, which appear in *Wolf*, 5–7.

Chapter 5 "Of Eldamar and the Princes of the Eldalië"

THIS CHAPTER TAKES ITS TITLE FROM THE EQUIVALENT CHAPTER IN THE "later *Quenta*," but a significant portion of it comes from the corresponding section of the *Annals of Aman*. Again the source material tends to switch back and forth between passages from the two primary sources, though it is not as convoluted as chapter 3. There are also a few inserts from the *Grey Annals* and other later works. There are again many small editorial changes that I pass over without comment here, but will discuss generally in the final chapter. The source materials are traced by paragraph in Table 6.

The first change of note in this chapter appears in the third paragraph ("But the Teleri. . ."; *Silm,* 57–58). This paragraph describes how the Teleri, the third and largest of the three kindreds of the Eldar, lingered on the coasts of Middle-earth and were befriended by Ossë and his spouse, Uinen. These were the Maiar who were the chief vassals of Ulmo. In the published text it states that Ossë instructed the Teleri and that they learned much from him of sea-lore and sea-music; this is based on an insert from LQ §36 (*MR,* 175). However, in the main source text for this chapter, *AAm* §66 (*MR,* 84), it is both Ossë and Uinen who taught the Teleri sea-lore and sea-music, not just Ossë. This small but significant change is the first of a number of occasions in which it appears that the roles of female characters are systematically lessened.

There is an interesting name change in paragraph 8 ("To these the . . ."; *Silm,* 59) of the name meaning "Pass of Light." The change from "Kalakiryan" to "Calacirya" is quite curious for two reasons. First, the spellings with no *n* at the end, such as "Kalakirya" (and before that, "Kalakilya"), were earlier forms that were replaced by the spelling with the *n* (see *MR,* 87 n. 7, 89, 102 n. 13, 180, 197). Second, although in one typescript of this chapter Tolkien emended "Kalakiryan" to "Calakiryan," in subsequent texts the name was consistently written with a *K,* including in the late essay *Quendi and Eldar* from which many of the final forms of names came (*WotJ,* 402). I suppose that Christopher wanted to keep this consistent with the other names written with a *C*

Table 6. Source Material by Paragraph for Chapter 5 "Of Eldamar and the Princes of the Eldalië."

Paragraph no.	Paragraph headwords	*Silm* page no.	Primary source	Secondary sources
1	"In time the hosts . . ."	57	LQ §34	AAm §63: "the Vanyar and the Noldor"
2	"Now Ulmo, by the . . ."	57	AAm §66	LQ §35: "who waited there, gazing on the dark waves," "anchored it," and "into which Sirion poured his waters"
				LQ §36: "the long shores beneath the Mountains of Aman; and they entered Valinor and were welcomed to its bliss" and "But the eastern horn of the island" (taken from a footnote)
				GA §11: final sentence from ". . . which was deed ground" to the end
3	"But the Teleri . . ."	57–58	AAm §66	LQ §36: "Long they remained by the coasts of the western sea" and "and Ossë instructed them, sitting upon a rock near to the margin of the land"
4	"When many years . . ."	58	AAm §70	GA §13: "the Noldor and of Finwë their king, who grieved at their long sundering from the Teleri and besought him to bring them to Aman," "to the coasts of Beleriand," and "his domain"
				LQ §36: "but great was the grief of Ossë when Ulmo returned to the coasts of Beleriand, to bear them away to Valinor" and "the Elves of the Falas"
				Quendi and Eldar (see *WotJ*, 378): "Falathrim"

(*continued*)

Table 6. Continued

Paragraph no.	Paragraph headwords	*Silm* page no.	Primary source	Secondary sources
5	"The kinsfolk and . . ."	58	AAm §71	GA §15: "remained in the Hither Lands, seeking him yet, though they would fain have departed to Valinor and the Light of the Trees, if Ulmo and Olwë had been willing to tarry longer" and the last sentence, except: *Quendi and Eldar* (*WotJ*, 379): "the desire of Aman" LQ §36: "at last the main host of the Teleri embarked on the isle, and Ulmo drew them far away"
6	"But when Elwë . . ."	58	GA §16	AAm §74: "and a high doom was before him" LQ §38: "Elvenhome"
7	"Now Ossë followed . . ."	58–59	AAm §§72 and 73	LQ §37: "But the island was not moved again, and stood there alone in the Bay of Eldamar; and it was called Tol Eressëa, the Lonely Isle" and "[by] that long sojourn apart in the Lonely Isle was caused the sundering of their speech from that of the Vanyar and the Noldor"
8	"To these the . . ."	59	LQ §38	AAm §72: "the dark waves to silver and gold"
9	"Upon the crown . . ."	59	LQ §39	LQ §16 (*MR*, 155): "Galathilion it was named in the Sindarin tongue" Footnote to LQ §17 (*MR*, 157): "Celeborn" and "Nimloth"
10	"Manwë and Varda . . ."	59–60	LQ §40	AAm §79: "and he and his people came often among them," "and in many things they soon

11	"The Noldor afterwards . . ."	60	LQ §41	surpassed their teachers" and the end of the paragraph from "for they had great love of words . . ." except:
12	"Finwë was King . . ."	60	LQ §41	"Lost" addition to the old QS typescript of §40 (see MR, 181): "And it came to pass that," "hills," and "and brought them forth in countless myriads"
13	"Fëanor was the . . ."	60	LQ §41	
14	"The seven sons . . ."	60	LQ §41	Editorial addition: "but the mother of Fëanor was Míriel Serindë, whereas the mother of Fingolfin and Finarfin was Indis of the Vanyar"
15	"The sons of . . ."	60–61	LQ §42	
16	"The sons of . . ."	61	LQ §42	Maeglin (WotJ, 317–18): "Aredhel" and "Ar-Feiniel"
17	"Here must be . . ."	61	LQ §43	"Lost" emendation that was made to the "earlier Quenta" (see MR, 183): the sentence beginning with "Therefore Ulmo" and ending with "strong-winged swans"
18	"There they dwelt . . ."	61	LQ §44	AAm §75: the last sentence
19	"As the ages . . ."	61–62	LQ §45	
20	"Fëanor and his . . ."	62	LQ §45	

Note: Chapter 5 of the "later *Quenta*" is given in *MR*, 173–84, and contains LQ §§34–45. The sections of the *Annals of Aman* used in this chapter are AAm §§63, 66, 70–75, and 79, which appear in *MR*, 83–86 and 92. The inserts from the *Grey Annals* come from *GA* §§11–16, which can be found in *WotJ*, 7–9. The other source materials are detailed where they are found.

instead of a *K*, but I cannot imagine why he would have removed the *n* at the end, and it is not explained in any of the *HoMe* texts. Perhaps, however, this change is explained in one of the many primarily linguistic texts that Tolkien wrote that were not included in the *HoMe* volumes.

It is also interesting that in the next paragraph, which describes the city Túna that the Vanyar and Noldor built, there are a few inserted names from a much earlier section in the "later *Quenta*." "Galathilion it was named in the Sindarin tongue" is an insertion based on LQ §16, where, however, the reference is to Telperion itself, not the Tree of Túna as it is used here. The names of the white Trees of Tol Eressëa ("Celeborn") and Númenor ("Nimloth") come from a footnote to LQ §17, in which "Celeborn" and "Nimloth" are also identified as alternate names for Telperion itself, and the name of the Tree in Tirion is described as "Galathilion the Less," implying that it was another name for Telperion (see *MR*, 155 and 157).

Then the following paragraph has a small but particularly unfortunate change. This paragraph describes which of the Valar each kindred of the Elves were associated with. After stating that the Noldor were beloved by Aulë, the "later *Quenta*" text that is the primary source for this paragraph added that they were also beloved by "Mandos the wise" (see *MR*, 176). This statement was replaced in the published text with a phrase from the *Annals* stating merely that Aulë and his people often came among the Noldor. The removal of the idea that the Noldor were beloved by Mandos is particularly disappointing, given the later events in which "the Doom of Mandos" is imposed on most of the Noldor after they follow Fëanor into exile, and becomes such an important element of the plot. It is unfortunate that this change was made, because this detail of the Noldor being beloved by Mandos adds an additional layer of significance to the later events. This is another occasion where it would be particularly helpful for Christopher to explain the reason for his editorial decision.

The next four paragraphs are all taken from LQ §41, which consists of one long paragraph that in the published text is broken into four paragraphs. But the second of those four paragraphs ("Finwë was King . . ."; *Silm*, 60) partly consists of an editorial addition. The statement that Finwë's sons were Fëanor, Fingolfin, and Finarfin comes from LQ §41, but the rest of that sentence, stating the name of the mother of each of those sons, was added in based on later events, since the history of Finwë's marriages was not yet set when this was written (as will be seen later).

The spelling of the name "Finarfin" is a curious matter. It is unclear to me at what point "Finarfin" replaced "Finarphin." In his commentary to LQ §41, Christopher states that as late as 1966, when the second edition of *The Lord of the Rings* was released, Galadriel was described as being of the royal house of Finarphin (*MR*, 181). This implies that the change from Finarphin to Finarfin was made some-time after 1966. However, in a footnote to the fourth version of the story of Finwë and Míriel (which Christopher dates as no later than the late 1950s; see *MR*, 199, 300) we see Tolkien already emending "Finarphin" to "Finarfin" (see *MR*, 262), whereas Christopher notes in his commentary that in the third version of that story not only is "Finarphin" so spelled, but his older brother's name is spelled "Fingolphin"! (See *MR*, 265.) There are numerous other instances of both spellings in texts dated from the late 1950s, including the *Quenta, Athrabeth Finrod Ah Andreth* (the *Athrabeth*), and the essay *Quendi and Eldar* (see *MR*, 276, 278, 304, 305, 311, 350; and *WotJ*, 179, 246, 383).

We find something of a way out of this tangled morass in Christopher's commentary to what became Chapter 7 "Of the Silmarils and the Unrest of the Noldor." He states that while "Finarphin" was spelled thus in the second edition of *The Lord of the Rings*, it was later changed on his suggestion to "Finarfin" (*MR*, 282). So apparently we have Christopher himself to thank for the final resolution of this confusion.

In the fifteenth paragraph ("The sons of . . ."; *Silm*, 60–61), which discusses the children of Fingolfin, the names of his daughter—Aredhel and Ar-Feiniel—come from the late work (around 1970) on Maeglin's story that is discussed in the short section in *The War of the Jewels* called *Maeglin*. There were two late versions of this work, which Christopher labels as B(i) and B(ii). Christopher notes that in some places his father changed the name Isfin to Areðel (Noble-elf), in other places he noted that it should be changed to Feiniel (White Lady), and in one place to Ar-Feiniel. Christopher concedes that there was no textual basis for his decision to combine them in the published text as "Aredhel Ar Feiniel," since they are actually competing names, and the final evidence seems to suggest that his father's final choice was Areðel (Aredhel) (*WotJ*, 317–18).

The description of Aredhel as "tall and strong" is changed from "she was greater and stronger than woman's wont." Perhaps this description was changed because it was too similar to the description of Galadriel in *The Fellowship of the Ring*, which says her voice "was deeper than woman's wont" (*LOTR*, 355).

The next paragraph, dealing with the children of Finarfin, is notable partly for the curious matter of the disappearing Orodreth. But perhaps more significantly, it also has a small edit that diminishes one of Tolkien's most beloved female characters.

In the first sentence of the paragraph, which refers to the sons of Finarfin, Tolkien had struck out the words "and Orodreth" and changed "four" to "three," indicating that he no longer considered Orodreth one of Finarfin's sons. There is an explanation of this in note 20 to "The History of Galadriel and Celeborn" in *Unfinished Tales*, where Christopher notes that his father had for some reason moved Orodreth back a generation in the same family. Christopher adds that this change was "never incorporated in the narratives of *The Silmarillion*" (*UT*, 255). However, we see here that this change was actually incorporated in one place in the narratives of "The Silmarillion," though it was not taken up in the published text. There is also one place in *AAm* §135 (when the Noldor are debating leaving Valinor) where Tolkien makes a marginal note "Names and relations now altered" and Orodreth's name was marked with an *X* (*MR*, 128). Also, in the *Shibboleth of Fëanor* section of *The Peoples of Middle-earth*, there is a text entitled "The parentage of Gil-galad" that expands further on Tolkien's thoughts on this matter. In this text, Christopher points out that his father first intended to make Orodreth Finrod Felagund's son, rather than his brother, but then decided that Orodreth should be Finrod's nephew, the son of Finrod's brother Angrod (see *PoMe*, 349–50).

It is difficult to question Christopher's decision not to attempt to incorporate these proposed changes in the narrative, given how uncertain this element of the genealogy was. However, there is a change that he made to this paragraph that is less explicable. In the source text (LQ §42), Finarfin's daughter Galadriel is described as "the most valiant" of the house of Finwë, as well as the most beautiful. For some unexplained reason, Christopher removed that description. Thus, even Galadriel, perhaps Tolkien's greatest female character (with the possible exception of Lúthien), is somewhat diminished by Christopher's edits to the text. I find this quite remarkable. Even in the unlikely event that this omission reflects some other text that was not printed in *HoMe*, it seems quite odd that Christopher would choose to omit such an unambiguous statement of her standing, particularly without any explanation.

In the next paragraph, the sentence describing how Ulmo sent Ossë to the Teleri to teach them the craft of shipbuilding comes from a "lost" emendation that was made to the "earlier *Quenta*" but not taken up in the "later *Quenta*," which has the alternative story that it was Ulmo himself who taught the Teleri the craft of shipbuilding (see *MR*, 178, 183). This provides a good example of the complex process that was used to create the published text, in which Christopher had to choose between different versions of the same story.

And that concludes chapter 5. Things begin to get more complicated from here, as material from the "second phase" of Tolkien's work on the "later *Quenta*" comes into play.

Chapter 6 "Of Fëanor and the Unchaining of Melkor"

As Christopher points out, the new "second phase" saw his father moving in the direction of a "much fuller mode of narrative" that would expand *The Silmarillion* back toward the level of detail in the original *Book of Lost Tales* (*MR*, 142). Unfortunately, much of this "reexpansion" is not reflected in the published *Silmarillion*. Indeed, as I indicated earlier, perhaps my largest complaint concerning Christopher's work on this project is that he did not include the expanded story of Finwë and Míriel, as was his father's clear intent.

One possible explanation for this is that Christopher felt that incorporating the "fuller mode of narrative" here would have contrasted too sharply with material that came before, which is not presented as fully. However, *The Silmarillion* as it is currently constituted is full of such contrasts. This is particularly evident with the stories of Beren and Lúthien and Túrin Turambar, which are much more fully treated than anything around them. Another argument against including this material is that it veers into philosophical speculation, rather than strictly advancing the plot. However, this is an important part of Tolkien's work, and should not be shied away from. *The Silmarillion* is no simple fantasy novel; it reflects the lifework of one of the most important thinkers of the twentieth century. These omissions have prevented a more complete appreciation and understanding of Tolkien's work and his thought on the nature of pride, love, and, most of all, death.

Tracing the source material for this chapter is complicated. Much of the chapter comes from the "second-phase" text that Christopher labels "FM" 4 (for "Finwë and Míriel 4"), which was the fourth and final version of the story of Finwë and Míriel that Tolkien wrote, but most of that text (and all the associated work in *Laws and Customs among the Eldar*), which represents the bulk of the expanded story of Finwë and Míriel, is omitted. This text was part of a chapter entitled "Of the Silmarils and the Darkening of Valinor" and had a subheading of "Of Finwë and Míriel" (*MR*, 256). There were then a series of other subheadings, which Tolkien decided to change into separate chapters (see *MR*, 299). All of these new chapters correspond to the chapters in the published *Silmarillion*, except that the separate chapter entitled "Of Finwë and Míriel" was not included.

In addition to the fourth version of Finwë and Míriel's story, some of the language in this chapter is taken from the essay *Laws and Customs among the Eldar*, and some comes from the first version of Finwë and Míriel's story. There are also portions that come from the "first-phase" version of chapter 6 in the "later *Quenta*," and some from the second-phase revisions of that chapter. Most of those second-phase revisions come from a "subchapter" that supplied the name of this chapter, "Of Fëanor and the Unchaining of Melkor." However, two paragraphs that are used at the end of this chapter actually are taken from the next sub-chapter, "Of the Silmarils and the Unrest of the Noldor." Finally, at the end of the chapter there are also a couple of inserts from the *Annals of Aman*. The source materials are traced by paragraph in table 7.

FM 4 provides the primary source for the first six paragraphs of the chapter. However, the third paragraph ("Míriel was the . . ."; *Silm*, 63) has one of the most complex textual histories in the whole book. The paragraph comes mostly from FM 4 §4, but with some language from no less than five additional sources: FM 4 §§3 and 8, LQ §46b, L&C A, and FM 1. I describe the sources of this paragraph in full to give another example of how complex the process sometimes could be.

The first phrase of the first sentence, "Míriel was the name of his mother," comes from both FM 4 §3 and LQ §46b, but the next phrase, "who was called Serindë, because of her surpassing skill in weaving and needlework" comes from L&C A (see *MR*, 236). The last phrase of the sentence, "for her hands were more skilled to fineness than any hands even among the Noldor," comes mainly from LQ §46b. However, the first word "for" comes from FM 4 §3, replacing "but," and "among" is also inserted from FM 4 §3, replacing "of" (the language in FM 4 §3 is "For her hands were more skilled to make things fine and delicate than any other hands even among the Noldor"). The next sentence and a half, beginning with "The love of" and continuing through "spirit and body," comes from FM 4 §4 (with "Míriel" coming from similar language appearing in L&C A, replacing "she"), but the next phrase, "and after his birth she yearned for release from the labour of living," comes from FM 1 (see *MR*, 206), with "release" changed from "rest" (the phrase "release from the labour of living" actually appears in FM 4 §8, which has "she yearned not only for sleep and rest but release from the labour of living"). This phrase replaces

Table 7. Source Material by Paragraph for Chapter 6 "Of Fëanor and the Unchaining of Melkor"

Paragraph no.	Paragraph headwords	*Silm* page no.	Primary source	Secondary sources
1	"Now the Three . . ."	63	FM 4 §1	FM 4 §2: second sentence
2	"In that time . . ."	63	LQ §46b (first phase)	FM 4 §3 and LQ §46b: "Miriel was the name of his mother" and "her hands were more skilled to fineness than any hands even among the Noldor" (see text)
3	"Miriel was the . . ."	63	FM 4 §4	L&C A (*MR*, 236): "who was called Serindë, because of her surpassing skill in weaving and needlework"
				FM 1 (see *MR*, 206): "and after his birth she yearned for"
				FM 4 §8: "release from the labour of living"
4	"Then Finwë was . . ."	63–64	FM 4 §§5 and 6 (which closely tracks the language in L&C A)	
5	"It is indeed . . ."	64	FM 4 §7 (which duplicates language in L&C A exactly)	
6	"She went then . . ."	64	FM 4 §§8 and 9	L&C A (*MR*, 236): "and passed in silence to the halls of Mandos"
7	"All his love . . ."	64	LQ §46c (first phase)	FM 4 §9: "All his love he gave thereafter to his son"
				LQ §46c (second phase): "and his dark hair raven-dark" (and perhaps "his eyes piercingly bright")

(continued)

Table 7. Continued

Paragraph no.	Paragraph headwords	Silm page no.	Primary source	Secondary sources
8	"While still in . . ."	64	LQ §46c (second phase)	FM 4 §22: "in the pursuit of all his purposes eager and steadfast" and "Few ever changed his counsel, none by force"
9	"Now it came . . ."	64–65	FM 4 §23, and the latter part of FM 4 §27	
10	"The wedding of . . ."	65	FM 4 §28	FM 2 (MR, 265): "for the sorrow and the strife in the house of Finwë is graven in the memory of the Noldorin Elves"
11	"Now even while . . ."	65	LQ §47 (second phase)	LQ §46c (second phase): the first sentence
12	"Before the gates . . ."	65	LQ §48 (second phase)	LQ §48 (first phase): "And Nienna aided his prayer; but Mandos was silent."
13	"Then Manwë granted . . ."	65–66	LQ §48 (second phase)	LQ §48 (first phase): "in a while," "he was given leave," and "and it seemed to Manwë" through "even as he" AAm §88: "he saw not to the depths of Melkor's heart"
14	"Now in his heart . . ."	66	LQ §§49 and 49a (second phase)	AAm §91: first two sentences AAm §92: "and had been instructed by him in the greatest of all his works; but he lied in his lust and envy" LQ §49a (first phase): "who first named him Morgoth"

Note: The fourth version of "Finwë and Míriel" is given in *MR*, 256–63 (with notes and commentary following) and is numbered FM 4 §§1–28. The passages taken from the essay *The Laws and Customs among the Eldar* come from the part of the manuscript that Christopher labels as "A" (which I abbreviate as "L&C A"), given in *MR*, 233–52. The first version of Finwë and Míriel's tale ("FM 1") can be found in *MR*, 205–7. There is also one passage that is taken from the second version of the tale, labeled "FM 2." The portion of Chapter 6, "Of the Silmarils and the Darkening of Valinor," from the first phase of the "later *Quenta*" that is used in this chapter is LQ §§46–49a is given in *MR*, 184–86, and the relevant second phase revisions to those sections can be found in *MR*, 272–74. Finally, the inserts from the *Annals of Aman* are from A*Am* §§88, 91, and 92 (*MR*, 93–94).

the phrase from FM 4 §4, "so that almost all strength seemed to have passed from her" (*MR*, 257).

In the fifth paragraph ("It is indeed . . ."; *Silm*, 64), in which Míriel responds to Finwë's grief at her exhaustion following the birth of Fëanor, there are two edits that are notable partly for their amusement value. In the first sentence, "It is indeed unhappy" is changed from "Unhappy it is indeed." Then "Rest now I must. Farewell, dear lord!" is omitted at the end of Míriel's statement. It appears that, as written by Tolkien, Míriel in her failing days spoke very much like Yoda from *Star Wars*. Actually, this type of archaic language is common in Tolkien's work. In an unsent draft of a letter to his friend Hugh Brogan dated September 1955, he defended his use of an archaic narrative style in *The Lord of the Rings*, including the use of the similar "backwards" construction "Helms too they chose" (see *Letters*, 225–26). As discussed in the final chapter, Christopher greatly reduced the use of archaic language in the published *Silmarillion*.

The beginning of the seventh paragraph ("All his love . . ."; *Silm*, 64) continues from FM 4 §9, but the rest of the paragraph comes from LQ §46c. The phrases describing Fëanor as having "piercingly bright" eyes and "raven-dark" hair and saying that he was "in the pursuit of all his purposes eager and steadfast" were added in. Yet Christopher says that the only difference between the original text and the second-phase text is that "Fëanor's hair is said to have been 'raven-dark'" (*MR*, 272). I have not been able to locate a source for the statement that his eyes were "piercingly bright," but I suspect that it might have been part of the same emendation with the "raven-black" hair that Christopher neglected to mention. The statement "in the pursuit of all his purposes eager and steadfast" is added from FM 4 §22, in which it is stated that "he pursued all his purposes both eagerly and steadfastly." However, this statement is somewhat contradicted in *The Shibboleth of Fëanor*, which states, "opposition to his will he met not with the quiet steadfastness of his mother but with fierce resentment. He was restless in mind and body, though like Míriel he could become wholly absorbed in works of the finest skill of hand; but he left many things unfinished" (*PoMe*, 333).

The following paragraph, which describes Fëanor's marriage, comes from a second-phase addition Tolkien made at the end of LQ §46c (see *MR*, 272–73). However, significant portions of this material are omitted, with the result of significantly lessening the character development of Fëanor and even more of his wife, Nerdanel.

The first omission consists of three sentences describing Nerdanel. In this omitted passage, it is noted that many were surprised at the union of Fëanor and Nerdanel, because she "was not among the fairest of her people." She is described instead as "strong, and free of mind, and filled with the desire of knowledge." It is further noted that she and Fëanor had met because, like him, she loved to wander by the sea and in the mountains, and that they were companions on many journeys. Another omitted sentence describes how Nerdanel would observe people by "listening to their words, and watching their gestures and the movements of their faces" (*MR*, 272).

These details regarding Fëanor and Nerdanel's relationship and her character are important, showing that Fëanor was not one to be influenced by surface charms; they give more depth to their relationship by showing how they met and what he saw in her. It is just the kind of character development that would have greatly added to the story. Nerdanel's character, in particular, would have been much more developed had this material not been deleted.

The statement that Fëanor learned much from his father-in-law, Mahtan,[1] about the making of things in metal and in stone is a complete deviation from the source material. In LQ §46c, it is *Nerdanel* who is described as learning much from her father about the making of things in metal and in stone, and it goes on to describe the images of the Valar and of others of the Eldar that she had made. They were so lifelike that their friends would speak to them. The passage also speaks of other wonderful things that she made "of her own thought in shapes strong and strange but beautiful" (*MR*, 272).

This change may have been made to match the passage later in the narrative where it is indicated that when Fëanor started making weapons, Mahtan rued the day that he had taught Fëanor the metalwork that Mahtan himself had learned from Aulë. However, I think it is an important detail that he taught these crafts to Nerdanel as well, and that it is unfortunate that Christopher changed the clear meaning of this passage. This is one of the most blatant examples of how Christopher's changes appear to weaken an important female character.

The next paragraph ("Now it came . . ."; *Silm*, 64–65) resumes from part of FM 4 §23 and the latter part of FM 4 §27. But omitted completely are §§10–22, which describe Finwë's plea to Manwë and then the Valar's discussion about what to do about his and Míriel's situation,[2] and part of §23 through the first half of §27, which deal with how Finwë and Indis came to be together (see *MR*, 258–62).

These extensive deletions are very unfortunate. The omitted material in §§10–22 not only greatly fleshes out the character of Míriel and her pride and stubbornness, as well as the nature of love and marriage among the Elves, but also introduces the critical concept of Melkor's "marring" of Arda and how death first entered into the world as a result of that marring. It contains one of the only clear illus-

The spirit of Míriel appearing before Mandos and Manwë, and taking a last look at Finwë. By Anushka Mouriño. Courtesy of the artist.

trations of the working of the Valar and their governance of Arda, and provides a good example of the interplay between fate and free will (it was ultimately Míriel's own choice not to return to the living, but Mandos points out to her that this "doom" that she takes upon herself will eventually become grievous not just to her, but to many others). Moreover, had these paragraphs been included, it would have been easier to justify the inclusion of the even more extensive exploration of this material contained in the essay *Laws and Customs among the Eldar* as an appendix.

I cannot accept the argument that including this material would have contrasted too sharply with the surrounding chapters in the level of detail. As stated above, *The Silmarillion* is already full of such contrasts, both before and after this chapter, and including this material would not have significantly increased that. As it stands now, this chapter at fourteen paragraphs and less than four printed pages is one of the shortest in the book. Had the full tale of Finwë and Míriel been included, this chapter still would not have been as long as some of the other chapters in the early part of the book, nor would it have been significantly more detailed than, say, the third chapter, "Of the Coming of the Elves."

Perhaps Christopher felt that these philosophical concepts were too complex to include. If so, he was both underestimating the audience and doing a disservice to his father's legacy. Twentieth-century literature is full of works that include significant philosophical diversions.[3] While it is true that this material is now available in *Morgoth's Ring* for those willing to wade through the dense scholarly commentary included in volumes of *The History of Middle-earth,* it was clearly meant by Tolkien to be part of *The Silmarillion,* and the omission of the bulk of Míriel's story makes it a lesser work.

The omissions from part of §23 through the first half of §27 are also unfortunate. The omission of the description of Indis as "exceedingly swift of foot" from §23 is another small example of the physical lessening of one of the female characters. Also removed from §23 is a description of the ways Indis was unlike Míriel. This is another detail that, in my opinion, should not have been omitted.

The omitted sections 24–26 tell of how Indis had long loved Finwë, of her own sadness, and how the two of them met and healed each other after Indis's brother Ingwë invited Finwë to spend some time in the full Light of the Trees. The portion of FM 4 §27 that was not used in the published text describes the wedding of Finwë and Indis, and the rejoicing of the Vanyar and the Noldor. It is a moving story, on a par with such tales as the meeting of Thingol and Melian, or Beren and Lúthien, and it should have been included.

Also removed is this warning: "In Indis was first proved true the saying: The loss of one may be the gain of another; but this saying also she found true: The house remembers the builder, though others may dwell in it after" (*MR*, 262). This is a particularly discerning observation, and it is shame that it was not included in the published text.

Finally, a reference to the "five children" of Indis and Finwë is removed. A footnote lists three daughters in addition to the sons Fingolfin and Finarfin (whose names are actually spelled that way): Findis, Finvain, and Faniel.[4] However, there is no mention of any of these daughters anywhere in the published *Silmarillion* (even in the genealogical table in the back). This is another small detail that shows how Christopher lessened the female presence in the tale.

The tenth paragraph ("The wedding of . . ."; *Silm*, 65) is the last taken from FM 4, with one phrase ("for the sorrow and the strife in the house of Finwë is graven in the memory of the Noldorin Elves") inserted from FM 2 (but very closely based upon L&C A; see *MR*, 239, 265 n. 11). The final four paragraphs are taken mainly from LQ §§46c–49a, mostly (but not entirely) as revised in the second phase.

We then find a curious and unfortunate example of older material replacing the newer version. Both the twelfth and thirteenth paragraphs ("Before the gates . . ." and "Then Manwë granted . . ."; *Silm*, 65–66) are taken from LQ §48, partly as emended in the second phase and partly as originally written in the first phase. The passage in which Manwë is shown to have been duped into believing that Melkor was cured because he did not comprehend Melkor's evil was taken from the older version, replacing a much longer, emended passage. The emended passage acknowledged that Melkor's evil was beyond full healing, but pointed out that since he was originally the greatest of the powers, his aid would, if he willingly gave it, do more than anything to heal the hurts he had caused. It goes on to state that Manwë judged that this was the path that Melkor was on, that he was treated fairly, and that Manwë was slow to perceive jealousy and rancor, since he himself did not experience these things (see *MR*, 273). Had the emended portion that was not used in the published version been taken up, things would have been a little clearer, and Manwë would not come across to many readers as being quite such a naive simpleton in his dealings with Melkor.

In a final twist, the first two sentences of the last paragraph come from *AAm* §91. The rest of the paragraph comes from part of the second-phase versions of LQ §§49 and 49a, which are actually the beginning of the next "subchapter" of the "later *Quenta*," "Of the Silmarils and the Unrest of the Noldor," except for another addition from *AAm*

§92 and one from the first-phase version of LQ §49a. It is curious that Christopher would chose to break the chapter at a different place than where his father designated. But we will see this type of thing occur several times again.

And that concludes chapter 6. Christopher's decisions to omit the bulk of the material on Finwë and Míriel and not include it as a separate chapter, as Tolkien clearly intended, and to remove other significant material regarding Nerdanel and Indis are very disappointing.

Chapter 7 "Of the Silmarils
and the Unrest of the Noldor"

As DISCUSSED ABOVE, THE CHAPTER ENTITLED "OF THE SILMARILS AND the Darkening of Valinor" in the second-phase version of the "later *Quenta*" was divided into subchapters (which Tolkien later indicated should become separate chapters). Most of this chapter comes from the second-phase subchapter that has the same title as this chapter. However, in one place the wording still comes from the earlier, first-phase version, and some of the language comes from the *Annals of Aman.* And of course, as already has been stated, the first paragraphs of the subchapter were already used in the previous chapter, and similarly the first two paragraphs of the next subchapter, "Of the Darkening of Valinor," are moved to the end of this chapter. The source materials are traced by paragraph in table 8.

In the first paragraph (*Silm*, 67), which describes the creation of the Silmarils and is taken from the second-phase version of the first paragraph of LQ §49b, the text reverts in part to the older version. In the first sentence, a phrase stating that the Silmarils were created "before Melkor was given his freedom within the land of Aman" was added in the second-phase revision (*MR*, 274), but is omitted from the published text so that the sentence matches the older text. This is not a major issue, but it is a good example of how Christopher sometimes appears to have ignored his father's explicit wishes.

The sixth paragraph ("In those days . . ."; *Silm*, 68) has a "tiny" change that is actually of great interest. In discussing how Melkor corrupted the Noldor by telling them about Mortal Man, and whispering that the Valar were holding the Elves captive in Valinor so that the Men could supplant them, it is mentioned that Melkor actually knew little of Men, because he paid small heed to the Third Theme of Ilúvatar. However, LQ §50 actually has "Second Theme," not "Third Theme." In his commentary, Christopher notes that in the *Ainulindalë* it is stated that the Children of Ilúvatar "came with the Third Theme" and that Manwë "was the chief instrument of the second Theme that Ilúvatar had raised up against the discord of Melkor" (see *MR*, 282). However, we see in author's note 1 to the commentary of

Table 8. Source Material by Paragraph for Chapter 7 "Of the Silmarils and the Unrest of the Noldor"

Paragraph no.	Paragraph headwords	*Silm* page no.	Primary source	Secondary sources
1	"In that time . . ."	67	First paragraph of LQ §49b	
2	"As three great . . ."	67	AA*m* §93	LQ §49b: "within the Kingdom of Arda," "darkness of the deepest treasury" and "marvellous"
3	"All who dwelt . . ."	67	AA*m* §94	LQ §49b: from "and Mandos foretold" to the end (except that "might touch" is taken from AA*m* §94)
4	"Then Melkor lusted . . ."	67–68	End of AA*m* §94 and AA*m* §95	First paragraph of LQ §50: "From that time forth, inflamed by this desire" and "and nothing of his malice could yet be seen in the semblance that he wore"
				Second paragraph of LQ §50: "and his lies passed" to the end of the paragraph (but "bitterly did the Noldor atone" is taken from the first-phase version)
5	"When he saw . . ."	68	Third paragraph of LQ §50	AA*m* §96: "defrauding the Elves of the inheritance of Ilúvatar"
6	"In those days . . ."	68	Fourth paragraph of LQ §50	LQ §50 (first phase): "kingdoms of Middle-earth" and "Small truth was there in this"
7	"Thus ere the . . ."	68–69	LQ §51	
8	"High princes were . . ."	69	LQ §52	AA*m* 98: "committed"

9	"And when Melkor . . ."	69	LQ §52b	LQ §52a: "And when Melkor saw that these lies were smouldering" AAm §97: "and that pride and anger were awake in the Noldor" through "vied one with another"
10	"Thus with lies . . . "	69	LQ §52c	
11	"Then there was . . ."	69–70	LQ §52d	
12	"But even as . . ."	70	LQ §52e	
13	"Fingolfin bowed before . . ."	70	LQ §52f	
14	"These words were . . ."	70	LQ §52g	
15	"Now the unrest . . ."	70–71	LQ §§52h, 53, 53a, 53b, and 53c	AAm §99: "he it was that had broke the peace of Valinor and drawn his sword upon his kinsman"
16	"Then Fingolfin said: . . ."	71	Beginning of LQ §53d	
17	"With him into . . ."	71	End of LQ §53d	AAm §99: from "and the Silmarils were shut . . ." to the end of the paragraph, except "though Fëanor by his own deeds had brought this thing to pass" (which comes from LQ §53d) and "and the bitterness that Melkor had sown endured" (which comes from the First-phase version of LQ §53)
18	"Now Melkor, . . ."	71	Beginning part of the first paragraph of LQ §54	AAm §100: "it seemed to the people of Valinor that the light of the Trees"
19	"It is told . . ."	71	The rest of the first paragraph and the second paragraph of LQ §54	AAm §101: "is yet free and bold as were his words"
20	"Now Fëanor's heart . . ."	71–72	Third paragraph of LQ §54	

(continued)

Table 8. Continued

Paragraph no.	Paragraph headwords	Silm page no.	Primary source	Secondary sources
21	"But his cunning . . ."	72	Fourth paragraph of LQ §54	Third paragraph of LQ §54: "But his cunning overreached his aim" / AAm §102: "his words touched too deep" through "eyes that," "and pierced the cloaks of his mind," "fierce," and "and he cursed" to the end of the paragraph
22	"Then Melkor . . ."	72	Fifth paragraph of LQ §54	AAm §103: "Finwë was filled" to the end
23	"Now the Valar . . ."	72	First paragraph of LQ §55, which was the first paragraph of the sub-chapter "Of the Darkening of Valinor"	AAm §104: "messengers came from Eldamar"
24	"Thus Melkor departed . . ."	72	Second paragraph of LQ §55	AAm §104: "But the Valar sought in vain for tidings of their enemy"

Note: The "later *Quenta*" subchapter "Of the Silmarils and the Unrest of the Noldor" from the second phase can be found in *MR*, 273–80, covering LQ §§49–54, and the two paragraphs from the next subchapter, "Of the Darkening of Valinor," are from LQ §55 (*MR*, 283). The first-phase sections from which some wording is taken are LQ §§50 and 53 (*MR*, 187 and 189). Otherwise, "LQ§x" refers to the second-phase version. The relevant sections from the *Annals of Aman* are AAm §§93–104, which are found in *MR*, 94–97.

the *Athrabeth* a reference to "the two new themes, representing the coming of Elves and Men, which were not in His first communication" (see *MR*, 336). Christopher speculates in discussing this reference that it probably indicates that his father had developed a new conception of the Music, in which the Elves came in the world with the Second Theme and only Men came with the Third Theme. He offers several other examples from the *Quenta* text and his father's letters that support this hypothesis (*MR*, 358 n. 10).

One cannot really question Christopher's decision to disregard this new conception and make this change here, however. Incorporating the idea that the Elves and the Men were introduced in separate themes in the Music would have required him to make drastic changes to the *Ainulindalë*. Also, while Christopher does not point this out, the statement that Melkor knew little of Men because he did not pay much attention to the Second Theme actually contradicts the idea that the Elves came with the Second Theme and Men came with the Third Theme. So it was appropriate that Christopher made this change.

However, the ninth paragraph ("And when Melkor . . ."; *Silm*, 69) has several major omissions that are less easily explained. The first half-sentence of this paragraph, which tells of how, after Melkor's lies had generated mistrust among the Noldor, he spoke to them of weapons, comes from LQ §52a. After that, a large amount of important material from the following paragraphs (LQ §§52a and 52b) is left out. This omitted material tells how Melkor went back and forth between the sons of Finwë speaking to them of weapons, and also describes the weapons that the Elves already had; these were made for them by Aulë and delivered to them in Middle-earth by Oromë as protection against the evils that beset them there, and as protection during the Great March to the shores of the Sea. Finally, another omitted detail is that the devices on the shields that the Noldor made were of silver and gold and gems (see *MR*, 276–77 for the omitted material).

There are a number of areas of significance in this omitted passage. First of all, the idea that Melkor went back and forth speaking with Fëanor and his half brothers makes the statement that was included the published text that "each believed that he alone had received the warning" more understandable. More significantly, the idea that the Quendi had previously had weapons that they had received from the Valar is quite interesting, and I think it is strange that Christopher chose to leave that out. The details of the Noldor's shields are a nice descriptive touch, which also seems strange to omit.

Part of the rest of the paragraph is taken from the *Annals* (*AAm* §97), but in a sentence omitted from that paragraph, a different story is told, in which Melkor spoke to the Elves about weapons, which they had never before known or possessed (*MR*, 96). Christopher notes that against this passage his father "wrote on the typescript: 'No! They must have weapons on the Great Journey'" (*MR*, 106). That shows how strange it is that Christopher left out of *The Silmarillion* the portion of the "later *Quenta*" describing how the Elves did have weapons on the Great Journey. This is, however, one area where Christopher gives a glimpse of his thinking. In his commentary on the second-phase revisions to the "later *Quenta*" chapter 6, he expresses the opinion that the material that his father added indicating that the Elves did have weapons on the Great March was a "somewhat mechanical narrative device" (*MR*, 281). Christopher's omission of this material shows how willing he was to "reconstruct" his father's work to fit his own vision.

Even more puzzling is the significant reduction of the critical twelfth paragraph ("But even as . . ."; *Silm*, 70), in which Fëanor confronts Fingolfin in front of their father, and draws his sword. In the first sentence, "Fëanor strode into the chamber" is reduced from "suddenly Fëanor appeared, and he strode into the chamber tall and threatening," and "A fire of anger was in his eyes" is removed before "and he was fully armed." The last sentence—"Then turning upon Fingolfin he drew his sword, crying: 'Get thee gone, and take thy due place!'"—is reduced from: "'He would not wait for the council, where all words would be heard by all, and answered. He would speak against me in secret. This I will not brook!' he cried, turning upon Fingolfin. 'Get thee gone, and take thy due place!' Then as a flash of flame he drew his sword. 'Get thee gone and dare my wrath no longer!'" (See LQ §52e; *MR*, 277–78.)

I cannot imagine why this crucial paragraph was reduced so greatly. It loses much without the added detail.

Similarly, the long fifteenth paragraph ("Now the unrest . . ."; *Silm*, 70–71), which combines LQ §§52h, 53, 53a, 53b, and 53c, has many fascinating details that are sadly lost. This paragraph describes how Fëanor was brought before the Valar for judgment after drawing his sword on his half brother Fingolfin and how the lies of Melkor were thus revealed, and it tells of the punishment imposed on Fëanor of twelve years of banishment. The first major omission is a sentence stating that perhaps it was the nature of Elves and Men as they grew to become "willful," to seek to escape from "tutelage," and to be ungrateful. Then a phrase describing the Valar as "perceiving that more was at work than the willfulness of youth" is omitted. Virtually all of LQ §53a was omitted. It describes how great a power and will would be necessary to lie before Mandos, but says that Fëanor was so "besotted" by Melkor's lies and so proud that he had no thought of lying, since he thought that he was completely justified. Another sentence describing how the evidence brought all the words and deeds "out of the dark into the light" is removed before "Then at last the root was laid bare." Christopher also removes another phrase indicating that all of Melkor's lies and half lies were exposed. Finally, another sentence is omitted, in which Mandos expresses the judgment that Fëanor's deed was all the more insolent for having taken place in the hallowed land of Aman (see *MR*, 278–79).

Once again, I cannot understand why this crucial passage was so greatly reduced. The loss of the statement that the Children perhaps would become willful as they grew "and [w]ould desire to escape from tutelage, remembering it with little gratitude" is particularly unfortunate. So many other important details are lost. This is such a critical part of the story, and it is a great shame that it is not fully told in the published text.

Paragraph 17 ("With him into . . ."; *Silm*, 71) also has a number of substantial details left out. The first is a sentence describing Fëanor's return to Túna before he left the city for his banishment. More significantly, a long passage is removed describing how Finwë would not be parted with him, but that Nerdanel would not go with Fëanor into exile and preferred to stay with Indis, with whom (to Fëanor's distress) she had good relations (see *MR*, 279). I particularly regret losing the latter detail. It is another example of the unfortunate reduction in the development of the female characters.

There continue to be minor reductions in the next two paragraphs, which describe how Melkor hides from Tulkas and the other Valar, and then reappears at Fëanor's fortress at Formenos, feigning friendship. The most significant detail lost is the fact that Melkor came to Formenos "in guise as a traveler that seeks for lodging" (*MR*, 280). Similarly, two paragraphs later ("But his cunning . . ."; *Silm*, 72) when Fëanor makes his angry reply to Melkor's overture, the word "gangrel!"[1] is omitted before "thou jail crow of Mandos!" This is another neat little detail showing just how fey Fëanor was (that he would call the strongest being in Arda a "gangrel"), which it seems strange to remove.

The last two paragraphs of this chapter are, as mentioned above, actually taken from the first two paragraphs of the next subchapter in the "later *Quenta*," "Of the Darkening of Valinor." It is a small but strange mystery that in both this chapter and the previous chapter, Christopher chose to move two paragraphs to the end of that chapter from the beginning of the next chapter (or "subchapter"). It seems strange that he would not respect the place where his father chose to divide these chapters. It is even more unfortunate that such significant details were omitted from this chapter. This is a trend that continues through the next several chapters.

Chapter 8 "Of the Darkening of Valinor"

THIS CHAPTER IS TAKEN MOSTLY FROM THE "OF THE DARKENING OF Valinor" subchapter of the long chapter entitled "Of the Silmarils and the Darkening of Valinor" from the second-phase version of the "later *Quenta*." However, there are even more important details lost in this chapter than in the previous chapter, particularly details related to the interaction between Melkor and Ungoliant, his partner in the darkening of Valinor.

Toward the latter part of the subchapter, the wording becomes nearly identical to that of the equivalent section of the *Annals of Aman*. Some of the language of the chapter is taken from that source. The source materials are traced by paragraph in table 9.

In his discussion about this subchapter, Christopher makes some particularly illuminating comments about his approach to creating the published *Silmarillion*. In his introductory comments, he notes that the relationship between the *Quenta* and the *Annals* "takes a new turn, and this is important for the understanding of the published *Silmarillion*, and its justification" (*MR*, 283). In his commentary regarding the subchapter, he further notes that at this point his father seemed to no longer regard the *Quenta* and the *Annals* as separate works, and he speculates that if his father "had continued this last version he would have 'cannibalized' the *Annals* where he chose to, regarding the latter now as no more than a constituent draft text for the sole work that was to emerge: *The Silmarillion*" (*MR*, 290–91).

That describes fairly well what Christopher himself did when faced with the task of producing a publishable version of *The Silmarillion*. I do not question his decision to combine portions of both sources; indeed, I do not see how he could have taken any other approach to publishing the work. However, I would have preferred he had taken an approach that erred on the side of being more inclusive, rather than less inclusive, as there are many details of great interest lost that in some cases significantly change the tone of what Tolkien wrote.

It appears that what he is saying is that because the language of the *Quenta Silmarillion* and that of the *Annals of Aman* converge at the end of this chapter, and for part of the next chapter, he was justified in using the language of the *Annals* to replace the language of the *Quenta Silmarillion* elsewhere. While this is often true, particularly where the *Annals* provided the most recent and/or the most complete version of a particular part of the story, it still does not explain why he left out important material that his father clearly intended to be part of the *Quenta Silmarillion*.

In the third paragraph ("In a ravine . . ."; *Silm*, 73) we see the first major omission from Ungoliant's story. This paragraph comes mostly from the *Annals* (*AAm* §105), though parts are from the portion of the "later *Quenta*" that covers the same material (LQ §55d). However, significant details from the "later *Quenta*" version are omitted altogether. After the statement that appears at the end of this paragraph stating that Ungoliant was "famished," most of two sentences are removed that describe the torment that Ungoliant was suffering as a result of her own webs shutting out all light (on which she fed) and her inability to leave her lair as a result (see *MR*, 284).

The next paragraph, which describes how Melkor sought out Ungoliant and enlisted her assistance, combines portions of LQ §§56, 56a, and 56c. However, great swaths of fascinating details are omitted, with most of LQ §56, almost all of LQ §56a, all of LQ §56b, and parts of LQ §56c and LQ §56d removed. The omitted passages tell of Ungoliant's fear at Melkor's approach, and of her inability to escape him in her weakened state. They describe how Melkor entices her to come assist him by alternating between threats and bribes, and how he finally entices her out of her lair with the lure of two green, shining gemstones. They further show him withholding this prize until she agrees to serve him, and once again calls him "master." And they tell of how she devoured many stones that he had stolen from Valinor, and how she began to grow and find new strength (see *MR*, 284–85).

Ungoliant is a particularly fascinating and important character; she provides a strong counterpoint to Melkor in Tolkien's depiction of evil, and losing these details is definitely a shame. They make Ungoliant's story much more interesting. But worse, there are many more even more significant details omitted in the following paragraphs.

The next paragraph tracks the rest of LQ §56d very closely, except for one small but significant change where material from *AAm* §107 replaces the wording from the "later *Quenta*." The statement in the first sentence that Ungoliant wove a cloak of darkness about herself and Melkor is based on *AAm* §107. In LQ §56d, she weaves the cloak only about herself (see *MR*, 285). This contributes to the lessening of her character. In the story as written by Tolkien in the "later *Quenta*," the cloak that she wove about herself only was directly related to the

Table 9. Source Material by Paragraph for Chapter 8 "Of the Darkening of Valinor"

Paragraph no.	Paragraph headwords	*Silm* page no.	Primary source	Secondary sources
1	"When Manwë heard . . ."	73	LQ §§55a and 55b	AAm §105: "That narrow land lay south of the Bay of Eldamar" and "and its long and mournful shores" through "Ungoliant had made her abode"
2	"Thus unseen he . . ."	73	LQ §55c	AAm §106: "and that in the beginning she was one of those that he corrupted to his service"
3	"In a ravine . . ."	73	AAm §105	LQ §55d: "In a ravine she lived" and "weaving her black webs in a cleft of the mountains"
4	"Now Melkor came . . ."	73–74	Portions of LQ §§56, 56a, and 56c	AAm §106: "came to Avathar and sought her out"
5	"A cloak of . . ."	74	LQ §56d	AAm §107: "about them when Melkor and Ungoliant set forth"
6	"But now upon . . ."	74	AAm §108	LQ §57: "But now upon the mountain-top dark Ungoliant lay"
7	"Now it was . . ."	74	AAm §109	
8	"Therefore Yavanna set . . ."	74–75	AAm §110	LQ §58: "upon Taniquetil"

#		Page		
9	"There came the . . ."	75	LQ §58b (virtually identical to AAm §111)	LQ §58a: "For though the escape" through "at this time Manwë"
10	"One thing only . . ."	75	AAm §112	Second paragraph of LQ §58c: "Valar and Eldar," "Formenos," and the final sentence
11	"Then Fëanor took . . ."	75	Third paragraph of LQ §58c	
12	"I hear thee,' . . ."	75	Fourth paragraph of LQ §58c	
13	"It is told . . ."	75–76	LQ §58d	AAm §113: "Melkor and," "and Melkor sprang upon the mound; and with his black spear he smote each tree to its core," "and their sap" through "till they were drained" and the final sentence
14	"So the great . . ."	76	AAm §114	
15	"Varda looked down . . ."	76	AAm §115 (which is virtually identical to LQ §59a)	LQ §59: first two sentences
16	"But Manwë from . . ."	76	LQ §59b	AAm §116: "But Manwë from his high seat looked out, and his eyes alone pierced through the night" and "a Darkness beyond Dark"
17	"Then the pursuit . . ."	76–77	AAm §116	LQ §59b: "achieved"

Note: The "later *Quenta*" second-phase subchapter "Of the Darkening of Valinor" (one of the subchapters divided from what had been chapter 6, as has been mentioned before) appears in *MR*, 283–89, and covers LQ §§55–59b (but §55 was already used in the previous chapter, as previously discussed). The relevant paragraphs from the *Annals of Aman*, AAm §§105–16, can be found in *MR*, 97–101.

increase in her strength described above. As will be seen, this change takes on more significance when considered with the even more extensive changes made in the following paragraphs.

The "later *Quenta*" tells a quite different story than that included in the next paragraph ("But now upon the . . .'; *Silm,* 74), which describes Melkor and Ungoliant's approach to the "Guarded Realm" and is taken directly from *AAm* §108. Critical details from LQ §57 and LQ §57a are omitted entirely, and again I do not understand why, for these passages say much about the characters of Ungoliant and particularly Melkor. The omitted portion of §57 describes how, when Ungoliant rested for a while "with eyes faint from labour[,] she saw the glimmer of the stars in the dome of Varda and the radiance of Valmar far away" and then how she crept down into the Blessed Realm once her lust increased and overcame her fear. Even more interesting is §57a, which tells how Melkor stood in the dark depths balanced "between evil hope and doubt" before heading down to the shore, cursing the Sea, "saying: 'Slime of Ulmo! I will conquer thee yet, shrivel thee to stinking ooze. Yea ere long Ulmo and Ossë shall wither, and Uinen crawl as mud-worm at my feet!'" (see *MR,* 286).

There are a number of important details lost as a result of the omission of this passage: Ungoliant's greed overcoming her fear of the Valar; Melkor's craven nature and the extent of his malice; and most of all, how he viewed Ulmo and his servants as his prime enemies, and how much he hated the Sea. Another important difference is that the two of them were not together when they approached the Guarded Realm. It will soon become clear why that is so significant.

These details absolutely should never have been deleted. By using the less developed version of the story from the *Annals* to replace the version written for the "later *Quenta*" itself, Christopher has cannibalized some of the most interesting features right out of the story.

It also should be mentioned that the reference to the "dome of Varda" in the omitted material shows that Tolkien might have been thinking about incorporating some changes to the physical properties of his invented universe. Such changes were discussed in the "Myths Transformed" texts in which he considered having Varda infuse the Two Trees with the holy Light, while also making a great dome out of mist or cloud, to keep out the spies of Melkor (see *MR,* 375–87). As I have indicated earlier, Christopher was wise not to try to incorporate this aspect of Tolkien's proposed revisions. However, the brief mention of the "Dome of Varda" certainly does not justify disregarding the whole new version of the darkening of Valinor.

In paragraph 8 ("Therefore Yavanna . . ."; *Silm,* 74–75) it is mentioned that the festival that was occurring when Melkor and Ungoliant approached was called by Manwë to heal the evil that had arisen. This paragraph mostly comes from *AAm* §110, some of the language of which is paralleled in the latter part of LQ §58 and LQ §58a. However, there are again some very significant details from the "later *Quenta*" that are unfortunately omitted.

In LQ §58, there is some more detail regarding the feast that was omitted; it describes how the greatest of feasts of Valinor took place upon Taniquetil[1] at the first gathering of fruits, when all the peoples of Valinor gathered in praise of Eru. Of greater note, in LQ §58a there is more detail about Manwë's summons to the Noldor and to Fëanor in particular: "'Fëanor son of Finwë, come and do not deny my bidding! In my love thou remainest and wilt be honoured in my hall'" (see *MR*, 286–87).

This certainly reflects better on Manwë than the bald statement that Manwë "commanded" Fëanor to come, which appears two paragraphs later. That paragraph ("One thing only . . ."; *Silm*, 75) comes mostly from *AAm* §112. Instead of just saying that Manwë commanded Fëanor to come to the festival (as does the passage from *AAm* §112 used in the published text), LQ §58c states that Fëanor "read the message of Manwë as a command" (*MR*, 287)—a small but important difference, particularly when taken in conjunction with the omitted statement quote above about Fëanor remaining in Manwë's love.

The end of the paragraph and the next two short paragraphs, however, do take up the greater detail contained in LQ §58c, which is not present in *AAm* §112. They contain the conversation between Fëanor and Fingolfin in which Fingolfin releases Fëanor and tells Fëanor that he will thenceforth consider him a full brother in heart and follow where he leads, but Fëanor says only, "I hear thee" and "So be it." I am thankful that Christopher did include this extra detail, though it does raise the question of why he included this but not much of the other new material.

The vast reduction of Ungoliant's story in this chapter from what Tolkien wrote in the "later *Quenta*" reaches its culmination in the following paragraph ("It is told . . ."; *Silm*, 75–76). This paragraph combines the language of LQ §58d with that of *AAm* §113. But a much more complete story, and in my opinion a more interesting one, is told in LQ §§58d, 58e, and 58f, which are left out completely.

In the story as included, of course, Melkor and Ungoliant arrive together, and it is Melkor who wounds each Tree with his spear; only then does Ungoliant finish them off by sucking up their sap, before draining the Wells of Varda and becoming so monstrous that even Melkor is afraid. In the "later *Quenta*" version, however, it is Ungoliant alone who destroys the Trees, with no assistance from Melkor at all! In fact, he is not even present. Here we see the significance of the omission of the earlier passages that indicate that she arrives alone and that only she was wrapped in the cloak of darkness.

In the omitted portion of §58d it is told how she herself pierces the Trees with her black beak, wounding them and sucking them dry. Then §58d describes how she drains the Wells of Varda, becomes huge and monstrous, and then hastens away "to the tryst that Melkor had made with her, and did not mean to keep." Then §58e tells how Melkor, the great Black Lord, lurked outside while Ungoliant alone did the dirty work of destroying the Trees, and only after the deed was done entered the Ring of Doom, cursed it, and "defiled the judgement seat of Manwë and threw down the thrones of the Valar." Finally, §58f describes how he then went to "his second mark, which he had kept secret in his mind," how Ungoliant overtook him on the way, and how she was so great that he could not escape her and "they went on together to the one place in the land of the Valar that he would have hidden from her"[2] (see *MR*, 288).

I see absolutely no justification for abandoning this much more complete version of the story of Melkor and Ungoliant, particularly since it was part of the last version of the *Quenta Silmarillion* that Tolkien wrote. The only possible explanation that I can think of is that Christopher wanted to include the version in which the main villain, Melkor, had a greater role in the destruction of the Trees. But the abandoned version is not only more complete—and clearly the version that Tolkien intended to include—but also much more subtle and interesting. Ungoliant is another strong female character (though of course a very evil one) whose role is particularly diminished by the edits and omissions made to the text of the last version of "The Silmarillion" as Tolkien wrote it (which, together with the weakening of other female characters, leaves the unfortunate impression that Christopher finds it difficult to accept such a primary role for a female character). Moreover, Melkor's own character—and how far he has already fallen (from being the most powerful entity in Arda to being a craven bully)—is much less clearly illuminated as a result of these omissions. It is very disappointing that Christopher chose to leave this important material out.

There are no additional changes or omissions worth noting in the last several paragraphs. However, this chapter reveals very significant changes from the story as Tolkien wrote it in his final work on the *Quenta Silmarillion*, which Christopher seems to try to justify based on his theory that the *Quenta* was increasingly cannibalizing the *Annals*. I believe, however, that the reductions and changes to the story of Ungoliant and Melkor are not justified.

Including these details would not have interrupted the flow of the narrative; on the contrary, they make it a far more compelling story. Nor would including this more extended narrative contrast sharply with the material that comes after it, since the following chapter is the longest one in the earlier part of the book (and, in fact, is the third-longest in the whole book, behind only the very long chapters "Of Beren and Lúthien" and "Of Túrin Turambar"). Moreover, including the more extended narratives that Tolkien created for these earlier sections of "The Silmarillion" would have, if anything, created a more balanced whole, since there *are* more extended narratives included in the later sections of the book. In addition, we have seen that Christopher did not hesitate to include additional detail in some places (such as the confrontation between Fëanor and Fingolfin), indicating that his main reason for excluding the greater detail regarding Ungoliant had more to do with his own preference as to what to include than any other factor.

Chapter 9 "Of the Flight of the Noldor"

IN CHAPTER 9, THERE ARE FOUR SEPARATE SOURCE MATERIALS THAT need to be looked at. In the first-phase work on the "later *Quenta*," "Of the Flight of the Noldor" was chapter 7 (it is chapter 9 in the published version, because the second-phase rewriting of chapter 6 resulted in three separate chapters). However, there are only fairly minor changes made to this chapter from what was chapter 5 in the "earlier *Quenta*," and so Christopher does not give the first-phase "later *Quenta*" text in full, but instead only notes the significant changes. It is thus necessary to compare some of the published text with the "earlier *Quenta*" (referred to as "QS"). Where the source material is clearly from the emended LQ texts, I will refer to them as "LQ §xx" (this is different from the material from the sixth chapter of the "later *Quenta*," where LQ usually referred to the second-phase work; but as will be seen, the second-phase work on chapter 7 is numbered differently). Where the source text is from the "earlier *Quenta*" with no changes noted to it in the discussion of LQ, I will refer to it as "QS §*xx.*"

I will need to refer to this older work, because the second-phase work extended only less than halfway through this chapter. The work that was done in the second phase on this chapter was broken into two "subchapters"—"Of the Rape of the Silmarils" and "Of the Thieves' Quarrel." However, unlike the "subchapters" from the second-phase work on chapter 6 of the "later *Quenta*," these "subchapters" were not used as chapter titles in the published work. Christopher was unable to relate the second-phase work on this material to the numbering of the "earlier *Quenta*," so he numbers it beginning with §1. Where this provides the source material, I refer to it as "LQ (Later Chap. 7) §xx." However, Christopher does not give the text in full where it "becomes scarcely distinct from that of *AAm*" (*MR*, 292). *The Annals of Aman* is of course, the fourth source. Indeed, the *Annals* prove to be the main source for this chapter.

In his introduction to the second-phase work to this chapter, Christopher further explains why he adopted the methodology of liberally replacing material from the "later *Quenta*" with material from the *Annals,* pointing out that here his father "again turned to the *Annals of Aman,* and in this case he adopted substantial parts of the older text so closely that the new is almost an exact copy, with only a word or two changed here and there" (*MR*, 292).

I point this out because I see in this statement confirmation of my earlier comments. It is clear from the words "of the older text" that the second-phase work on the "later *Quenta*" was later than the work on the *Annals of Aman*. So not only does that work represent the latest work on what Tolkien himself designated to be the *Silmarillion* text, it was the latest work on this material, period. Where elements were introduced in that later work that did not exist in the earlier work, I do not see how the cannibalization process (or, as Christopher refers to it here, the "amalgamation" process) can justify the omission of those elements (except where there is a compelling reason to exclude details, such as the reference to "the Dome of Varda" discussed in the previous chapter).

Moreover, Christopher goes on to state that in this second-phase work on the "later *Quenta*" his father "also introduced a new element into the narrative: the attack by Melkor on Formenos reported by Maedhros" (*MR*, 292). However, that "new element" itself was excluded from the published version. That provides further evidence that the omission of material had more to do with Christopher's own preferences as to what should be included and what should not be included than it did with anything else—particularly since, for long stretches in this chapter, Christopher does include the version with a greatly expanded narrative. In fact, including the expanded narrative in the previous several chapters would have more closely matched the level of detail in this chapter, contributing to the goal of keeping *The Silmarillion* on a consistent narrative keel, rather than interfering with it.

The source materials are traced by paragraph in table 10.

The first paragraph (*Silm*, 78), which finds the Valar sitting in darkness in a great concourse after the destruction of the Trees, combines language from *AAm* §117 with language from LQ (Later Chap. 7) §1 (some of which is identical). However, there is a passage from the beginning of LQ (Later Chap. 7) §1 that is omitted. This omitted passage tells that after what would have been one more day of the Trees ("but time was blind and unmeasured"), the Valar returned to the Ring of Doom and sat on the ground, "for their thrones were defiled" (see *MR*, 292–93). Since the story of Morgoth defiling the thrones of the Valar is not included in the previous chapter, this passage would have made little sense had it been included. This is an example of how some cuts required further omissions.

The next several paragraphs describe the conversation of Yavanna and other Valar about saving the Trees by using the Light preserved

Table 10. Source Material by Paragraph for Chapter 9 "Of the Flight of the Noldor"

Paragraph no.	Paragraph headwords	*Silm* page no.	Primary source	Secondary sources
1	"After a time . . ."	78	LQ [Later Chap. 7] §1	AAm §117: first sentence, "Then" and "then many voices were lifted up in lamentation"
2	"Yavanna spoke before . . ."	78	AAm §118	
3	"Then Manwë spoke . . ."	78	AAm §119	
4	"There was long . . ."	78	Second and third paragraphs of AAm §119	
5	"But Aulë the Maker . . ."	78	Fourth paragraph of AAm §119	
6	"But Fëanor spoke . . ."	78	LQ (Later Chap. 7) §4	
7	"'Not the first,' . . ."	78–79	AAm §121	
8	"Then Mandos said: . . ."	79	LQ (Later Chap. 7) §6	
9	"But even as . . ."	79	AAm §122	
10	"Then Fëanor rose . . ."	79	LQ (Later Chap. 7) §11	LQ §60 (first phase): "and by that name only was he known to the Eldar ever after"
11	"Many there grieved . . ."	79	LQ (Later Chap. 7) §12	
12	"Meanwhile Morgoth . . ."	80	LQ (Later Chap. 7) §§13 and 14	AAm §125: "and he crossed over"
13	"'Blackheart!' she said. . . ."	80	First paragraph of LQ (Later Chap. 7) §15	
14	"What wouldst thou . . ."	80	Second paragraph of LQ (Later Chap. 7) §15	
15	"Not so much,' . . ."	80	Third paragraph of LQ (Later Chap. 7) §15	

16	"Then perforce Morgoth . . ." 80	Sixth and seventh paragraphs of LQ (Later Chap. 7) §15	AAm §125: "Huger and darker yet grew Ungoliant"
17	"In his right hand . . ." 80	LQ (Later Chap. 7) §16	AAm §126: "Ered Gorgoroth"
18	"But Ungoliant had . . ." 80–81	LQ (Later Chap. 7) §§17, 18, 19, and 20	GA §34 (see *Wolf*, 15): "and even after Ungoliant herself departed, and went whither she would into the forgotten south of the world, her offspring abode there and wove their hideous webs"
19	"And thus the fear . . ." 81	AAm §§127 and 128	LQ (Later Chap. 7) §21: the first sentence GA §35 (see *Wolf*, 15): "above their gates he reared the threefold peaks of Thangorodrim, and a great reek of dark smoke was ever wreathed about them" QS §63: "and the anger of the pain" and "seldom indeed did he leave the deep places of his fortress, but governed his armies from his northern throne"
20	"For now, more . . ." 81–82	AAm §128	
21	"Now when it was . . ." 82	AAm §129	QS §64: "and mourned for the darkening of their fair city" and "Through the dim ravine of the Calacirya"
22	"Then suddenly Fëanor . . ." 82	AAm §§130 and 131	QS §65: "and the hill and all the stairs and streets that climbed upon it were lit with the light of many torches that each one bore in hand"

(*continued*)

Table 10. Continued

Paragraph no.	Paragraph headwords	*Silm* page no.	Primary source	Secondary sources
23	"Why, O people . . ."	82	First part of *AAm* §132	QS §66: "but he was distraught with grief for the slaying of his father, and with anguish for the rape of the Silmarils"
24	"Here once was . . ."	82–83	The rest of *AAm* §132	
25	"Long he spoke . . ."	83	*AAm* §133	
26	"Then Fëanor swore . . ."	83	QS §67	
27	"Thus spoke Maedhros . . ."	83–84	*AAm* §134	
28	"At length after . . ."	84	*AAm* §136	
29	"Little foresight could . . ."	84	*AAm* §137	
30	"And indeed when . . ."	84	*AAm* §§138 and 139	QS §68: "upon their bitter road" Note made by Tolkien on a late copy of LQ §68 (see *MR*, 197): "upon their bitter road"
31	"But even as the . . ."	85	*AAm* §140	
32	"But Fëanor laughed . . ."	85	*AAm* §141	
33	"Then turning to . . ."	85	*AAm* §142	
34	"In that hour . . ."	85	*AAm* §143	
35	"Now Fëanor led . . ."	85–86	*AAm* §§144 and 145	QS §69: "But as the mind of Fëanor cooled and took counsel he perceived," "yet it would need long time and toil to build so great a fleet, even were there any among the Noldor skilled in that craft" and "and in his rebellion he thought that thus the bliss of Valinor might be further diminished and his power for war upon Morgoth be increased"

36	"But the Teleri . . ."	86	AAm §146	
37	"Then Fëanor grew . . ."	86	AAm §147	
38	"But Olwë answered: . . ."	86	AAm §148	
39	"Thereupon Fëanor left . . ."	87	AAm §149	
40	"Thus at last . . ."	87	AAm §150	
41	"Nonetheless the greater . . ."	87–88	AAm §151 and part of AAm §152	QS §71: "Much it foretold" and "but all heard the curse that was uttered upon those that would not stay nor seek the doom and pardon of the Valar"
42	"Tears unnumbered . . ."	88	The rest of AAm §152 and AAm §153	
43	"Ye have spilled . . ."	88	AAm §154	
44	"Then many . . ."	88	AAm §155	QS §71: "cowardice, from cravens or the fear of cravens"
45	"But in that hour . . ."	88–89	AAm §156	
46	"The Noldor came . . ."	89	AAm §157	
47	"Therefore Fëanor halted . . ."	89	AAm §§158 and 159	
48	"But when they . . ."	90	AAm §160	
49	"Then Fëanor laughed . . ."	90	AAm §§161 and 162	AAm §163 and QS §73: "they knew that they were betrayed"
50	"Then Fingolfin seeing . . ."	90	AAm §163	QS §73: "left to perish in Araman and return" Handwritten note made to AAm §163, and an essay on the names of the descendants of Finwë: "There Elenwë the wife of Turgon was lost"

Note: The relevant sections to this chapter from the *Annals of Aman* are *AAm* §§117–63, which appear (including notes and commentary) in *MR*, 106–28. The "second-phase" work on chapter 7 of the "later *Quenta*" can be found in *MR*, 292–99, and its sections are numbered LQ (Later Chap. 7)§§1–21. Chapter 5 in the "earlier *Quenta*" ("QS") appears in *Lost Road*, 232–39, and the changes made to this chapter in the first phase of the "later *Quenta*" are noted in *MR*, 193–97. In both LQ and QS the relevant portions are §§60–73.

in the Silmarils. There are no significant differences between *AAm* §§118–20 and LQ (Later Chap. 7) §§1–4, until we get to Fëanor's response to the request for the Silmarils in the sixth paragraph ("But Fëanor spoke . . ."; *Silm*, 78), where he states that breaking the Silmarils would break his heart and he would "be slain." This language comes from LQ (Later Chap. 7) §4; *AAm* §120 has "die" instead of "be slain." Christopher notes that the change of "I shall die" to "I shall be slain" resulted from the emergence of the story of Míriel (see *MR*, 268–69, 293).

However, the next paragraph continues from *AAm* §121 without taking up a related and important difference in LQ (Later Chap. 7) §5. In the first sentence of that paragraph, Mandos replies to Fëanor's statement that he would slain if the Silmarils were broken by saying that he would not be first, referring to the fact that unbeknownst to those there, Finwë had already been slain by Melkor. In his discussion about the story of Finwë and Míriel, Christopher notes that in LQ (Later Chap. 7) §5, after "but they did not understand his word" in the first sentence, appeared the further words "thinking that he spoke of Míriel" (see *MR*, 269, 293). The omission of this in the published text is another small example of the downplaying of Míriel's importance.

With the ninth paragraph ("But even as . . ."; *Silm*, 79) we see another major omission. This paragraph comes from *AAm* §122, and briefly tells of how messengers come from Formenos and report that Melkor has slain Finwë and stolen all the jewels of the Noldor kept there, including the Silmarils. However, there is a very significant expansion of this part of the story in LQ (Later Chap. 7) §§7–10 that is (very unfortunately) not included in the published *Silmarillion*.

Instead of some anonymous messengers (as in the published version), it is the sons of Fëanor who come from Formenos to report the evil news. First, §7 tells of their arrival, of Maedhros reporting that Finwë was slain and the Silmarils taken, and of Fëanor reacting by falling on his face and lying as one dead. Then, in §8, Maedhros tells of how a darkness approached the house of Fëanor, and in §9 he describes how they heard the sound of great blows, heard one piercing cry, and saw a sudden flame of fire. He tells of how their horses cast them to the ground and flew away, while they lay "blind and without strength," and how afterward they realized that Melkor had been there, along with some other power that had robbed them "of all wit and will." Finally, §10 tells of their discovery of Finwë alone in the house, with his head "crushed as with a great mace of iron" and his sword "twisted and untempered as if by lightning-stroke," and of how all the treasuries were emptied, and the Silmarils taken (*MR*, 293–94).

Maedhros reporting on the death of Finwë and the rape of the Silmarils to Manwë. By Anushka Mouriño. Courtesy of the artist.

This is the "new element" introduced in the final work on this chapter that Christopher refers to in the quote that I cite at the beginning of this chapter. Its omission is difficult to understand, given that it was clearly intended by his father to be part of the *Quenta Silmaril-lion,* and that it is an immensely more interesting and moving version of the story. The descriptive detail and the fact that the story is told by a close member of Finwë's family both make it far more compelling than the version included in the published text. But unfortunately, no real explanation for this puzzling decision is given.

Curiously, the next paragraph is taken from LQ (Later Chap. 7) §11, which is similar but not identical to *AAm* §123. The first words of the paragraph, "Then Fëanor rose," do not really make sense without the omitted portion discussed above in which Fëanor fell upon his face and lay as one dead.

It is also worth noting that one addition to this paragraph comes from the first-phase work on this chapter, which was not included in this second-phase work. The phrase "and by that name only was he known to the Eldar ever after" (referring to Fëanor giving Melkor the name "Morgoth") comes from a late first-phase addition to LQ §60. No similar phrase appears in either LQ (Later Chap. 7) §11 or *AAm* §123.

The next paragraph continues from LQ (Later Chap 7) §12, but with a couple of important details omitted, including the culmination of the "new element" in which Maedhros and his brothers bring the news of Finwë's death and of the rape of the Silmarils. At the end of the previous paragraph, it is told how Fëanor fled from the Ring of Doom into the night after hearing the evil news. There is then a sentence omitted from the beginning of this paragraph in which Maedhros and his brothers, who did not realize he had been present when they brought the news of his father's death, chased after him in haste because they feared that he would now slay himself (MR, 295).

Fëanor's sons' worry that he would slay himself illustrates his grief at his father's death far more clearly than the seemingly pro forma question included in the previous paragraph, "who among sons, of Elves or of Men, have held their fathers of greater worth?" Fëanor is also made less sympathetic with the omission of the statements contained in LQ (Later Chap. 7) §12 that those who saw his grief "forgave all his bitterness" and that later events might have been different if he had "cleansed his heart ere the dreadful tidings came" (see MR, 295).

This paragraph ends the subchapter in LQ (Later Chap. 7) called "Of the Rape of the Silmarils." The next paragraph ("Meanwhile Morgoth . . ."; Silm, 80) is taken from the beginning of the subchapter called "Of the Thieves' Quarrel." This paragraph combines LQ (Later Chap. 7) §§13 and 14. The much-expanded version of the story "Of the Thieves' Quarrel" (§§13–21, compared to only §§125 and 126 in AAm) is taken up in the published Silmarillion almost in its entirety. It is odd that this one element of the expansion of the story of Morgoth and Ungoliant's interactions is taken up in the published text, when all the rest was omitted.

There is one puzzling change in this paragraph in which the phrase "and he crossed over" (referring to Morgoth crossing the Helcaraxë, or grinding ice) is taken from AAm §125 and replaces "they crossed over" (referring, of course, to both Morgoth and Ungoliant). This makes little sense, because (unlike in the story as told in AAm §125) earlier in that sentence it is already stated that "Morgoth and Ungoliant passed in haste" and came to the Helcaraxë. Fortunately, this is one of only a few occasions where the process of combining different sources resulted in such a blatant contradiction.

The following three short paragraphs are taken from the first three paragraphs of LQ (Later Chap. 7) §15 and contain the discussion between Ungoliant and Morgoth in which she challenges him to make good on his promise to give her the treasure taken from Formenos "with both hands." These paragraphs have a couple of small but significant changes worth noting. After she calls him "Blackheart!" the parenthetical phrase "(calling him 'Master' no longer)" is omitted, and then "thy" and "thou" replace "your" and "you" where

Ungoliant is addressing Morgoth. This is actually quite puzzling. As Christopher notes in his commentary, "Ungoliant no longer calls Morgoth 'Master,' but she continues to address him as a superior, using 'you,' whereas Morgoth calls her 'thou' as previously" (*MR*, 298). It is a shame to lose this subtle point, presumably in the name of consistency.

We find the last major reduction of the story of Ungoliant and Morgoth in the next paragraph ("Then perforce . . ."; *Silm*, 80), which is taken from the sixth and seventh paragraphs of LQ (Later Chap. 7) §15. The fourth and fifth paragraphs are omitted entirely. The two omitted paragraphs describe how Morgoth tries to claim that Ungoliant has already had her half of the treasure taken from Valinor, because he had reluctantly let her feast upon the gems of Fëanor to keep her busy while he claimed the Silmarils (*MR*, 296).

The following paragraph ("But Ungoliant had . . ."; *Silm*, 80–81) completes the story of Ungoliant. This very long paragraph for some reason combines LQ (Later Chap. 7) §§17, 18, 19, and 20 into one paragraph. In addition to some small additions from *AAm* §126, it has a short passage added from *The Grey Annals* (*GA* §34; see *WotJ*, 15) regarding Ungoliant's departure into the "forgotten south of the world." The portion used here from *GA* §34 is omitted from chapter 10, paragraph 15.[1]

The beginning part of the next paragraph comes from LQ (Later Chap. 7) §21, which is the final section of the subchapter "Of the Thieves' Quarrel" and is as far as the second-phase work on the "later *Quenta*" reached. The rest of the paragraph comes from *AAm* §§127 and 128, which are closely related to LQ (and QS) §62 and 63, though a significant portion is omitted, as discussed below. There are a couple of additions that come from QS §63 (the first that we have seen that come directly from the "earlier *Quenta*") and another addition from *GA* §35.

The passage that comes from *GA* §35, describing the "threefold peaks of Thangorodrim" (see *WotJ*, 15), replaces a longer passage describing Morgoth's fortress from *AAm* §127. In a bizarre twist, the portion of *AAm* §127 that is replaced here is then itself used to replace the passage from *GA* §35 used in chapter 10, paragraph 15 (for which *GA* §35 partly provides the primary source)! There does not seem to be any good reason why these descriptions of Thangorodrim switched places in this way.

The large portion of *AAm* §127 that was omitted deals with the problematic question of the origin of the Orcs. The portion that was omitted by Christopher repeats twice that the Orcs were "bred" by Morgoth "in envy and mockery of the Eldar" and "in hatred." After describing them further, it goes on to say that though they "were strong and fell as demons," they were not of demonkind, but rather children of the earth that had been corrupted by Morgoth. But then there was an additional portion of the passage that was subsequently struck out by Tolkien himself, which includes the story of the Orcs originally being Elves that were captured by Melkor and ruined in captivity. It then quotes Ælfwine reporting Pengoloð as saying that after the Ainulindalë Melkor could not make anything of his own "that had life or the semblance of life" and that this was even truer after his evil actions in Valinor (see *MR*, 109–10).

Christopher notes that the section discussing the origin of the Orcs in *AAm* §45 was added after his father wrote the above passage.[2] Christopher further speculates that the portion that his father struck out was eliminated either because he realized that it had been superseded by the earlier passage and was not in the right place, or because he no longer accepted the theory of the Orc's origins (*MR*, 124).

Christopher observes that it was likely that the note that his father wrote beside *AAm* §43 that said "Alter this. Orcs are not Elvish" applied here as well (*MR*, 127–28). Still, as I noted earlier in chapter 3, one cannot really blame Christopher for leaving in the impression that Orcs were in fact of Elvish origin, since his father left so much confusion regarding the whole issue of the origin of the Orcs.

The *Annals of Aman* is the primary source for the rest of the chapter (paragraphs 20–50; *Silm*, 81–90), though with additions from the *Quenta* in different places. This makes sense, as the *Annals* contain the last written version of this part of the story. They also contain the most extended narrative of this part of the story. This is particularly true of the twelve paragraphs from paragraph 23 ("'Why, O people . . .'"; *Silm*, 82) through paragraph 34 ("In that hour . . ."; *Silm*, 85). These paragraphs come almost exclusively (with one major exception) from *AAm* §§132–43 and tell of how Fëanor inflamed the bulk of the Noldor in rebelling against the Valar and heading to exile in Middle-earth. This material is covered in the "earlier *Quenta*" in the last two sentences of §66 and in §§67 and 68 (with virtually no changes to it in the "later *Quenta*"). The story is pretty much exactly the same in these sections of the *Annals of Aman* and the "later *Quenta*," but it is told in much greater detail in the *Annals*. Thus, we see that Christopher was willing to include the more expansive version of parts of the story, where he so chooses.

The single exception that I refer to occurs in the twenty-sixth paragraph ("Then Fëanor swore . . ."; *Silm*, 83), which introduces the Oath of Fëanor, one of the most important elements of "The Silmarillion," haunting different characters throughout the rest of the work. The first two sentences of this paragraph come from *AAm* §134, with minor changes, but the bulk of the paragraph, describing the oath, comes from QS §67, disregarding the much more complete version in *AAm* §134, where the full text of the oath is given.

Here is the full text of the oath as it is given in *AAm* §134:

> Be he foe or friend, be he foul or clean,
> brood of Morgoth or bright Vala,
> Elda or Maia or Aftercomer,
> Man yet unborn upon Middle-earth,
> neither law, nor love, nor league of swords,
> dread nor danger, not Doom itself,
> shall defend him from Fëanor, and Fëanor's kin,
> whoso hideth or hoardeth, or in hand taketh,
> finding keepeth or afar casteth
> a Silmaril. This swear we all:
> death we will deal him ere Day's ending,
> woe unto world's end! Our word hear thou,
> Eru Allfather! To the everlasting
> Darkness doom us if our deed faileth.
> On the holy mountain hear in witness
> and our vow remember, Manwë and Varda!
>
> (*MR*, 112)

It is difficult for me to express how remarkable I find it that Christopher chose to leave out this incredibly powerful text, which was after all the final version that his father wrote regarding the oath (since the *Annals* was written after this first-phase work on the "later *Quenta*"), and to replace it with the older version in which the oath is simply described in bald terms. This is particularly so since the text then picks right back up with the rest of the text of *AAm* §134 in the next paragraph and continues with the *Annals of Aman* thereafter, and this is the only place in these twelve paragraphs where that greater detail is not included in the published book.

This is most disappointing. The actual words of the oath ooze power and dread, so much more so than the short summary that is used in the published text.

In the next paragraph, there is an omission that does make sense. After the passage talking about Galadriel being eager to go into exile, a sentence is removed that states that as the youngest of Finwë's House she was born in Valinor and knew little of "the unguarded lands" (*MR*, 113). Christopher correctly notes that that was a strange sentence "because all the progeny of Finwë were born in Aman (*AAm* §§78, 81–82)" (*MR*, 125).

The next item of note is not until the thirty-seventh and thirty-eighth paragraphs, which contain the conversation between Fëanor and Olwë, lord of the Teleri, in which Fëanor demands the Teleri's help and Olwë refuses it (*Silm*, 86). This conversation is taken from *AAm* §§147 and 148. However, in the "earlier *Quenta*" (and the scarcely edited "later *Quenta*") this conversation does not take place. In QS §70 the text states simply, "But the Teleri would not join the Noldor in flight, and sent back their messengers" (*Lost Road*, 236). This is another indication that where he chose to, Christopher was perfectly willing to include the more detailed version of the story.

There is a curious change made in the forty-first paragraph ("Nonetheless the . . ."; *Silm*, 87–88), which tells of the appearance of Mandos before Noldor after they have stolen the ships of the Teleri in a bitter fight. In this meeting he foretells their Doom. This paragraph comes mostly from *AAm* §151 and part of *AAm* §152, but omits the first part of Mandos's speech to the Noldor, in which he tells them to turn back and seek pardon from the Valar before their curse falls upon them (*MR*, 117). But then at the end of the paragraph the phrase "but all heard the curse that was uttered upon those that would not stay nor seek the doom and pardon of the Valar" is added from QS §71 (with minor changes; see *Lost Road*, 237), essentially summarizing the portion of Mandos's actual words that had been removed.

In the next paragraph, Mandos's statement "but if ye go further, be assured that" is removed before he says that the Valar will shut the Noldor out of Valinor. However, other than these puzzling omissions, the words of Mandos are included almost intact in this paragraph and the next one, as is Fëanor's reply in the paragraph after that. Mandos's speech is merely described in QS and LQ §71, and the part about not suffering from cowardice is the only part of Fëanor's reply to Mandos that is given in QS and LQ §71. Christopher wisely included the more complete version of this part of the story. I wish he had done the same with the Oath of Fëanor.

The forty-fifth paragraph ("But in that hour . . ."; *Silm*, 88–89) comes from *AAm* §156, which is almost identical to LQ §72 (one of the few paragraphs in this chapter rewritten from QS), except for one significant difference. In LQ §72 it specifies that Fingon and Turgon had no part in the Kinslaying of the Teleri (*MR*, 196). Christopher points out, however, that it is clear that the writing of this passage in the "later *Quenta*" preceded its writing in the *Annals of Aman* from the fact that the passage in the "later *Quenta*" as originally drafted had "Elwë" instead of "Olwë", whereas in the *Annals of Aman* "Olwë" was written as such from the beginning.[3]

Christopher admits some confusion over the question of the spelling of the name "Endor" that appears in the subsequent paragraph, defined there as "Middle-earth." In the *Ambarkanta,* "Endor" referred to the midpoint of Middle-earth, not Middle-earth itself (*SoMe,* 241). Christopher notes that in *The Lord of the Rings* the Quenya word "Endóre" is given as meaning Middle-earth itself, not the midpoint, and that in Letter 297, his father refers to "Endor" as meaning Middle-earth. Christopher also notes that while in the manuscript here and at several subsequent points, the form "Endar" is clearly written, in some places the typist typed "Endor" and in others "Endar," and his father let both stand. Christopher says that he "hesitantly" used the form Endor in the published *Silmarillion* (*MR,* 126).

It is worth noting here that there exists a version of the story of the burning of the ships at Losgar alternative to the one from *AAm* §§158–62, that appears in the published text (*Silm,* 89–90). The alternative version appears in a short essay printed in the *Shibboleth of Fëanor* section of *The People of Middle-earth* entitled "The Names of the Sons of Fëanor with the Legend of the Fate of Amrod."

In this essay, he notes that Amrod and Amras, the youngest of Fëanor's sons, were twins, and that their mother, Nerdanel, originally gave them both the same mother-name, Ambarussa (Top-Russet) because they were both red-haired and they were much alike. When Fëanor requested that their names be different, Nerdanel gave him a strange look and then said that one should be called Umbarto (Fated), "'but which time will decide.'" Fëanor was disturbed by this ominous name and changed it to "Ambarto."

The essay then describes how when "Fëanor became more and more fell and violent, and rebelled against the Valar," he and Nerdanel became estranged. When it became clear that Fëanor was leaving Valinor forever and taking their sons with him, she begged that he leave with her the two youngest, or at least one of them. Fëanor responded that if she had been a true wife (as she had been until she was "cozened by Aulë") she would have kept all of her children, since she would have gone with them, and all of their sons were determined to go. Nerdanel then prophesied that one of them would never set foot in Middle-earth, and they parted in anger.

The essay then tells how Fëanor, "filled with malice," aroused Curufin and a few of those closest to him and set the ships of the Teleri aflame, to the dismay of all but a few, since many possessions were still on board, and the ships would have been useful for further journeying. Then when the host was mustered the following morning, only six of Fëanor's seven sons could be found. The older twin "went pale with fear" and asked his father whether he had roused his brother, who had slept aboard the ship. Some (including Fëanor) suspected that Ambarto planned to sail his ship back and rejoin his mother, because he was shocked by his father's deeds. "'That ship I destroyed first,' said Fëanor (hiding his own dismay). 'Then rightly you gave the name to the youngest of your children,' said Ambarussa, 'and Umbarto "the Fated" was its true form. Fell and fey are you become.' And after that no one dared speak again to Fëanor of this matter" (see *PoMe*, 353–55).

This essay was written later than the material used in the published text of *The Silmarillion*, and there is little indication that Tolkien intended for it to be included in *The Silmarillion*. However, at one place in the material that would be used in Chapter 17, "Of the Coming of Men into the West" a reference is made to the "lands of Diriol" (the original name of Fëanor's son Amras) (see *WotJ*, 218). This suggests that Tolkien may have already eliminated one of the twins at the point this was written, since previously they had always been designated as holding the land together.

Finally, there are two items of note in the last paragraph (*Silm*, 90), which describes the crossing of the grinding ice of the Helcaraxë by Fingolfin and the others of the Noldor left behind by Fëanor.

First, the description of Galadriel as "the valiant and fair" (*MR*, 120) is removed. This recalls the earlier edit where the description of her as "the most valiant" of the House of Finwë was also removed, and is yet another small example of the seemingly systematic weakening of female characters.

Second, there is an insert regarding the fate of Turgon's wife, Elenwë, that comes partly from a handwritten note made to *AAm* §163 and partly from an essay on the names of the descendants of Finwë described above. The insert simply names her and says that she was "lost." It comes from a marginal note that Tolkien made here, which in addition to stating that she was lost adds that Turgon then only had a daughter and no other heir, that he himself nearly lost his life trying to rescue her, and that as a result of this, he "had less love for the Sons of Fëanor than any other" (*MR*, 128). It is unfortunate that these additional details were not included.

The name "Elenwë" is not given in this note, however. In the section on Maeglin in *The War of the Jewels*, Christopher notes that it stated "Turgon had no heir: for his wife, Alairë, was of the Vanyar and would not forsake Valinor." He further indicates that the inclusion of the name "Elenwë" in *The Silmarillion* was based on corrections made to Elvish genealogies created in 1959 in which the name "Anairë" (defined as a Vanya "who remained in Túna") was changed to "'Elenwë who perished in the Ice'" (*WotJ*, 323). But Elenwë is named in the essay entitled "The Names of Finwë's Descendants," where it tells the story of her death, with the added detail that Turgon was able to rescue his daughter when both she and her mother had been cast into the "cruel sea" by the "treacherous" ice, a detail that Christopher notes appears nowhere else (*PoMe*, 345–46, 363).

Thus ends chapter 9. This chapter demonstrates that Christopher was willing, when he wanted to, to include the more extended narratives that his father wrote. But it also contains several very puzzling omissions, particularly the story of Maedhros telling of Finwë's death and the actual words of the Oath of Fëanor.

Chapter 10 "Of the Sindar"

IN BOTH THE "EARLIER *QUENTA*" AND THE "LATER *QUENTA*," THE NEXT chapter is "Of the Sun and the Moon and the Hiding of Valinor," and in the *Annals of Aman,* too, that is the next (and last) material covered. However, in the published work, Christopher inserted the new chapter "Of the Sindar," taken mostly from *The Grey Annals.* There are also some additions from other sources, including chapter 13 of the "later *Quenta*," "Concerning the Dwarves." For ease of reference, I will refer to that section as LQ (CtD). The source materials are traced by paragraph in table 11.

There is a certain logic to including this material here, since describing the situation with the Sindar back at Middle-earth helps to set the stage for the events to come, all of which take place in Middle-earth (until the final chapter of the *Quenta*). However, while that may be a more traditional storytelling device, Tolkien may well not have wanted to set the stage, preferring to leave the reader in a state of anticipation. There are a number of examples in *The Lord of the Rings* of this type of storytelling, such as Merry and Pippin describing the sack of Isengard to Aragorn, Legolas, and Gimli after the fact (*LOTR,* 564–75). In *The Road to Middle-earth* Tom Shippey discusses some other examples of Tolkien's use of this technique. As he points out, this offers "the assurance that there is more to Middle-earth than can immediately be communicated."[1] Ironically, Flieger observes that Tolkien wrote in a letter to Christopher himself that "it is the untold stories that are the most moving" (*Letters,* 110).[2]

Other than the oddness of inserting this material here as a new chapter, there are far fewer major changes here than in the previous four chapters. However, there are a number of items worth noting.

In the first paragraph (*Silm,* 91), which combines *GA* §§18 and 17 (oddly, in that order), there are two significant omissions from *GA* §17. First, there is the statement that it was not known to Elves or Men when Lúthien came into the world (*WotJ,* 9). It is perhaps understandable that Christopher would want to make the time of Lúthien's coming into the world more certain, but this may be another example of a move toward a more traditional storytelling style from Tolkien's tendency to leave some things more vague or open. The second omission

116

is the statement that Thingol and Melian's child would be the "fairest of all the Children of Ilúvatar that were or shall be" (ibid.). This statement had already been made at the end of Chapter 4 (taken from the *Annals of Aman*), and so it did not need to be repeated.

The source material of the next paragraph is quite complex, and worth tracing in detail. The first sentence, describing the arrival of the Dwarves in Beleriand, is based on *GA* §19 but with a number of changes (see *WotJ*, 9, for comparison). The next sentence, detailing the names that the Dwarves called themselves and were called by the Sindar, comes from LQ (CtD) §7, but again with significant changes (see *WotJ*, 205). The final part of the sentence in which the Sindar are described as calling the Dwarves "Gonnhirrim, Masters of Stone" is a significant departure, as LQ (CtD) §7 has "the exiled Noldor . . . called them . . . the Gonnhirrim masters of stone." This change is based on the "Excursus on the languages of Beleriand" that Christopher prints in the middle of *The Grey Annals* (*WotJ*, 19–29), in which Tolkien completes the transition of his conception of linguistic history, so that essentially what had been Noldorin (or Gnomish) became Sindarin, native to Beleriand, displacing the former Ilkorin.[3] The next two sentences, describing the realms of the Dwarves, blend the language of *GA* §19 with that of LQ (CtD) §7, which has "Gabilgathol and Tumunzahar, which are interpreted in the Gnomish tongue . . . Belegost Mickleberg, and Nogrod the Hollowbold" (see *WotJ*, 9–10 and 205–6, for comparison). Finally, the last sentence, beginning with "Greatest of all the mansions" (talking of Moria, of course) comes from LQ (CtD) §7, except that the name "Hadhodrond" comes from the essay *Quendi and Eldar* and replaces "Nornhabar" (see *WotJ*, 389 and 414), and the last part of the sentence, from "and to the Eldar" to the end (describing how Moria was only a rumor and a name to the Elves), is also inserted from *Quendi and Eldar*, which has "was known to the Eldar only by name" (see *WotJ*, 389).

The next paragraph ("From Nogrod and . . ."; *Silm*, 91–92), which speaks of the relationship between the Dwarves and the Elves, is even more complex. This long paragraph comes from a dizzying mishmash of passages from *GA* §§19, 20, and 21 and LQ (CtD) §§4 and 7. The first sentence comes from the end of *GA* §19, and the next two sentences come from the beginning of *GA* §20. The ensuing sentence comes from LQ (CtD) §7. After that the following sentence returns to *GA* §20, but most of the next two sentences come from LQ (CtD) §4 (though in reversed order). But the final part of the last sentence (after "with stone") telling of the Dwarves' love of copper and iron, comes from *GA* §21.

Table 11. Source Material by Paragraph for Chapter 10 "Of the Sindar"

Paragraph no.	Paragraph headwords	*Silm* page no.	Primary source	Secondary sources
1	"Now as has been . . ."	91	GA §§18 and 17 (in that order)	
2	"It came to pass . . ."	91	LQ (CtD) §7	GA §19: first sentence (see text); most of the third sentence *Quendi and Eldar* (see *Wolf*, 389 and 414): "Hadhodrond" and "and to the Eldar came but as a name and a rumour from the words of the Dwarves of the Blue Mountains" Excursus on the languages of Beleriand (*Wolf*, 19–29): "and Gonnhirrim, Masters of Stone"
3	"From Nogrod and . . ."	91–92	GA §§19, 20, and 21	LQ (CtD) §7: "Few of the Eldar" through "where battle after befell" LQ (CtD) §4: "But the Naugrim" through "and with stone" (with the two sentences reversed)
4	"Now Melian had . . ."	92	GA §22	
5	"Therefore the Naugrim . . ."	92–93	GA §23	

6	"But the Elves . . ."	93	*GA* §24	
7	"And when the . . ."	93	First part of *GA* §25	
8	"But as the . . ."	93	Rest of *GA* §25	
9	"And ere long . . ."	93–94	*GA* §§26 and 27	
10	"Therefore Thingol took . . ."	94	*GA* §28	
11	'At this time . . ."	94	*GA* §29	
12	'Now as has been . . ."	94	*GA* §30	
13	'Of the long years . . ."	94–95	First part of *GA* §31	"Excursus on the languages of Beleriand" (*WotJ*, 20–21): "and the Naugrim" through "and passed into the knowledge of many peoples"
14	"In Beleriand in . . ."	95	Rest of *GA* §31	
15	"But it came to . . ."	95–96	*GA* §§32, 33, 34, 35	*AAm* §127: "and above its doors he reared the reeking towers of Thangorodrim"
16	"Now the Orcs . . ."	96	*GA* §§37 and 38	*GA* §30: "and they were called" through "colour of leaves" except: *Quendi and Eldar* (*WotJ*, 385): "the Laiquendi"
17	"But the victory . . ."	96	*GA* §39	
18	"And when Thingol . . ."	96–97	*GA* §40	
19	"But new tidings . . ."	97	*GA* §41	

Note: The sections of the *Grey Annals* used this chapter are *GA* §§ 17–41, which appear in *WotJ*, 9–16. Chapter 13 of the "later *Quenta*," "Concerning the Dwarves," can be found in *WotJ*, 203–6. It is numbered LQ (CtD) §§1–8. Other sources are detailed as they appear.

There are also a couple of omissions worth noting. Omitted from the end of the first sentence of LQ (CtD) §4 is a statement that the Dwarves' works had little beauty until they encountered the Noldor "and learned somewhat of their works" (see *WotJ*, 204). It would have been nice to have retained this detail of the relationship between the Dwarves and the Noldor. Also, the bulk of *GA* §21 deals with the origin of the Dwarves (see *WotJ*, 10), but since that was already covered in great detail in chapter 2, it is rightly omitted here.

The rest of the chapter comes almost entirely from *GA* §§22–41. As in the rest of the book, there continue to be a multitude of small editorial changes, but there are no major changes until the twelfth paragraph ("Now as has been . . ."; *Silm*, 94), which describes the coming of the people known as the Nandor (the followers of Denethor, son of Lenwë) into Beleriand. This paragraph comes from *GA* §30, but is significantly reduced (although part of what is omitted here is used later, in two different places, as will be seen). At the end of this paragraph, two long sentences are omitted. This passage describes the land where the Nandor lived: Ossiriand, the Land of Seven Rivers, and also explains why they are called the Green-elves (see *WotJ*, 13).[4]

The next paragraph comes from the first part of *GA* §31, with an insert regarding the Dwarves' use of the Runes of Daeron that comes from the "Excursus on the languages of Beleriand" referred to above, which appeared at the end of the first version of the *Grey Annals* (*WotJ*, 20–21). A revised version of the "excursus" appeared in the second version of the *Grey Annals*, but the part from which the insertion comes was removed from that version (see *WotJ*, 19–29).

It may be recalled that paragraph 15 ("But it came to . . ."; *Silm*, 95–96) was mentioned in the previous chapter. This long paragraph, which tells of the return of Melkor and Ungoliant to Middle-earth, combines *GA* §§32, 33, 34, 35, and 36. There is also one insert that comes from *AAm* §127. As discussed in chapter 9, above, a significant portion of *GA* §34 regarding Ungoliant is used in paragraph 18 of that chapter, and it is omitted here. And, as is also discussed in that chapter, the passage used in this paragraph from *AAm* §127 ("and above its doors he reared the reeking towers of Thangorodrim") replaces the passage from *GA* §35 describing Thangorodrim, while that passage appears in chapter 9, paragraph 19, replacing the segment from *AAm* §127 that is used here. This switch has got to be one of the oddest twists in the whole complex weave that makes up the published *Silmarillion*.

As discussed above, part of *GA* §30 is used in the seventeenth paragraph ("But the victory . . ."; *Silm*, 96). This paragraph, telling of the death of Denethor and the rout of the Green-elves by the Orcs, comes mostly from *GA* §39, but with an insertion about the name "Green-elves" from *GA* §30.[5] However, the name "the Laiquendi" for the Green-elves is inserted from the essay *Quendi and Eldar* (see *WotJ*, 385). Then, with the final sentence, the text returns to *GA* §39.

Finally, the last paragraph (*Silm*, 97), which references the coming of Fëanor and the burning of the ships at Losgar, is taken from *GA* §41, which begins a new section of the *Grey Annals*: "Of the coming of the Noldor." This is another example of Christopher moving paragraphs from the beginning of one section to the end of a previous section. As a result, this paragraph feels out of place, as if it were just thrown in at the end the chapter. As in fact it was.

The narrative continues in the "Of the coming of the Noldor" section of the *Grey Annals,* but it is not picked up again in the published text of *The Silmarillion* for three more chapters, until Chapter 13, "Of the Return of the Noldor."

Chapter 11 "Of the Sun and the Moon and the Hiding of Valinor"

"OF THE SUN AND THE MOON AND THE HIDING OF VALINOR" WAS THE title of chapter 8 in the "later *Quenta*," and chapter 6 in the "earlier *Quenta*," having been pushed back an additional chapter by the insertion of chapter 9, "Of the Sindar." However, very little of this chapter actually comes from the *Quenta* texts; the bulk of the actual text of the chapter is taken from the final section of the *Annals of Aman*, subtitled "Of the Moon and the Sun. The lighting of Endar, and the Hiding of Valinor" (the subtitle is two sentences). Once again, the *Annals of Aman* contains the more detailed version of this part of the tale, and presumably the latest written, and so it seems appropriate that it provides the text for the published version. There are also additions detailing the first rising of the Sun from the *Grey Annals*. The source materials are traced by paragraph in table 12.

As mentioned above in the discussion regarding the *Ainulindalë*, this chapter would have required major changes in order to incorporate the vast reconception of elements of the legendarium described in the texts printed in the "Myths Transformed" section of *Morgoth's Ring*. It is not only the part of "The Silmarillion" with which Tolkien was perhaps most dissatisfied, but also one of the parts that changed the most in tone from the original story. Christopher too expresses dissatisfaction with this chapter, stating, "This chapter does not seem of a piece with much of the rest of the work, and could not be made to be so" (see *BoLT1*, 202). Ironically, it is one of my favorite chapters in *The Silmarillion*. I am thankful that Tolkien did not make the fundamental changes to his legendarium that he indicated he believed were necessary (and that Christopher did not attempt to incorporate them). But I am equally glad that he toned down the original, highly "primitive," and even absurd *Tale of the Sun and the Moon* from the original *Lost Tales*. I think that the tone that is captured in this chapter in the published text is just right.

Christopher says of the original tale that the "last outpourings of life from the dying Trees are utterly strange and 'enormous'". He points out that even the Valar are nervous about how bright and hot the Sun is, and some are even angry and distressed at it, recognizing that they have unleashed "a terrible and unforeseen power" (*BoLT1*, 201).

As the legendarium evolved, this description evolved into the "succinct and beautiful" language that survives in the published *Silmarillion*, which nonetheless "cannot entirely suppress a sense that there emerges here an outcropping, as it were, uneroded, from an older level, more fantastic, more bizarre" (*MR*, 372). I love the sense of hope being born out the depths of quiet melancholy that is captured in this chapter. This is the divine plan working in harmony: Eru inserts the finger of God to bring forth Light when all hope is seemingly gone, and the Valar take Eru's gift and bring its radiance to "the world," rather than keeping it in "heaven," as was the case with the Trees.

However, Tolkien came to feel that this conception was too "astronomically absurd" and should be abandoned. In the "Myths Transformed" section of *Morgoth's Ring*, there are several examples of his attempts to alter this fundamental part of the story.[1] These efforts were highly unsuccessful in my eyes, and I am grateful that Christopher did not attempt to incorporate them.[2] Christopher's response to his father's scornful assertion that the story of the making of the Sun and the Moon is astronomically absurd is that "it is in conception beautiful, and not absurd; but it is exceedingly 'primitive'" (*MR*, 371).

I agree that it is in conception beautiful. And, I would argue, in execution as well. The two short paragraphs that survive in the published *Silmarillion* from the original's far more detailed (and far more bizarre and fantastic) description of the creation of the Sun and the Moon wonderfully capture the sense of mystery and awe that makes Tolkien's work so special.

And, as Tolkien himself notes,[3] if this "absurd" business of the making of the Sun and Moon were to be abandoned, it would cause the loss of such dramatic elements as having the first incarnate beings, the Elves, wake in a starlit world, or the Noldor returning to Middle-earth "and unfurling their banners at the *first* rising of the Moon" (*MR*, 370).[4]

Those losses alone would be enough to outweigh any benefits of making the change.

The first paragraph (*Silm*, 98) tells of the Valar's sadness after hearing of Fëanor's spurning of their message to turn back. This long paragraph combines *AAm* §164 with most of §165, with one change of some significance. The statement that describes the marring of Fëanor as one of Melkor's most evil works was changed from a more absolute statement that it was "the most wicked" (see *MR*, 129). As is

The birth of the Sun and the Moon. By Anushka Mouriño. Courtesy of the artist.

Table 12. Source Material by Paragraph for Chapter 11 "Of the Sun and the Moon and the Hiding of Valinor"

Paragraph no.	Paragraph headwords	*Silm* page no.	Primary source	Secondary sources
1	"It is told that . . ."	98	AAm §164 and most of AAm §165	
2	"But Mandos said: . . ."	98	Concluding paragraph of AAm §165	
3	"But when at . . ."	98–99	AAm §§166 and 167	
4	"These Yavanna took . . ."	99	AAm §168	
5	"These things the . . ."	99	AAm §§169 and 170	
6	"Isil the Sheen . . ."	99	AAm §171	QS §75: "the Heart of Fire, that awakens and consumes"
7	"The maiden whom . . ."	99–100	AAm §172	
8	"Isil was first . . ."	100	AAm §173	GA §53: "and even as" to the end
9	"Tilion had traversed . . ."	100	GA §§54 and 55	AAm §173: "Tilion had traversed" through "arose in glory, and the" and "and there was the sound of many waterfalls"
10	"Now Varda purposed . . ."	100	AAm §174	
11	"Because of the . . ."	100–101	AAm §175	
12	"Varda commanded the . . ."	101	AAm §176	
13	"Therefore by the . . ."	101	AAm §177	
14	"Still therefore . . ."	101	AAm §178	
15	"But Morgoth hated . . ."	101–2	AAm §179	
16	"But seeing the . . ."	102	AAm §180	Probable editorial addition: "and in the city of Tirion upon the green hill" AAm §156: "Finarfin yet ruled the remnant of the Noldor" QS §79: "in the deep cleft of the mountains"
17	"And in that time . . ."	102	AAm §181	

Note: The relevant sections from the *Annals of Aman* are AAm §§164–81, which appear in *MR*, 129–38. Chapter 8 in the "later *Quenta*" can be found in *MR*, 197–99 and chapter 6 in the "earlier *Quenta*" in *The Lost Road*, 239–45. It covers §§74–80 in both LQ and QS. The additions from the *Grey Annals* come from GA §§53–55 (see *Wolf*, 30).

so often the case, Christopher gives no explanation for this curious change, but perhaps he was simply trying to avoid contradicting other instances where his father describes Melkor's actions in similar terms.[5]

The two paragraphs referenced above regarding the actual creation of the Sun and the Moon (*Silm*, 99) come from *AAm* §§167 and 168. This is among the least changed passages in the book. It is well that Christopher retained this "succinct and beautiful language" with little interference.

There is a bit of confusion in the sixth paragraph ("Isil the Sheen . . ."; *Silm*, 99) regarding the names that the Sun was given. In the published text, which is taken mostly from *AAm* §171, "Anar" is the name given the Sun by the Vanyar (distinguished from the names given the Sun by the Noldor). However, in QS §75, "Anar" is one of the names given the sun by the Eldar (distinguished from the name given by the "gods"), and it means "the Heart of Fire, that awakens and consumes." In LQ §75 that name was changed to "Naira" with the translation changed slightly to "the heart of flame, that awakens and consumes," and it is still a name given by the Eldar, as distinguished from the name given by "the gods." However, in *AAm* §171 the name is "Vása," which is translated only as "The Consumer" (see *Lost Road*, 240; and *MR*, 130, 136, 198). In the published text, Christopher uses the name and context (as a Noldorin name) from *AAm* §171, but uses the translation that goes back to QS §75.

The text continues to be taken mainly from the *Annals of Aman*, but in another example of the constant cutting and pasting of material from different sources, in the eighth paragraph ("Isil was first . . ."; *Silm*, 100) there is an addition from *GA* §53, replacing a similar passage from *AAm* §173. The language between the two passages is quite similar, with the main difference being that the passage used from *GA* §53 contains the statement that Fingolfin "let blow his silver trumpets" and the passage replaced from *AAm* §173 does not (compare *WotJ*, 30 with *MR*, 131). It should be noted, however, that an earlier passage from *AAm* §163, which does reference Fingolfin's people blowing their trumpets upon their return to Middle-earth at the first rising of the Moon, was used in the last paragraph of chapter 9 (see *Silm*, 90; and *MR*, 120), so including it here might have been considered redundant.

More interesting is the fact that later in *AAm* §173 appears the passage describing Fingolfin unfurling his banners at the first rising of the Sun (not the Moon, as Tolkien seemed to think later when he wrote the "Myths Transformed" text referred to earlier) and that that passage is also removed (see *MR*, 131). However, the unfurling of Fingolfin's banners does appear later in the published text in chapter 13 (see *Silm*, 108); it was taken from the *Grey Annals*. That is actually a much nicer passage, and Christopher made the right choice to include it, rather than the one here.

Then the next paragraph, describing the first rising of the Sun, blends language from *AAm* §173 with language from *GA* §§54 and 55. Omitted from the portion from the *Annals of Aman* is a description of the snow on the mountains glowing as with fire, and omitted from the portion taken from the *Grey Annals* is a similar statement that "all the mists of the world smoked and glowed liked gold" (see *WotJ*, 30; and *MR*, 131). This is exactly the type of descriptive details that often seems to be missing from the published work.

Meanwhile, in two places Christopher removes references to the beauty of Arien, the "maiden" who was chosen to guide the vessel of the Sun. Back in the seventh paragraph ("The maiden whom . . ."; *Silm*, 99–100) a statement was removed regarding how fair Arien was to behold. In the tenth paragraph ("Now Varda purposed . . ."; *Silm*, 100), where it states that Tilion (who steered the vessel of the Moon) was drawn to her "splendour," this replaces "the splendour of her beauty" (see *MR*, 131 for both references). It is odd that these two references are removed, and perhaps this fits with the pattern of reducing the role of female characters that I described earlier.

At the end of the fourteenth paragraph ("Still therefore . . ."; *Silm*, 101), after the statement that the Light of the Trees lives on only in the Silmarils (not in the Sun and the Moon), an additional statement that the Silmarils "are lost" is removed (see *MR*, 132). This omission makes sense, since one of the Silmarils is not really lost but becomes the morning star of Eärendil. However, this is one place where the "later *Quenta*" has a significantly expanded story that does not appear in the *Annals*. In LQ/QS §79, after it states that the Light of the Trees lives only in the Silmarils, it goes on to state that someday their fire may be used to regenerate the "ancient joy and glory." It then describes how Ulmo foretells that this would only take place with the help of Men, and that only Manwë heeded his words, because the rest of the Valar were angry at the Noldor on account of their ingratitude and the Kinslaying or were afraid of Morgoth's might and cunning (see *MR*, 198–99; and *Lost Road* 242–43).

This passage would have provided additional insight into the minds of the Valar and particularly well illustrates the statement in the *Ainulindalë* that "Manwë and Ulmo have from the beginning been allied, and in all things have served most faithfully the purpose of Ilúvatar" (*Silm*, 19). It seems clear that the failure to include this passage relates to Christopher's decision not to include at the end of the *Quenta Silmarillion* the "Second Prophecy of Mandos" that predicts the remaking of the Earth after the last battle, when the Silmarils are recovered and used to rekindle the Two Trees.[6] This omission may have also been influenced by the decision not to include the *Athrabeth* as an appendix, as Tolkien directed,[7] since the idea that appears in this omitted passage of the importance of the role of Men in the healing of Arda is particularly emphasized in that work (see, e.g., *MR*, 318).

There is another odd reduction in paragraph 15 ("But Morgoth hated . . ."; *Silm*, 101–2). This paragraph talks about how Morgoth attempts to attack Tilion as he guides the vessel of the Moon (Morgoth being too afraid of Arien to assail the Sun). The bare statement that Tilion was victorious is reduced from a more developed statement that implied that the attacks did not completely stop, and that while Tilion would always be victorious, "the pursuing darkness overtakes him at whiles" (see *MR*, 133). It seems strange that this "explanation" of lunar eclipses is eliminated, but the "explanation" of solar eclipses (that Tilion was drawn to Arien and sometimes his shadow cuts off her brightness, causing darkness during the day; see *Silm*, 101) is retained.

In the next paragraph ("But seeing the . . .; *Silm*, 102) there appears to be a rare editorial addition. This paragraph tells how, after the assault on Tilion, the Valar fortified their land. After the statement that the only pass that they left open was at the Calacirya, the words "wherein still stood forsaken the green hill of Túna" are omitted (see *MR*, 133). But then after the further statement that the Valar did not close that pass because of the "Eldar that were faithful," a longer passage is added that points out that Finarfin ruled the remnant of the Noldor in the city Tirion on the green hill, in a deep cleft in the mountains. The portion regarding Finarfin ruling the remnant of the Noldor could be said to be taken from *AAm* §156 (repeating what was already said in chapter 9 after Finarfin and his people forsook the march to Middle-earth following the Kinslaying; *Silm*, 88). And the portion regarding their living in a deep cleft in the mountains comes from QS §79 (see *Lost Road*, 242). However, I am unable to find a source for the statement that they lived in Tirion upon the green hill. It is not unreasonable to assume that that was where Finarfin and his people lived after they forsook the march, except that it seems to contradict what Tolkien wrote in the omitted statement referenced above in which he describes the green hill of Túna (where Tirion is located) as "forsaken."

The final paragraph of this chapter comes from *AAm* §181, which ends *The Annals of Aman*. Indeed, this is the end of the material from *Morgoth's Ring* that appears in the published *Silmarillion* (save for a couple of additions here and there).

And that ends chapter 11. Despite Christopher's own quibbles about this chapter, I think it works very well in the published text.

Chapter 12 "Of Men"

WITH CHAPTER 12 THE NARRATIVE RETURNS TO THE "LATER *QUENTA*," coming mainly from the equivalently named chapter 9, which in turn only has a few changes from the "earlier Quenta" (in which it was chapter 7). Where the source material comes from the "earlier *Quenta*" and is unchanged in the "later *Quenta*," I designate it simply "QS §*xx*." Where there are specific changes cited (and thus both sources need to be consulted to check the citation), I refer to it as "LQ/QS §*xx*." Where the passage comes from a place where the "later *Quenta*" has been completely revised, I designate it as "LQ §*xx*," of course. There is also one paragraph that is taken mostly from *The Grey Annals*. The source materials are traced by paragraph in table 13.

This short chapter has a number of puzzling omissions. In the very first paragraph (*Silm*, 103) a statement that none of the Valar except Manwë and Ulmo gave any further thought to the exiled Noldor after they gave Light to Middle-earth is removed (see *Lost Road*, 245). It seems exceedingly strange that Christopher would eliminate the idea that Manwë kept the exiled Noldor in mind, as did Ulmo (later in the paragraph the statement that Ulmo kept the exiles most in mind is retained). It seems to unnecessarily contribute to the lessening of the character of the chief Vala.

The second paragraph is an important paragraph, discussing the difference between the "Years of the Sun" and the "Years of the Trees" and how "the air of Middle-earth became heavy with the breath of growth and mortality" (setting the stage for the coming of mortal Men). This paragraph actually comes mostly from GA §56, with a small portion from QS §82 added in. However, highly critical related material from QS §82 (which was not changed or eliminated in the "later *Quenta*") is left out. This material describes how "measured time had come upon earth" and also tells of how with the coming of the Sun the waning of the Elves began (see *Lost Road*, 245). This omitted passage had great importance in Tolkien's mythology, particularly the beginning part. Perhaps Christopher omitted it because it seemingly conflicts with the idea that time was already "measured" during the Years of the Trees, but since the Light of the Trees did not extend to Middle-earth, the statement that measured time came

Table 13. Source Material by Paragraph for Chapter 12 "Of Men"

Paragraph no.	Paragraph headwords	*Silm* page no.	Primary source	Secondary sources
1	"The Valar sat . . ."	103	LQ/QS §81	QS §82: "the air of Middle-earth became heavy with the breath of growth and mortality," "life teemed upon the soil and in the waters," and "beneath the new Sun"
2	"For this time . . ."	103	GA §56 (*WotJ*, 30)	GA §57: "The Atani they were named" Footnote to §14 of "Of the Coming of the Men into the West" (see *WotJ*, 191): "The Second People" (see also *MR*, 39, where Christopher describes his father writing on the title page to the *Ainulindalë* version D "Atani [Second] Followers = Men") *Quendi and Eldar* (see *WotJ*, 387): "Apanónar, the After-born"
3	"At the first . . ."	103–104	LQ/QS §§82 and 83 (including footnote)	
4	"Morgoth had then . . ."	104	QS §84	
5	"But the dawn . . ."	104	LQ/QS §85	
6	"Immortal were the . . ."	104–5	LQ/QS §§85 and 86	
7	"In after days . . ."	105	LQ §87	

Note: Chapter 7 of the "earlier *Quenta*" is given in *Lost Road*, 245–48. The "later *Quenta*" changes are given in *The War of the Jewels*, 173–75. The relevant sections are §§81–87.

upon earth with the coming of the Sun is literally true. More importantly, this deleted material makes it clear that time as we know it started with the rising of the Sun and the waning of the Elves. This omitted passage helps make these myths relevant to the modern world.

In short, it should never have been omitted.

The next paragraph is another one with a complex textual history. It combines the remaining portion of LQ/QS §82 with LQ/QS §83, including inserting a long footnote to that section into the text, with a changed name coming from *GA* §57 (as Christopher notes) and another name inserted from the essay *Quendi and Eldar.* Another insertion comes from a footnote to the later chapter "Of the Coming of the Men into the West."

One point of confusion in this paragraph relates to the location of Hildórien, the place where Men first arise. QS §82 put it as "in the uttermost East of Middle-earth that lies beside the eastern sea" (see *Lost Road,* 245). This was changed in the first version of LQ §82 to "in the midmost parts of Middle-earth beyond the Great River and the Inner Sea, in regions which neither the Eldar nor the Avari have known" (*WotJ,* 173). In the second version of LQ §82 most of this revised passage is absent, and it just has "in the midmost part of Middle-earth," but Christopher speculates that this might have been an error of the typist. However, *GA* §57 has "in the mid-most regions of the world," whereas in the older *Annals of Valinor* it was stated that "Hildórien was in the further east of Middle-earth but it was in the middle regions of the world," which is consistent with the *Ambarkanta* map IV (see *WotJ,* 173–74). Christopher seems to have compromised between these varying views by stating that Hildórien is "in the eastward regions of Middle-earth."

Then the sixth paragraph ("Immortal were the . . ."; *Silm,* 104–5) omits altogether a very critical long section of the *Quenta Silmarillion* regarding the mortality of the Elves. The omitted material describes how the Elves could perish from wounds or grief. More importantly, it describes what happens to their spirits if their bodies do die: that they go to the halls of Mandos to await return, either as spirits or reborn into their own children (see *Lost Road,* 246–47).

One possible explanation for this deletion is that Christopher concluded that so much information regarding the fate of the Elves did not belong in a chapter entitled "Of Men". Another possibility is that he removed it because his father expressed doubts about the concept of the Elves being reborn in their children in a hastily written manuscript associated with the *Athrabeth* entitled "Reincarnation of the Elves" (see *MR,* 363–64). But even there, Tolkien explicitly states that the reincarnation of the Elves was "an essential element in the tales."

In a later text he again rejects the idea of Elvish rebirth as a child, but indicates that it could be retained in *The Silmarillion* as a false notion of Mannish origin (*PoMe*, 390 n. 17). In any event, the essential element of Elvish reincarnation (whether through rebirth as children or some other means) is a critical element of Tolkien's mythology, which appears nowhere else in the published text, and so it is unfortunate that it was removed here. As Verlyn Flieger points out, Tolkien described death and immortality as the "real theme" of his work. She stated that it "went to the heart of what became, as the mythology grew, the most important aspect of his invented world. To put it as simply as possible: Men die and leave the world; Elves do not. Men are mortal; Elves are immortal. This is a huge difference and Tolkien clearly intended that it be the major, albeit largely unstated dividing line between his two peoples."[1] We see here that it was not intended to be quite as unstated as it appears from the published text.

And thus ends chapter 12. Despite the short length of the chapter, there are a couple of quite disturbing omissions.

Chapter 13 "Of the Return of the Noldor"

CHAPTER 13 COMBINES WHAT WAS CHAPTER 10 IN THE "LATER *QUENTA,*" "Of the Siege of Angband"—which is edited from chapter 8 of the "earlier *Quenta*"—with significant portions of *The Grey Annals.* I continue to adopt the convention of referring to those passages where the source material comes from the "earlier *Quenta*" and is unchanged in the "later *Quenta*" as "QS §xx" (with the continued presumption that, unless otherwise stated, these passages were not changed in the "later *Quenta*"). Where there are such specific changes cited (and thus both sources need to be consulted to check the citation), I continue to refer to it as "LQ/QS §xx." And where the passage comes from a place where the "later *Quenta*" has been completely revised, I continue to designate it as "LQ §xx," of course. The source matcrials are traced by paragraph in table 14.

The first paragraph (*Silm,* 106) comes from the first paragraph of LQ §88, which was completely rewritten from QS. It has one omission that is worth noting mostly because Christopher seems to deny making it. This paragraph tells how Fëanor and his sons arrived back in Middle-earth first of the exiles, at the place called "Lammoth, the Great Echo" where Morgoth had made his great cry when he was assailed by Ungoliant.[1] It describes how the Noldor's own cries were echoed in the hills. However, a sentence is removed that explains that it had received its name because it was situated "between the Sea and the walls of the echoing mountains of the Eryd Lómin" (see *WotJ,* 176). Christopher notes that this paragraph contradicts the story of the name of the Lammoth that was given in the second-phase work on the "later *Quenta,*" chapter 7,[2] where it is said that the name came from Morgoth's cry. He adds that both "traditions" were included in the published work (ibid.). However, this seems to disregard the fact that he actually removed the sentence in this paragraph in which the source of the name is specifically stated. It seems that even when "including both traditions" he could not tolerate including such a seeming contradiction.

The fourth and fifth paragraphs ("Yet cause he had . . ." and "Then his sons . . ."; *Silm,* 107) describe Fëanor's death, and are taken entirely from *GA* §§45 and 46. The material in these three paragraphs is cov-

Table 14. Source Material by Paragraph for Chapter 13 "Of the Return of the Noldor"

Paragraph no.	Paragraph headwords	*Silm* page no.	Primary source	Secondary sources
1	"It has been told . . ."	106	LQ §88	
2	"Now the flames of . . ."	106	GA §42	Second paragraph of LQ §88: "Under the cold stars before the rising of the Moon" and "the great land" through "bore the same name"
3	"Under the cold . . ."	106–7	GA §§43 and 44	Third paragraph of LQ §88: "aroused by the tumult of Lammoth and the light of the burning at Losgar" QS §88: "and it is renowned in song"
4	"Yet cause he had . . ."	107	GA §45	
5	"Then his sons . . ."	107	GA §46	
6	"Now in Mithrim . . ."	108	GA §§48 and 47, in that order	*Quendi and Eldar* (see *WotJ*, 378, 410): "Now in Mithrim there dwelt Grey-elves, folk of Beleriand that had wandered north over the mountains" Unknown: "From the Elves of Mithrim the Noldor learned of the power of Elu Thingol, King in Doriath, and the girdle of enchantment that fenced his realm"
7	"But even in the . . ."	108	QS §89	GA §50: "But the sons of Fëanor knew that Morgoth would betray them, and would not release Maedhros, whatsoever they might do; and they were constrained also by their oath, and might not for any cause forsake the war against their Enemy"
8	"Then the brothers . . ."	108	QS §90	

9	"Now rumour came . . ."	108–9	QS §91	GA§51: "Therefore Morgoth took Maedhros" GA §52: "and the ages of the stars were ended" GA §55: "unopposed" and "and Maedhros" to the end
10	"But Fingolfin, . . ."	109	GA §§58 and 59, and the first part of §60	QS §92: "for the agony of those that endured the crossing of the Ice had been great"
11	"Thus because of . . ."	109	GA §60	QS §92: "hesitated, and the dread of light was new and strong upon the Orcs" QS §93: "But Morgoth arose from thought, and seeing the divisions of his foes he laughed" and "A wind came" LQ §93: "and afar off they could be seen in Mithrim, staining the bright airs in the first mornings of the world"
12	"Then Fingon the . . ."	109–10	GA §60	QS §94: "Then" (the first word in the paragraph) and "High upon the shoulders" to the end LQ §94: "Long before" through "friendship with Maedhros"
13	"Thus Fingon found . . ."	110	LQ §95	
14	"His prayer was . . ."	110	QS §§96 and 97	
15	"There Maedhros in . . ."	110–11	QS §98	GA §61: "and the hatred between the houses of Fingolfin and Fëanor was assuaged" End of GA §69: "saying to Fingolfin: 'If there lay no grievance between us, lord, still the kingship would rightly come to you, the eldest here of the house of Finwë, and not the least wise'"

(continued)

Table 14. Continued

Paragraph no.	Paragraph headwords	*Silm* page no.	Primary source	Secondary sources
16	"Therefore even as . . ."	111	GA §62	LQ §98: the first sentence LQ/QS §99: "and Angband was beleaguered from west, and south, and east"
17	"Now King Thingol . . ."	111	GA §63	GA §47: "Now King Thingol welcomed not with a full heart the coming of so many princes in might out of the West, eager for new realms" QS §99: "and he would not open his kingdom, nor remove its girdle of enchantment, for wise with the wisdom of Melian he trusted not that the restraint of Morgoth would endure"
18	"Angrod son of . . ."	111–112	GA §63 and GA §64	
19	"Now the lords of . . ."	112	First sentence of GA §65 and GA §66	
20	"But Caranthir, who . . ."	112	GA §67	
21	"Then Angrod was . . ."	112	GA §§68, 70 and 71	GA §69: "But Maedhros restrained his brothers"
22	"Now the people . . ."	112–113	GA §114	QS §122: "they climbed the heights of Ered Luin and looked eastward in wonder, for"
23	"When twenty years . . ."	113	GA §72	QS §99: "in the spring," "and there came also" through "out of Doriath there came but" LQ/QS §99: "The joy of that feast" through "Feast of Reuniting"
24	"At Mereth Aderthad . . ."	113	QS §99 (see text)	GA §72: beginning of the first sentence through "friendship" and "and all the land" to the end

25	"And when again . . ."	113–114	LQ/QS §100	GA §73: "and it is told that at this feast" GA §74 (based on the year count of the annal): "And when again thirty years had passed"
26	"Now on a time . . ."	114	LQ §101	GA §75: "his sister," "their kinsman," and "Therefore he opened" through "called Nargothrond" "The Dwarvish origin of the name Felagund" (*PoMe*, 351–52): "In that labour" through "princes of the Noldor" Editorial invention: "And in that time" through "the Necklace of the Dwarves" *The Nauglafring* (*BoLT2*, 247): "It was a carcanet of gold, and set therein were gems uncounted from Valinor; but it had a power within it so that it rested lightly on its wearer as a strand of flax, and whatsoever neck it clasped it sat always with grace and loveliness."
27	"There in Nargothrond . . ."	114	LQ §101	Marginal note: "he was named in the tongue of the Dwarves" and "But Finrod Felagund was not the first to dwell in the caves beside the River Narog" GA §75: "[hewer] of Caves" ("hewer" from *The* "Dwarvish origin of the name Felegund" (*PoMe*, 352)
28	"Galadriel his sister . . ."	115	LQ §101	*Concerning Galadriel and Celeborn* (see *UT*, 234): "for in Doriath dwelt Celeborn" *The Lord of the Rings*, appendix B (Introduction to Second Age), (1082): "kinsman of Thingol"

(*continued*)

Table 14. Continued

Paragraph no.	Paragraph headwords	Silm page no.	Primary source	Secondary sources
29	"But Turgon remembered . . ."115		End of LQ §101	GA §75: "and there was great love between them" (but see text) GA §76: "And in the next year" (based on) and "a city after the manner" to the end
30	"Now Morgoth, believing . . ."115		GA §77	QS §102: "Orcs poured forth" through "of the Blue Mountains" and "and while others" through "Angband's gates" LQ/QS §102: the last sentence
31	"A victory it was . . ."	115–16	GA §§78, 81 and 82	QS §102: "For a long time" through "lords of the Noldor" QS §103: "Yet the Noldor" through "regain the Silmarils"
32	"When nearly one . . ."	116	GA §115	QS §103: "When nearly one hundred years had run since the Dagor Aglareb," "by the route that Fingolfin followed from the Grinding Ice," "and Fingon fell upon them," and "for the Orcs were not in great number, and only a part of the people of Hithlum fought there"
33	"Again after a . . ."	116–17	GA §116	LQ/QS §104: "Again after a hundred years" and "Fingon won great praise" through "of this new thing"

Note: Chapter 10 in the "later *Quenta*" "Of the Siege of Angband" is printed in *WotJ,* 175–80. Chapter 8 of the earlier *Quenta* appears in *Lost Road,* 248–58. The relevant sections in LQ and QS are §§88–104. The portions from *The Grey Annals* used in this chapter pick up from §42, right after where it left off at the end of chapter 10, and continue through §82 (except for a couple of paragraphs that are moved to chapter 17), with additional portions coming from §§114–16. These can be found in *WotJ,* 17–38 and 45–47.

ered in much less detail in the remaining part of LQ/QS §88 (see *Lost Road*, 249). I am pleased that Christopher included the more extensive version from the *Grey Annals*. After all, Fëanor is one of the most important characters in *The Silmarillion*, and it is proper that his death should be fully described.

In the seventh paragraph ("But even in the . . ."; *Silm*, 108) there is one change of some significance. This paragraph (which comes almost directly from QS §89) describes the meeting between Maedhros and Morgoth's emissaries, resulting in Maedhros being captured. The statement in the description of Morgoth's forces "there were Balrogs" is changed from "they were Balrogs" (suggesting that as written by Tolkien, Morgoth's entire embassy consisted of Balrogs; see *Lost Road*, 249). This change is consistent with Tolkien's intention to reduce the number of Balrogs that existed to no more than three to seven.

The ninth paragraph ("Now rumour came to"; *Silm*, 108–9) details the arrival of Fingolfin and the reaction of Morgoth's servants to the rising of the Sun.[3] This paragraph comes mostly from QS §91 (at one point using language from the older version instead of the replacement that Tolkien had written in the "later *Quenta*"), with additions from *GA* §§52 and 55.[4] There are a number of omissions from this paragraph worth noting.

The first omission is a sentence stating how the Orcs were amazed at the rising of the Moon as Fingolfin set foot on Middle-earth (see *Lost Road*, 250). I suppose that Christopher considered this redundant, but the Orcs' amazement at the rising of the Moon would have provided a good setup for their terror at the rising of the Sun.

The description of the Sun as rising "flaming in the West" comes from the older QS §91; in the final version of LQ §91 this was amended to "flaming above the shadows" (see *WotJ*, 177), but this change was not taken up in the published text. Although this is a minor matter, it seems strange that Christopher would disregard such a specific change.

The next omission from this paragraph worth noting is a sentence describing the time of growth following the rising of the Sun, and included the phrase "and good was made of evil, as happens still" (see *Lost Road*, 250). The first part, describing the time of growth, repeats what was stated earlier, and therefore its omission is understandable. However, the latter part about good being made of evil is a nice summary of an important tenet of Tolkien's philosophy and should not have been deleted.

Finally, there is also a statement describing Morgoth's fear and wrathful pondering that is omitted from this paragraph (*Lost Road*, 250). This is another odd detail to remove, again reducing the sense of what a craven bully Morgoth had become.

The twelfth paragraph ("Then Fingon the . . ."; *Silm*, 109–10) begins the story of Fingon's valiant rescue of Maedhros. The first half of this paragraph comes from *GA* §60 (except that the first word comes from QS §94 and there is an insert taken from LQ §94 describing the history of friendship between the two). But then the rest of this paragraph and the next three paragraphs all are taken from LQ/QS. *GA* §61 simply states "In the *Quenta* it is told . . ." and then sums up in two sentences what is stated in those three and a half paragraphs. This is an interesting switch, since for the past several chapters it was the *Annals* that told the story in greater detail than the *Quenta*. Needless to say, I am glad that Christopher included the extended narrative here.

The fifteenth paragraph ("There Maedhros in . . ."; *Silm*, 110–11) mostly continues from the *Quenta* (most of QS §98), but it does have one insertion from *GA* §61, and another, interestingly, from *GA* §69. This insert consists of the words of Maedhros to Fingolfin when he cedes to him any claim to the kingship of the Noldor. As will be seen, this conversation takes place somewhat later in the narrative in the *Grey Annals* than it does in the *Quenta*, or in the published *Silmarillion*.

Conversely, the first part of the first sentence of the seventeenth paragraph ("Now King Thingol . . ."; *Silm*, 111), describing Thingol's displeasure at having so many mighty new princes looking for realms in Beleriand, is taken from *GA* §47, which is much earlier in the narrative. The rest of that sentence comes from the second-to-last sentence of QS §99. It does not, however, include the addition made to the end of this sentence in the "later *Quenta*," indicating that Thingol would also never completely forget the Kinslaying, because of his kinship with Olwë, the lord of the Teleri at Alqualondë. Once again, it is difficult to understand why a specific addition like this would be left out; I see no reason why it should not have been included.

In the nineteenth paragraph ("Now the lords of . . ."; *Silm*, 112) there is another long passage omitted. This paragraph introduces the council that the Noldor held in Mithrim. The beginning of the first sentence comes from *GA* §65, but the rest of that section is omitted and the remainder of this paragraph comes from *GA* §66. The omitted portion of *GA* §65 describes the reason they called the council: to decide how they would deal with the Grey-elves and to conduct their war against Morgoth. It also points out that many of them found the northlands "chill" and found the southern countries "fairer" and were more interested in finding new homes where they could live in peace far away from the "camps of war" (*WotJ*, 33). It seems a strange passage to leave out, but certainly does not strike me as having the same degree of significance as some of the other omissions that I have commented on.

Another fairly long passage is omitted from paragraph 21 ("Then Angrod was . . ."; *Silm*, 112), but the material that was removed here was partially covered already earlier in the chapter. This paragraph combines *GA* §§68, 70, and 71, with one small insert from *GA* §69. It will be recalled that a part of that section was already used in paragraph 15 of this chapter, but the rest of it is omitted. The portion of *GA* §69 that is not used either here or back in paragraph 15 tells of how, when the council discussed choosing who would be their chief prince, almost all chose Fingolfin. It goes on to describe how this brought Mandos's prediction that the House of Fëanor would be forever called "the Dispossessed" to the recollection of all of those present. It also says that this only added to the unhappiness of the sons of Fëanor at the choice of Fingolfin, except for Maedhros himself, "though it touched him the nearest" (*WotJ*, 33–34).

In the published text, of course, the decision to make Fingolfin the high king was made earlier in the narrative, when the Noldor are first reunited after Maedhros's rescue by Fingon and Mandos's prediction and the dissatisfaction of Maedhros' brothers are briefly referred to. That part of the story was taken mostly from the older version contained in the *Quenta Silmarillion*. This is an example of the dangers of constantly switching back and forth between different sources. Christopher would have done better here to have included the *Grey Annals* version intact.

Even more interestingly, the next paragraph—describing the people of Caranthir and their relationship with the Dwarves—is inserted here from much later in the narrative, coming from *GA* §114 (with an insert taken from QS §122, also much later in the narrative). It seems strange that this paragraph was moved to this spot, instead of remaining where it was written among what would become Chapter 15, "Of the Noldor in Beleriand." However, an explanation for this move is suggested by another insertion made in the twenty-sixth paragraph ("Now on a time . . ."; *Silm*, 114), as will be seen shortly.

Several serious issues arise in that paragraph, which describes Finrod's founding of his kingdom at Nargothrond. The first part of this paragraph comes from LQ §101 (which was rewritten from QS), with some language inserted from *GA* §75. There is also an insert that comes from a note to *The Shibboleth of Fëanor.* But the latter part of the paragraph contains the first major editorial invention in the book. It is in fact closely related to the most extensive (arguably the only truly extensive) editorial invention in the book.[5] Part of this passage, however, is actually based on a passage that goes all the way back to the tale *The Nauglafring* in *The Book of Lost Tales 2*.

The insert described above is the statement in this paragraph that the Dwarves assisted in the building of Nargothrond. There is no such indication in either the "later *Quenta*" or the *Grey Annals*, only a note that Tolkien wrote next to the name "Felagund" in LQ §101 saying, "This was in fact a Dwarvish name; for Nargothrond was first made by Dwarves as is later recounted." The only reference to a later account that Christopher refers to is a comment of Mîm's in a constituent text to the *Narn* in which he says, "Elves have caused the end of his race, and taken all their mansions, especially Nargothrond" (see *WotJ*, 179–80). However, there is an explicit statement that Finrod had the Dwarves' assistance in building Nargothrond in a note entitled "The Dwarvish origin of the name Felagund" dated December 1959 (*PoMe*, 351–52).

It is possible that this addition of the statement that the Dwarves assisted with the creation of Nargothrond is the reason that Christopher moved the description of the relationship of Caranthir and his people with the Dwarves to paragraph 22 of this chapter from what was to become chapter 15. This way there was already some precedent for the Noldor having dealings with the Dwarves before the creation of Nargothrond. This is an example of how complicated the process of the creation of this text was, and how changes required additional changes.

In his commentary to the original "lost tale," *The Nauglafring*, Christopher notes that the idea that the Rodothlim (the precursors of the Noldor of Nargothrond) possessed treasures coming out of Valinor persisted throughout the development of this part of the story all the way to the published *Silmarillion*, where it states that Finrod brought more treasures to Middle-earth than any of the other princes of the Noldor (*BoLT2*, 246; and *Silm*, 114). In fact, the statement regarding Finrod's treasures was never part of the *Quenta Silmarillion* as written by Tolkien; it was inserted by Christopher and comes almost directly from the note entitled "The Dwarvish origin of the name Felagund" described above.

Most importantly, there is no indication in any of Tolkien's writings that (as is stated in this paragraph) the Dwarves created a great necklace for Finrod (whether called the "Nauglamîr" or anything else), or that anything called the "Necklace of the Dwarves" (under any name) was ever created before Thingol had the Dwarves create the version of the Nauglamîr that included the Silmaril Beren and Lúthien took from Morgoth. The Dwarves' first creating the Nauglamîr for Thingol is the story as it existed from the original Lost Tale, *The*

Nauglafring, and Tolkien never changed it, despite the important role that this preexisting Necklace of the Dwarves plays in the published text of *The Silmarillion.*

Christopher does comment on this curious matter. At the end of Section V of *The War of the Jewels,* there is a short section entitled "A Note on Chapter 22 Of the Ruin of Doriath in the published *Silmarillion*" in which Christopher acknowledges that he created this version of this story (*WotJ,* 354–56).[6]

Finally, the last sentence of the paragraph, describing the Nauglamîr, is based closely on a passage describing its predecessor, the Nauglafring, from the original Lost Tale *The Nauglafring* (*BoLT2,* 228).

The next paragraph comes partly from LQ §101, but it is changed based on the marginal note cited in the previous paragraph regarding Nargothrond being first made by Dwarves. The statement that Finrod was named Felagund "in the tongue of the Dwarves" is based on the portion of the marginal note in which Tolkien wrote beside the name Felagund, "This was in fact a Dwarvish name" (*WotJ,* 179). The last sentence, stating that Finrod Felagund was not the first to dwell at Nargothrond, is apparently based on the rest of the marginal note cited above, which reads "for Nargothrond was first made by Dwarves as is later recounted" (ibid.).

The following paragraph ("Galadriel his . . ."; *Silm,* 115) combines language from *GA* §75 and LQ §101, but with a fundamental change that does not appear at all in either the *Quenta* or *Annals* traditions, but instead appears to come from the text entitled *Concerning Galadriel and Celeborn* published in the "History of Galadriel and Celeborn" section of *Unfinished Tales.* The first part of the first sentence, "Galadriel his sister went not with him to Nargothrond," seems to be based mostly on LQ §101, which has "Yet Galadriel his sister dwelt never in Nargothrond" (*MR,* 178.) *GA* §75 simply states that she "did not depart from Doriath" (*MR,* 35). The statement that she never dwelt in Nargothrond contradicts, however, a statement in *GA* §108 that is included later in the published text[7] that when Nargothrond was completed "Galadriel came from Doriath and dwelt there a while" (*WotJ,* 44). The next part of the sentence, "for in Doriath dwelt Celeborn, kinsman of Thingol," is an addition that appears to be based on the comment in *Concerning Galadriel and Celeborn* that "[i]n Doriath she met Celeborn, grandson of Elmo the brother of Thingol" (see *UT,* 234; see also the introduction to the Second Age portion of appendix B of *The Lord of the Rings,* where Celeborn is specifically described as "kinsman of Thingol"). The final part of the sentence, "and there was great love between them," is taken from *GA* §75 (*WotJ,* 35). But in *GA* §75 the "them" refers to Galadriel and

Melian, not Galadriel and Celeborn, as is the implication in the published text.

There is a significant amount of material that was either moved to later in the narrative, or omitted altogether from the thirty-first paragraph ("A victory it was . . ."; *Silm*, 115–16), describing the siege of Angband. This paragraph comes from *GA* §§78, 81 and 82.[8] There are also three sentences from *GA* §81 that are not used here. One, from the middle of the section, describes how Morgoth used the lore and skill of captured Noldor for his own purposes, took pleasure in tormenting them, and also learned of the deeds of his enemies. The other two are at the end of that section and describe how Morgoth would release some of these captured Elves to work treason among their fellows, thus helping to fulfill Mandos's curse (see *WotJ*, 37).[9] There is also a very interesting passage in *GA* §82 that is omitted here and not used anywhere else in the published text. This passage tells of how the Elves learned that the Silmarils still existed and were set in Morgoth's iron crown, because some of the Noldor that he captured were too mighty for him to daunt, and therefore often became his mightiest foes when they escaped (see *WotJ*, 38). I believe that this passage should have been retained to balance the statement included in the published text regarding how many of the released Noldor were still under Morgoth's control and were used as his spies.

Then the next and final paragraph skips all the way to *GA* §115.[10] That brings us to the end of chapter 13.

Chapter 14 "Of Beleriand and Its Realms"

CHAPTER 14 COMES MAINLY FROM THE "LATER *QUENTA*" CHAPTER 11 OF the same name, which in turn was edited from chapter 9 in the "earlier *Quenta*." The chapter also takes some of its language from the *Grey Annals*. The source materials are traced by paragraph in table 15.

There is a long discussion associated with this chapter in *WotJ*, 180–91, regarding the history of the *Silmarillion* maps. Included with this discussion is a reproduction of the second and last map of Middle-earth west of the Blue Mountains in the Elder Days, with all of the alterations and additions that Tolkien penciled onto it over the years, in four separate drawings (Northwest, Northeast, Southwest, and Southeast). Christopher then exhaustively describes the alterations that his father made.

Christopher then created two new maps, one that appears at the end of the published work, entitled "Map of Beleriand and the Lands to the North," and one that appears in chapter 14 entitled "The Realms of the Noldor and the Sindar." Both of these maps are based on the map published in *The War of the Jewels*. The one that appears at the end of the text has all of the names of the various princes and kings removed from the places where they ruled, whereas the one that appears in this chapter has much less geological detail (and covers much less territory). There are a number of other changes made to those maps, but I am not going to attempt to analyze those changes here.

There is relatively little to say about the text of this chapter (although the minor editorial changes are particularly heavy here). The second paragraph (*Silm*, 118), which describes Morgoth's realm, has a couple of significant omissions. The first gives additional geographical details, including the location of Utumno at the midpoint of his northern realm, as well as changes that occurred as a result of his war with the other Valar (see *Lost Road*, 259). The other omission is a footnote that was added to the "later *Quenta*" quoting Ælfwine as stating that this material does not come from Pengolod but instead was added in by Ælfwine from the *Dorgannas Iaur* (*WotJ*, 191–92). This is another example of the context within which the story was framed

Table 15. Source Material by Paragraph for Chapter 14 "Of Beleriand and Its Realms"

Paragraph no.	Paragraph headwords	*Silm* page no.	Primary source	Secondary sources
1	"This is the . . ."	118	*GA* §83	LQ/QS §105: "This is the" through "ancient days"
2	"In the north . . ."	118	LQ/QS §105 (as changed in LQ2)	
3	"To the west of . . ."	118–19	LQ/QS §106	*Quendi and Eldar* (see *WotJ*, 400): "Hithlum it became in the tongue of the Sindar that dwelt in those regions" QS §106: "and the most part" through "Mountains of Mithrim"
4	"Fingolfin and Fingon . . ."	119	*GA* §83	Footnote that was changed on the late typescript of LQ 2: "that signifies" through "and Mount Taras" QS §116: "the wise, son of Fingolfin"
5	"West of Dor-lómin . . ."	119	LQ/QS §106	
6	"South of Ard-galen . . ."	119–20	LQ/QS §106	LQ/QS §117: "From the northern slopes of Dorthonion Angrod and Aegnor, sons of Finarfin, looked over the fields of Ard-galen" and "their people were few, for the land was barren, and the great highlands behind were deemed to be a bulwark that Morgoth would not lightly seek to cross" *GA* §85: "and were the vassals of their brother Finrod, lord of Nargothrond"

7	"Between Dorthonion and . . ."	120	Last sentence of LQ/QS §106	LQ/QS §117: first sentence
8	"Now the great and . . ."	120	LQ/QS §109	LQ/QS §107: first two sentences
9	"But the realm of . . ."	120–21	See secondary sources	QS §109: beginning of the first sentence, through "Narog" GA §85: "to the River Nenning, that reached the sea at Eglarest" LQ/QS §119: "and Finrod became" through "only in the Falas" GA §90: "There dwelt those" through "make war by sea" except that "Barad Nimras" comes from LQ §120 (with the "Barad" actually added in from the map) and "western" is added in before "sea" from QS §120 QS §120: the final sentence
10	"Thus the realm . . ."	121	QS §120	
11	"Upon the left . . ."	121	LQ/QS §110	Maeglin (Wolf, 333 and 338 n. 7): "That way was made long before, in the time ere Morgoth returned to Middle-earth," "where still there stood in the days of the Siege the stone bridge of Iant Iaur" and "and crossing the Arossiach (which signifies the Fords of Aros)"
12	"Southward lay the . . ."	121–22	QS §110	QS §121: "the guarded woods of Doriath, abode of Thingol the Hidden King, into whose realm none passed save by his will"

(continued)

Table 15. Continued

Paragraph no.	Paragraph headwords	Silm page no.	Primary source	Secondary sources
13	"In the south-west . . ."	122	LQ/QS §§ 111 (excluding the first sentence, which is used later in the chapter), LQ/QS §112, and part of LQ/QS §113	
14	"This dividing fall . . ."	122–23	LQ/QS §113	GA §39: "Upon Amon Ereb" QS §115: "died Denethor" through "starlit peace of Beleriand" QS §108: "tangled forest" through "Dark Elves wandering"
15	"Gelion was a . . ."	123	LQ/QS §114	LQ §113: "far green country"
16	"In Ossiriand dwelt . . ."	123	LQ/QS §115	Footnote to LQ §108: "wherefore the Noldor" to the end
17	"East of Dorthonion . . ."	123–24	QS §118	Footnote to LQ §118: the final sentence
18	"Between the arms . . ."	124	LQ/QS §118	GA §86: "in the greenwoods," "But there" through "even from afar," and the final sentence
19	"Thus the sons . . ."	124	QS §119	

Note: Chapter 11 of the "later *Quenta*" appears at *WotJ*, 191–98, and chapter 9 in the "earlier *Quenta*" is printed in *Lost Road*, 258–72. The relevant sections are §§105–121. I continue to follow the protocol of referring to "QS" where there are no specific changes cited in the "later *Quenta*," and referring to "LQ/QS" where there are such specific changes cited. There are two sets of edits noted by Christopher, which he designates as "LQI" and "LQ2," but I do not make this distinction. The language from the *Grey Annals* comes from *GA* §§83–90 (*WotJ*, 38–40).

being removed from the text, resulting in the loss of the sense of this being a work compiled from different sources.

Another odd point is that, while the fifth, sixth, and seventh paragraphs (*Silm*, 119–20) are all taken mostly from LQ/QS §106, the fifth paragraph ("West of Dor-lómin . . .") has an insert from QS §116, and the next two paragraphs both have significant language blended in from LQ/QS §117. I have no idea why this material was moved up ten and eleven paragraphs like this.

In the next paragraph ("Now the great . . ."; *Silm*, 120) describing the lands bordering the rivers Sirion, Teiglin, and Narog, it is strange that the text states that the distance that Sirion flows is "one hundred and thirty leagues," because Christopher specifically notes that the distance that Sirion flowed was changed from 121 leagues in the "earlier *Quenta*" to 131 in the "later *Quenta*" (*WotJ*, 193). It also should be noted that this paragraph is taken from the first half of LQ/QS §107 and most but not all of LQ/QS §109, skipping half of §107 and all of §108. It loses additional details describing the tributaries of Sirion and the lands bordering Beleriand (see *Lost Road*, 260–61; and *WotJ*, 193).[1]

The next paragraph ("But the realm . . ."; *Silm*, 120–21) describes the realm of Nargothrond. It was one of the most difficult ones for me to track down. The beginning of the first sentence, through "Narog," comes directly from QS §109. The next part, "to the River Nenning, that reached the sea at Eglarest," is based on a statement in *GA* §85 (see *WotJ*, 39).[2] From "and Finrod became" it picks up from LQ/QS §119, through the next sentence. Then the following three sentences come from *GA* §90. The name "Barad Nimras" comes from LQ §120 (with the "Barad" actually added in from the map; it does not appear in the "later *Quenta*" text) and "western" added in before "sea" from QS §120. Finally, the last sentence is taken from QS §120. This is a good example of how much cutting and pasting Christopher and Guy Kay did from different sources at certain places in this endeavor.

The next paragraph continues from QS §120, but the following paragraph ("Upon the left . . ."; *Silm*, 121), describing East Beleriand, jumps back to LQ/QS §110. It also has several inserts that come from the late (approximately 1970) material associated with the text *Maeglin* that formed the basis for chapter 16. The first of these inserts states that the pass through Nan Dungortheb to Doriath had been made before Morgoth returned to Middle-earth. The second insert describes how the stone bridge of Iant Iaur was still standing on that path during the days of the Siege. The last of the inserts from the *Maeglin* material adds a reference to "crossing the Arossiach (which signifies the Fords of Aros)" (see *WotJ*, 333, 338 n. 7).

The fourteenth paragraph ("This dividing fall . . ."; *Silm*, 122–23) comes mostly from the rest of LQ/QS §113, but with significant inserts from QS §§108 (regarding a "tangled forest" in which only a few Dark Elves wandered; see *Lost Road*, 261) and 115 (regarding the death of Denethor in the first battle with the Orcs that "broke the starlit peace of Beleriand"; *Lost Road*, 263), and another small insert that comes from *GA* §39 (*WotJ*, 16).[3] There is also a reference in LQ/QS §115 to "when the Orcs were first made" that is eliminated. As Christopher notes, it quite interesting that his father never changed this statement (see *WotJ*, 195). However, Christopher really had no choice but to remove it, because it so clearly contradicted what is said elsewhere about the origin of the Orcs.[4]

Then the sixteenth paragraph ("In Ossiriand dwelt . . ."; *Silm*, 123) comes from bits and pieces of the portion of LQ/QS §115 not previously used in the fourteenth paragraph. The final portion of the paragraph is added in mostly from a footnote to LQ §108.

This ends chapter 14. With the high degree of minor editorial changes, in addition to the cutting and pasting from different sources, a considerable amount of work went into preparing a chapter that Tolkien himself stated a reader could skip (see *WotJ*, 196).

Chapter 15 "Of the Noldor in Beleriand"

CHAPTER 15 IS TAKEN PARTLY FROM A SHORT NEW CHAPTER THAT WAS inserted at this point into the "later *Quenta*" called "Of Turgon and the Building of Gondolin." Since there is no corresponding material to this new chapter in the old *Quenta Silmarillion,* it has no section numbering to relate it back to that document. However, since Christopher only prints four paragraphs of it, I will simply refer to "the first paragraph of 'Of Turgon and the Building of Gondolin,'" "the second paragraph of 'Of Turgon and the Building of Gondolin,'" and so on.

Christopher notes that the rest of this new chapter followed the *Grey Annals* (*GA,* §§111–13) virtually word for word, and that his father actually noted that those sections should be moved to the *Silmarillion* (see *WotJ,* 120, 199). The first three paragraphs of "Of Turgon and the Building of Gondolin" that Christopher prints come before that portion, whereas the fourth paragraph printed comes after those sections.

The balance of the chapter comes from *GA,* §§91–110. The events described in these sections are not covered in the "later *Quenta*" (or the "earlier *Quenta*") at all. Christopher clearly made the right decision in adding these passages to the published version of *The Silmarillion.* The source materials are traced by paragraph in table 16.

There is again comparatively very little to be said about this chapter. However, at the end of the second paragraph (*Silm,* 125) there is what appears to be a very surprising editorial change. This paragraph tells of how Turgon founded the hidden city of Gondolin, and quotes Ulmo's words to him when he was ready to go dwell there. The last part of the paragraph (including Ulmo's words) is taken from *GA* §111, which is part of the passage from the *Grey Annals* that Christopher says followed almost word for word the chapter "Of Turgon and the Building of Gondolin." In the final sentence, where Ulmo cautions Turgon to "love not too well the work of thy hands and the devices of thy heart" after telling him that Gondolin will last longest of all of the Elves' realms, those words are expanded from simply "love it not too well" (see *WotJ,* 44).[1]

Table 16. Source Material by Paragraph for Chapter 15 "Of the Noldor in Beleriand"

Paragraph no.	Paragraph headwords	*Silm* page no.	Primary source	Secondary sources
1	"It has been told . . ."	125	First paragraph of "Of Turgon and the Building of Gondolin"	
2	"Now after the . . ."	125	Second and third paragraphs of "Of Turgon and the Building of Gondolin"	Footnote to the third paragraph: "It is said that Turgon" through "the Hidden Rock"
				GA §111: "And he said:" to the end, except: Possibly loosely based on *Quenta Noldorinwa* (*SoMe*, 140): "love not too well the work of thy hands and the devices of thy heart"
3	"And Ulmo warned . . ."	125–26	*GA* §112	
4	"Then Ulmo returned . . ."	126	*GA* §113	
5	"Through many long . . ."	126	"Fourth" paragraph of "Of Turgon and the Building of Gondolin"	
6	"Now while the . . ."	126–27	*GA* §91 and the first paragraph of *GA* §92	
7	"For that woe . . ."	127	Second paragraph of *GA* §92	

8	"Then Melian looked . . ."	127	GA §93
9	"'Near,' said Galadriel . . ."	127	First part of GA §94
10	"Then Galadriel spoke . . ."	127	The rest of GA §94 and GA §95
11	"And Melian spoke . . ."	127	GA §96
12	"Then Thingol was . . ."	127–28	GA §97
13	"But Melian said: . . ."	128	GA §98
14	"And Thingol answered: . . ."	128	First paragraph of GA §99
15	"Their swords and . . ."	128	Second paragraph of GA §99
16	"It was not long . . ."	128	GA §100
17	"It chanced that at . . ."	128	GA §101
18	"But Finrod answered: . . ."	128	GA §102
19	"I marvel at you, . . ."	128	GA §103
20	"Then Finrod was . . ."	129	First part of GA §104
21	"Then Angrod spoke . . ."	129	The rest of GA §104
22	"Yet the shadow . . ."	129	GA §§105 and 106
23	"Then the sons of . . ."	129	GA §107
24	"It came to pass . . ."	130	GA §108
25	"But it is said . . ."	130	GA §109

Note: "Of Turgon and the Building of Gondolin" is printed in *WotJ*, 198–201. *GA* §§91–113 can be found at *WotJ*, 40–45.

It is quite surprising that this iconic statement was so significantly an editorial expansion. The only possible source that I can find for this expansion is a statement in a replacement text of chapter 15 of the *Quenta Noldorinwa* (the precursor to the *Quenta Silmarillion*) in which it states that the people of Gondolin "grew to love that place, the work of their hands, as the Gnomes do, with a great love" (*SoMe*, 140). I suppose it is also possible that the language "the work of thy hands and the devices of thy heart" was actually included in the part of "Of Turgon and the Building of Gondolin" that was not published in *The War of the Jewels*, but I can hardly believe that Christopher would have stated that at that point the "Of Turgon and the Building of Gondolin" material followed the *Grey Annals* text here "almost word for word" (see *WotJ*, 199) if there had been such a significant difference. There can be little doubt, however, that whoever wrote it, the change improves the text. In fact, Flieger cites this statement as enunciating an important theme of Tolkien's at the very culmination of *Interrupted Music*, her book on the making of his mythology.[2]

In the sixth paragraph ("Now while the . . ."; *Silm*, 126–27) which is taken from *GA* §§91 and 92, there is a small change that relates back to one of the changes in the previous chapter. This paragraph begins describing Galadriel's conversation with Melian in Doriath. The statement that she dwelt "in Thingol's realm in Doriath" replaces a statement that she dwelt "with Melian, and was dear to her" (see *WotJ*, 40). It may be recalled that in chapter 13, paragraph 28, the statement that there was great love between Galadriel and Melian was replaced with the statement that there was great love between Galadriel and Celeborn. This is a small but interesting example of the domino effect that changes can have.

The text continues with very, very light editorial changes the rest of the way. There is one curious change in the fifteenth paragraph ("'Their swords and . . .'"; *Silm*, 128). Where Melian tells Thingol that the "swords and counsels" of the Noldor will have two edges, "swords" replaces "words" (see *WotJ*, 42). I cannot help but wonder whether this is a typographical error, either in the published text or originally in *The War of the Jewels*, but in any event "swords" is definitely an improvement over "words" here.

And that concludes chapter 15. The changes made in this chapter are among the smallest anywhere in the published text.

Chapter 16 "Of Maeglin"

CHRISTOPHER HAS ALREADY DONE MY WORK FOR ME IN THIS CHAPTER. In part III of *The War of the Jewels, Maeglin* (316–39), he details the history of the story of Maeglin and his coming to Gondolin, culminating in some of the latest work (around 1970) that Tolkien did on the *Silmarillion* material. In this part, rather than give the texts in full, Christopher uses the text of chapter 16 from the published *Silmarillion* for reference, and describes the changes that he made to the source text paragraph by paragraph. There is no need for me to copy out all of the changes noted by Christopher; that would be simply duplicating his work, with no real possibility of adding any kind of insight to what Christopher has already stated. Nor would a table tracking the source material paragraph by paragraph be either possible or necessary. I refer the reader to *WotJ*, 317–30.

Chapter 17 "Of the Coming
of Men into the West"

Cʜᴀᴘᴛᴇʀ 17 ᴄᴏᴍᴇꜱ ꜰʀᴏᴍ ᴀ ɴᴇᴡ ᴄʜᴀᴘᴛᴇʀ ɪɴ ᴛʜᴇ "ʟᴀᴛᴇʀ *ǫᴜᴇɴᴛᴀ*" that was created in around 1958 (see *WotJ*, 213, 215). This was a major expansion of the "Edain" portion of what had been called "Of the Naugrim and the Edain" (and before that "Of Men and Dwarfs"), which had been chapter 10 in the "earlier *Quenta*."[1]

The new chapter on the Edain had two alternate titles. Typed as a heading to the text was "Of the Coming of Men into the West and the Meeting of the Edain and the Eldar," but there was a separate title page that had "Of the Coming of the Edain & their Homes and Lordships in Beleriand." The text is numbered consecutively from 1 to 34, but the numbers mostly do not correspond directly to the paragraphs in the published text. I refer to the source paragraphs as "CMW [for "Coming of Men into the West"] §*x*." There are also two paragraphs that are taken from the *Grey Annals*, one from §§79–80 and the other from §§130–31. The source materials are traced by paragraph in table 17.

Fortunately, despite the fact that most of this chapter appears in the published text, Christopher elected to print it in full. He comments, "To show the editorial alterations and insertions in the published text takes much space, and it is difficult to make them clear . . ." (*WotJ*, 215). In fact, the changes seem to be quite clear. There are a number of debatable changes and omissions that are made in this chapter, which in some cases alter the sense of what Tolkien wrote.

In the second paragraph (*Silm*, 140) when Finrod Felagund comes upon the first Men to come into the West, the first signs he sees are "lights in the evening" and "the sound of song" (two of Tolkien's most common symbols). However, a description of their voices as "fair, though untutored in music" is removed after the statement that they used a tongue that Finrod was not familiar with and was not a tongue of Dwarves or Orcs (*WotJ*, 216).

The reasons for this omission are difficult to comprehend. I have always found it strange when reading this paragraph that Finrod would not be able to tell that the voices of the Men who came into the West were not those of Orcs, who I have always imagined as sounding very rough and harsh. Retaining this omitted material would have eliminated that confusion. I cannot think of any reason for removing the description of their voices as fair, though untutored in music. Again, it would be helpful to have Christopher's explanation for a decision like this. It may well be that there is some textual or other basis for it not included in *HoMe,* but absent such an explanation we can only speculate as to the reason.

Then, before the next paragraph, most of CMW §3 is omitted entirely (the first sentence is used at the end of the second paragraph). The omitted portion describes these newcomers as "tall, and strong, and comely, though rude and scantily clad" and their camp as "well-ordered." It also states that there were fair women and children among them (see *WotJ,* 216).

Again, I see no justification at all for the omission. The omitted material makes it clearer why love stirred in Finrod's heart when he saw these strange new people. Why would Christopher want to obscure that? There is nothing in Tolkien's late writings about the Edain published in *HoMe* that would seem to justify the omissions from these two paragraphs of the statements describing the people whom Finrod first encountered as being fair of voice and appearance (see, e.g., *Of Dwarves and Men* in *PoMe,* 303, 307–8).

In the sixth paragraph ("Thus it was . . ."; *Silm,* 141), the names "Nóm" and "Nómin" that Men called Finrod and his people are inserted from a footnote that is otherwise not included, in which it is explained that these words for "Wisdom" and "The Wise" come from an ancient language of Bëor's people, and that this language was forgotten when they learned the language of the Elves, though they kept many names. Another footnote indicating that Bëor's name meant "Vassal" in that tongue is also omitted. But a third footnote indicating that since these Men had had dealings with the Dark-elves, their language was similar to the Elven-tongues is incorporated into the text of the next paragraph (see *WotJ,* 217, for each footnote). It seems odd that the one footnote was included, another only partly included, and the third left out entirely.

There is an interesting reversal in the ninth paragraph ("Now Felagund . . ."; *Silm,* 142) in which Bëor tells Finrod of the other two houses of the Edain that were also crossing into the West. In the published text, he states that the speech of the Haladin is sundered from that of his people, and the tongue of the people of Marach is more like theirs. These statements are reversed from the text of CMW §10, where Bëor states that the Haladin speak the same tongue that they do, and the people of Marach speak a different tongue (see *WotJ,*

Table 17. Source Material by Paragraph for Chapter 17 "Of the Coming of Men into the West"

Paragraph no.	Paragraph headwords	*Silm* page no.	Primary source	Secondary sources
1	"When three hundred . . ."	140	CMW §1	
2	"In a valley among . . ."	140	CMW §2 and the first sentence of §3	
3	"Now these were . . ."	140	CMW §4	
4	"Long Felagund watched. . ."	140	CMW §5	
5	"Now men awoke . . ."	140–41	CMW §6	
6	"Thus it was . . ."	141	CMW §7	Footnote: "Nóm" and "Nómin"
7	"Now the Eldar . . ."	141	CMW §§8 and 9	Footnote to §8: "It is said also" through "many words and devices"
8	"But it was said . . ."	141–42	GA §§79–80	
9	"Now Felagund learned . . ."	142	CMW §10	*Of Dwarves and Men* and *The Problem of Ros* (*PoMe*, 308, 326 n. 49, 368 and 372 n. 4): "a people from whom we are sundered in speech" and "of a different speech"
10	"Now the Green-elves . . ."	142	CMW §11	
11	"Then by the advice . . ."	142	CMW §12	Footnote: "and the name of that land thereafter was Estolad, the Encampment" Editorial addition: "Amrod and"
12	"Soon after the . . ."	142–43	CMW §13	
13	"Felagund himself often . . ."	143	CMW §14	Footnote: second sentence
14	"Fingolfin, as King . . ."	143	CMW §14	
15	"The Edain did not . . ."	143	CMW §§15 and 16	
16	"It is said that . . ."	143–44	GA §§129–30	
17	"But many Men . . ."	144	CMW §17	
18	"The leaders of . . ."	144	CMW §18	

19	'Then a council . . .'	144	CMW §19	
20	'To this Bereg . . .'	144–45	CMW §20	
21	'Then those that . . .'	145	CMW §21	
22	'But *SoMe* still . . .'	145	CMW §22	
23	'During this time . . .'	145	CMW §23	
24	'Now the Haladin . . .'	145–46	CMW §24	
25	'Haldad had twin . . .'	146	CMW §25	
26	'Then Caranthir looked . . .'	146	CMW §26	
27	'But Haleth was . . .'	146	CMW §27	
28	'But they remained . . .'	146–47	CMW §28	Genealogical table (see *Wolf*, 228, 238): "Haldan son of Haldar"
29	'Now Brethil was . . .'	147	CMW §29	
30	'In this way it . . .'	147	CMW §30	
31	'Now Hador Lórindol, . . .'	147–48	CMW §31	*Athrabeth* (see *Wolf*, 228 and 233–35; *MR*, 305): "Lórindol" Footnote: "and from it came the common tongue of Númenor"
32	'The sons of Hador . . .'	148	CMW §32	Genealogical table of the house of Bëor (see *Wolf*, 231): "and the sons of Bregolas were Baragund and Belegund"
33	'All of these were . . .'	148	CMW §33	GA §133: "their hope was high" through "movements of the Enemy" GA §135: "His people were of great strength" through "Morwen of the House of Bëor" except "quick to anger and to laughter" and "the Children of Ilúvatar in the youth of Mankind"
34	'The years of the . . .'	148–49	CMW §34	GA §144: "grief" and "the swift waning of the life of Men and"
35	'Nonetheless the . . .'	149	Last sentence of CMW §34	

Note: The text of "Coming of Men into the West" appears in *Wolf*, 215–25. GA §§79–80 appears in *Wolf*, 36–37, and §§130–31 at *Wolf*, 49–50.

217–18). Christopher says this reversal is based on "late and very express statements of my father's" (*WotJ*, 226). He gives no further details there, but there are actually two late texts published in *The Peoples of Middle-earth*, *Of Dwarves and Men* and *The Problem of Ros*, that both describe the languages of the houses of Bëor and Hador as similar and the language of the Folk of Haleth as unrelated and unintelligible to the other two houses of the Edain (see *PoMe*, 308, 326 n. 49, 368, 372 n. 4). These must be the "late and very express statements" that Christopher refers to.

In the eleventh paragraph ("Then by the advice . . ."; *Silm*, 142) there is a small but noteworthy addition. In the original text, Bëor and his folk are said to take up their abode in the lands of Diriol (the original name of Amras, one of Fëanor's two twin sons) (see *WotJ*, 218). As mentioned in the discussion of chapter 9, this suggests that the story of the death of one of the twins at the burning of the ships at Losgar may have already been in existence at this time. Christopher changed the text to add in both the names Amrod and Amras, since he did not incorporate the story of the death of one of the twins into the published text.

The statement in the thirteenth paragraph ("Felagund himself . . ."; *Silm*, 143) that the Elves originally gave men the name "Atani"—which in Beleriand became "Edain"—but that that name was used only for the three houses of the Elf-friends is added from a footnote to the text. However, an additional two sentences from the footnote giving the other names that the Elves called Men are omitted (see *WotJ*, 219).

In paragraph 15 ("The Edain did . . ."; *Silm*, 143) Tolkien marked "Magor" to be changed to "Hador," intending those names to be switched so that "Hador" would come earlier in the genealogy. This change was apparently taken up in the *Athrabeth*, where Adanel is the sister of Hador Lorindol, not of Magor (see the discussion in *WotJ*, 235).

The text continues with no major changes until the thirtieth paragraph ("In this way it . . ."; *Silm*, 147), which has one sentence strangely omitted. This paragraph describes the alliance between the people of the three houses of the Edain and the Elves. However, a sentence stating that the only condition imposed on the Edain was that they consider Morgoth to be their enemy and not deal with him was inexplicably omitted (see *WotJ*, 223).

In paragraph 33 ("All of these were . . ."; *Silm*, 148), the following descriptive phrases regarding the people of Hador from CMW §33 are omitted: "tall and strong, . . . fierce in battle, generous to friend and to foe, swift in resolve, fast in loyalty, joyous in heart" (see *WotJ*,

224). Again, without an explanation from Christopher, it is difficult to understand why these were omitted.

This concludes chapter 17. Contrary to Christopher's assertion, it was not terribly difficult to make the editorial alterations and insertions clear. I cannot help but speculate that what he really meant was that it would have been difficult for him to make clear the reasons for some of the omissions that he made, particularly in the second and third paragraphs.

Chapter 18 "Of the Ruin of Beleriand and the Fall of Fingolfin"

CHAPTER 18 IS BASED MAINLY ON THE CHAPTER IN THE "LATER *QUENTA*" with the same name, which was the last chapter in which substantial changes were actually made to the text from the "earlier *Quenta.*" The relevant sections are §§132–56. Once again (and for the last time), where there is no specific change noted in the "later *Quenta,*" I designate the source material as "QS"; where there are changes noted but some of the source goes back to the earlier work I designate the source material as "LQ/QS", and where the source material is completely from the new work, I designate it as "LQ."

Not surprisingly, some of the language is filled in from the portion of *The Grey Annals* that covers the same time period. This is *GA*, §§133 and 145–66. There are also several paragraphs that are taken partly from material that was otherwise published for the first time in the recently released *The Children of Húrin.* The source materials are traced by paragraph in table 18.

In the second paragraph (*Silm,* 150) the reference to the "sixth generation of Men after Bëor" is changed from "fifth generation," correcting an erroneous change that Tolkien made in amending this paragraph in response to the major changes to the history and genealogy of the Edain in the last chapter (in the "earlier *Quenta*" it read "the sons of the sons of the Fathers of Men"; *Lost Road,* 280). In discussing this change, Christopher points out that the statement "not yet come to full manhood" is not really appropriate for Baragund and Belegund, who were two of the men in that generation and were at this time thirty-five and thirty-three years old, respectively (see *WotJ,* 241–42). He nonetheless let that language stand.

In the fourth paragraph ("In the front of . . ."; *Silm,* 151) there is a significant omission. This paragraph briefly describes Morgoth's triumph in the Dagor Bragollach (the Battle of Sudden Flame). At the end of the paragraph, after the statement that the battle was deemed to have ended with the coming of spring, a significant portion of QS §135 is omitted. This omitted passage describes how Morgoth saw that he had not gathered sufficient forces, nor accurately judged the

Table 18. Source Material by Paragraph for Chapter 18 "Of the Ruin of Beleriand and the Fall of Fingolfin"

Paragraph no.	Paragraph headwords	*Silm* page no.	Primary source	Secondary sources
1	"Now Fingolfin, King . . ."	150	QS §132	*GA* §133: "Morgoth was free to labour in his deep mines, devising what evils none could foretell ere he should reveal them"
2	"But when the sixth . . ."	150	LQ/QS §133	
3	"There came a time . . ."	150–51	LQ/QS §134	*GA* §145: "Anfauglith the Gasping Dust"
4	"In the front of . . ."	151	QS §135	*GA* §145: "in his full might"
5	"Thus ended the . . ."	151	QS §136	
6	"The sons of . . ."	151–52	LQ/QS §137	*GA* §146: "and a great part" through "the Pass of Sirion" and "the bravest of his"
				LQ/QS §138: the final sentence
7	"So great was . . ."	152	LQ/QS §140	*GA* §147: "the Tall"
8	"For the war had . . ."	152–53	LQ/QS §§141 and 142	
9	"Now news came to . . ."	153	*GA* §155	LQ/QS §144: first sentence and "and he sounded his horn" to the end
10	"That was the last . . ."	153	The rest of LQ/QS §144	*GA* §148: "great fortress"
11	"Then Morgoth hurled . . ."	154	QS §145	*GA* §156: "and the cries echoed in the Northlands"
12	"But at the last . . ."	154	QS §146	
13	"Thus died Fingolfin . . ."	154	LQ/QS §147	*GA* §157: "marred his face"
14	"Great was the . . ."	154	*GA* §157	QS §148: first sentence through "became known"
				Penciled addition: "but his young son" to the end, except:
				"The names of Finwë's descendants" (see *PoMe*, 347–48, 351, 364): "Ereinion"
15	"Now Morgoth's power . . ."	154–55	LQ/QS §§138 and 139	*GA* §158: first sentence through "Northlands"

(continued)

Table 18. Continued

Paragraph no.	Paragraph headwords	Silm page no.	Primary source	Secondary sources
16	"For nigh on two . . ."	155–56	LQ/QS §§143, 148 (other than the first sentence, part of which was used in paragraph 14), and 149	GA §159: "At last so desperate" through "until at last," "whose names were long remembered in the songs," "fled," and the final sentence GA §153: "and Orodreth was driven out, and fled to Nargothrond"
17	"To Men Morgoth . . ."	156–57	First part of QS §150	
18	"It is told that . . ."	157	The rest of QS §150 and LQ/QS §151	GA §173: "their hair was dark as were their eyes" GA §174: "But Maedhros" to "new-come Men"
19	"There was small . . ."	157	LQ/QS §152	GA §160: "then Beleg Strongbow" through "for many years after" (except "Halmir and Beleg")
20	"At this time . . ."	158	GA §161	UT, 57: "In the days before the Dagor Bragollach" through "Halmir lord of the Haladin" (see also CoH, 33) CoH, 35: "over the Brithiach" through the end
21	"There Turgon the . . ."	158	CoH, 35–36	
22	"But Húrin and Huor . . ."	158–59	CoH, 36	
23	"But Maeglin, the . . ."	159	CoH, 36–37	
24	"Then Húrin answered . . ."	159	CoH, 37	GA §166: "and in time" to the end
25	"Now when Turgon . . ."	159	QS §154	GA §151: first sentence, through "leaguer of Angband" QS §153: "for he deemed that Gondolin was strong, and the time not yet ripe for its revealing" (loosely based)

26	'Rumour came to . . .'	160	QS §155	GA §152: "into the uttermost West" through "aid of the Valar"; QS §135: "and that he had not measured rightly the valour of the Noldor nor the might in arms of the Men that fought beside them"
27	"When seven years . . ."	160	GA §171	GA §170: "Great though his victory" through "regain what they had lost"; GA §170: "Morgoth renewed his assault"; QS §156: "and he sent a great force against Hithlum," "by an arrow," "Húrin his son" through "mind and body" and "heavy slaughter from Ered Wethrin"; Apparent editorial insertion based on paragraph 7: "and in that same place his father Hador Lórindol died but a little time before"
28	"But King Fingon . . ."	160	GA §172	
29	"Thereafter Húrin son . . ."	160–61	GA §171	QS §156: "and served Fingon"; Late addition to GA §171: "Húrin was of" through "Hareth of the Haladin"; GA §187: "His wife was Morwen Eledhwen, daughter of Baragund of the house of Bëor"; GA §159: "she who fled from Dorthonion with Rían daughter of Belegund and Emeldir the mother of Beren"
30	"In that time . . ."	161	End of QS §156	

Note: The changes made to this chapter in the "later *Quenta*" are detailed in *Wolf,* 238–43, and the original chapter in the "earlier *Quenta*" is given in *Lost Road,* 279–91. The relevant sections are §§132–56. *GA* §§133 and 145–66 are given in *Wolf,* 50 and 52–60.

valor of the Noldor, and that when he learned of the Noldor's new allies, the Edain, "a new anger possessed his heart, and he turned to thought of further evil" (see *Lost Road*, 281). There does not seem to be any good reason to omit this passage here. And, in fact, it is not fully omitted, since part of it is actually inserted into a much later part of this chapter.[1]

Similarly, there is more cutting and subsequent pasting at the end of the sixth paragraph ("The sons of . . ."; *Silm*, 151–52). This paragraph describes the defeat of the sons of Finarfin and the rescue of Finrod Felagund by Barahir, the father of Beren. It combines language from LQ/QS §137 with that from *GA*, §146, and also includes the first sentence of LQ/QS §138. But the rest of that section and all of LQ/QS §139 (which tell of the fate of Barahir and his people) are moved to later in the chapter, as again will be seen.[2]

There is then an odd change in the eighth paragraph ("For the war had . . ."; *Silm*, 152–53), which tells of how the war went ill with the sons of Fëanor. The statement that Celegorm and Curufin sought harbor with Finrod Felagund is a change from the statement that they sought harbor with both Orodreth and Finrod. The latter statement is itself changed from the statement in the "earlier *Quenta*" that they sought harbor with "their friend Orodreth" (see *Lost Road*, 283; and *WotJ*, 239, 240). Removing Orodreth from this passage seems an odd choice, particularly given how pleased Celegorm and Curufin are in the following chapter when Finrod gives his crown to Orodreth when he leaves Nargothrond to help Beren. This is another example of a small change that has ramifications further along in the narrative.

The first sentence of the next paragraph comes from LQ/QS §144 (skipping, for now, §143). Then it turns to the first sentence of *GA*, §155. However, after stating that Fingolfin was "filled with wrath and despair" and before stating that he mounted his horse and rode off alone, some further phrases describing his "silver arms," his "white helm," his "sword Ringil," and his "blue shield set with a star of crystal" are omitted (*WotJ*, 55). This is just the kind of descriptive detail that makes Tolkien's writing so vivid, and I do not understand why it would be omitted. The paragraph continues from *GA* §155 through the middle of the penultimate sentence, but the final part, in which Fingolfin challenges Morgoth and Morgoth responds, returns to QS §144. This is another unfortunate example where the less detailed version is used. Omitted from *GA* §155 are the actual words used by Fingolfin in challenging Morgoth, which are worth noting here in full: "and smote upon it once again, and sounding a challenge upon his silver horn he called Morgoth himself to come forth to combat, crying: 'Come forth, thou coward king, to fight with thine own hand!

Den-dweller, wielder of thralls, liar and lurker, foe of Gods and Elves, come! For I would see thy craven face'" (*WotJ*, 55).

As with the words of the Oath of Fëanor, the actual words that Fingolfin uses are far more evocative than the bare statement that he challenged Morgoth to come forth.

Finally, there is a strange change in this paragraph in which "Dor-nu-Fauglith" replaces "the Anfauglith" (see *WotJ*, 55). Christopher notes in the index of *The War of the Jewels* that the former is the earlier name of the latter (see *WotJ*, 124, 435). Indeed, earlier in this chapter "Anfauglith" replaces "Dor-nu-Fauglith."[3] In the published text, "Dor-nu-Fauglith" does appear one other time: in the next chapter, where it appears that it was not changed from an earlier source. But "Anfauglith" appears at least a dozen times. I could understand accidentally leaving it unchanged, but it seems quite strange to me to actually change it from the new name back to the old one in this one instance.

The fourteenth paragraph ("Great was the . . ."; *Silm*, 154) tells of the reaction to Fingolfin's death. It is a short one-sentence paragraph that combines language from the beginning of the first sentence of QS §148 with that from the end of GA §157, including incorporating a late penciled addition to that paragraph on one of the most debated questions in all of Tolkien's work: the ancestry of Gil-galad. The statement at the end of the single sentence, regarding Fingon's son being sent to the Havens, comes from the late penciled addition, with "Ereinion (who was after named Gil-galad)" changed from "(?Findor) [*sic*] Gilgalad" (*WotJ*, 56). The name "Ereinion" comes from the third note to *The Shibboleth of Fëanor*, entitled "The names of Finwë's descendants" (see *PoMe*, 347–48, 351, 364 n. 47).

The history of Gil-galad's parentage is fascinating. Christopher points out that at one point in the development of this chapter (and the following chapter) there were several notes in which his father was exploring the possibility of making Gil-galad the son of Finrod (and therefore changing the part of the story in which Finrod had no wife). These notes were, however, rejected (see *WotJ*, 242–43). Christopher further observes that he adopted the story of Gil-galad being Fingon's son in the published text from the penciled addition noted above, but that this was "adopted after much hesitation" and was by no means his father's last word on the subject (*WotJ*, 243).

At one point in the development of appendix B of *The Lord of the Rings* and *Of the Rings of Power*, Tolkien actually considering making both Gil-galad and Galadriel children of Finrod, with Galadriel as his elder sister (see *PoMe*, 174, 185). Christopher includes a long discussion on "The Parentage of Gil-galad" in the *Shibboleth of Fëanor* section of The *Peoples of Middle-earth* (see 349–51). It appears that the final solution that Tolkien came up with was to make Gil-galad the son of Orodreth. However, as mentioned earlier, Orodreth is another character with a greatly changing history. At the point that this decision was made, Orodreth was apparently considered the son of Finrod's brother, Angrod.[4] So Gil-galad was therefore Angrod's grandson (and Finrod's grandnephew, and Finarfin's great-grandson). Christopher points out that to reflect this change, he actually changed the name in the letter Gil-galad sends to Meneldur in the tale *Aldarion and Erendis* in *Unfinished Tales* from "Finellach Gil-galad of the House of Finarfin" to "Ereinion Gil-galad son of Fingon," as well as removed "Finellach" from the reference to "King Gil-Galad" in *A Description of Númenor* (see *UT,* 168, 199; and *PoMe,* 351.) Christopher admits that a "much closer analysis of the admittedly extremely complex material" than he made when creating *The Silmarillion* "makes it clear that Gil-galad as the son of Fingon was an ephemeral idea" (*PoMe,* 351).

It is, nonetheless, difficult to argue that Christopher would have done better to attempt to adopt the later idea of Gil-galad as Finrod's nephew. A good case could be made that this was just as much an ephemeral idea. This well illustrates the particular difficulties that Christopher faced in the task of completing a publishable version of *The Silmarillion*. In cases like this, Christopher truly was between a rock and hard place.

The next two paragraphs are two of the longest in the book. Paragraph 15 ("Now Morgoth's power . . ."; *Silm,* 154–55) deals with the fate of Barahir and his folk, going back to the unused portion of LQ/QS §138 and §139, which as noted above were skipped earlier. Significant portions of this long paragraph are mixed in from *GA* §§158 and 159. Then paragraph 16 ("For nigh on two . . ."; *Silm,* 155–56) combines LQ/QS §§143, 148 (other than the first sentence, part of which was used in paragraph 14), and 149. It also has one small addition from *GA* §153. One has to wonder why Christopher and Guy Kay artificially created two such long paragraphs back-to-back; it does make for difficult reading.

One omission from the sixteenth paragraph is worth noting. The addition from *GA* §153 states that Orodreth was driven out of Tol Sirion (which he oversaw for his brother, Finrod) and flees to Nargothrond. However, omitted from that passage is the further information that Orodreth was rescued from death by Celegorm and Curufin and their riders (see *WotJ,* 54). This is particularly interesting, given the history of the scorn the brothers later show to Orodreth, as told in the next chapter on Beren and Lúthien.

In the eighteenth paragraph ("It is told that . . ."; *Silm*, 157) we see the introduction of a different class of Men: the Easterlings or "Swarthy Men," who play such a pivotal role in Morgoth's eventual triumph. This paragraph combines part of QS §150 with LQ/QS §151, with a couple of inserts from *GA* §§173 and 174. There are two omissions worth noting.

First, the final sentence of QS §150 is removed. This sentence describes how Morgoth was happy with the arrival of the Easterlings, thinking that they would be easier to manipulate and that they would help him to hurt the Elves (*Lost Road*, 286). This would have provided a good foreshadowing of what was to come, for in fact the Easterlings do provide Morgoth with invaluable assistance against the Elves. But perhaps Christopher wanted to avoid revealing that before it happened.

Later in the paragraph, when the Easterlings are being described, a statement from QS §151 that they were "not uncomely" is removed (see *Lost Road*, 286). It seems unfortunate to me that Christopher elected to omit this statement. There is a similar statement in *GA* §173 (see *WotJ*, 60), so it clearly was always Tolkien's intention to make this point. One of the criticisms that is sometimes leveled against Tolkien's writings is that his heroes are all too good-looking and his villains all too ugly. This omission only serves to exacerbate that criticism.

The twentieth paragraph ("At this time . . ."; *Silm*, 158) through the twenty-fourth paragraph ("Then Húrin answered . . ."; *Silm*, 159) describe the sojourn of Húrin and Huor in Gondolin. These paragraphs are mostly taken from the *Grey Annals*. Tolkien never emended this part of the *Quenta Silmarillion*, so the "later *Quenta*" typescripts retain the old story that it was Húrin and "Haleth the Hunter" who were brought to Gondolin. However, even though Christopher specifically states that the published text of this portion of the chapter is taken from *GA* §§161–66 (see *WotJ*, 241), there is another source from which much of the language of these paragraphs is taken. Christopher indicates in both *The War of the Jewels* and *Unfinished Tales* that a version of the story of Húrin and Huor in Gondolin was removed from the version of the *Narn I Chîn Húrin* published in *Unfinished Tales* (with the erroneous title *Narn I Hîn Húrin*).[5] Christopher describes but does not print this passage in *WotJ*, 169–70 (see also *UT*, 146 n. 1). However, this omitted portion of the *Narn* is included in the newly published *The Children of Húrin*. So it has now become possible to more closely trace the sources of these paragraphs.

The twentieth paragraph comes partly from *GA* §161, but much of it more closely follows the *Narn* text, partly that published in *Unfin-*

ished Tales but mostly the portion published only in *The Children of Húrin,* as will be seen.

Tracking down the source of the text at the beginning of the paragraph regarding the "great feast" where the son and daughter of Hador marry the daughter and son of Halmir, respectively, is tricky. Christopher mentions an addition that he calls the first reference to the double marriage in the commentary to *GA* §171 (*WotJ,* 128). However, the addition that he refers to does not really say anything about the "double marriage"; it just refers to Húrin's mother as the daughter of Haleth (*WotJ,* 60). I do not know whether something is left out, or whether Christopher is making more of a leap than the text seems to really support. In the commentary to *GA* §161, Christopher notes that back in *GA* §140 there is reference to Haleth's son Hundor marrying Hador's daughter Glorwendil and that in *GA* §171 the genealogy is further extended with the marriage of Galion to Haleth's daughter (see *WotJ,* 126). Similarly, in his discussion of the genealogical tables in conjunction with great change in the history of the Edain in the chapter, Christopher again refers to the "double marriage" of Hador's daughter and elder son (*WotJ,* 233–35). But though it can be determined from looking at the table that those individuals married each other, there is still no reference to a text that refers to a double marriage at which both couples got married.

In fact, the only text that I can find that does refer to this double wedding is the beginning of the *Narn,* where it states, "His [Hador's] daughter Glóredhel wedded Haldir son of Halmir, lord of the Men of Brethil; and at the same feast his son Galdor the Tall wedded Hareth, the daughter of Halmir" (*UT,* 57; see also *CoH,* 33).

As for the statement in the next sentence that "the sons of Galdor were fostered in Brethil by Haldir their uncle," prior to the publication of *The Children of Húrin* I suspected that it comes from the part of the *Narn* that was not published in *Unfinished Tales,* and that suspicion was confirmed once *The Children of Húrin* was released. Indeed, most of this paragraph follows the language in that text more closely than that in *GA* §161 (compare *CoH,* 35 with *WotJ,* 57).

The next paragraph almost directly matches the text published in *The Children of Húrin.* The language is significantly different from that of *GA* §162, though the meaning is basically the same. The only significant difference between the text in *The Silmarillion* and that in *The Children of Húrin* concerns the reference in *The Silmarillion* to "messages and dreams" coming to Turgon from Ulmo up Sirion. In the *Children of Húrin* text it only states that Ulmo had "counseled" him. However, since both texts were edited by Christopher, it is impossible to determine which is the original reading. I have not been able to locate any alternative source for this statement, and otherwise the paragraphs are virtually identical.

The next paragraph is completely identical to the text of *The Children of Húrin*. Whether that indicates that they were edited in the same way or that they simply match the source text is impossible to say. The equivalent material is covered in *GA* §§163 and 164, with fewer differences than the previous two paragraphs had, but still significant variations in the language.

The beginning of the next paragraph, describing Maeglin's reaction to King Turgon's granting leave to the brothers to leave Gondolin, continues to follow the *Children of Húrin* text. However, Maeglin's actual words at the end of the paragraph are taken from *GA* §165. As Christopher notes in his discussion about the text of the version of the story of Húrin and Huor in Gondolin in the *Narn*, a significant difference in the story of the brothers in Gondolin between the *Narn* version and the one in the *Grey Annals* (and the published *Silmarillion*) is that in the *Narn* version Maeglin's words are much fiercer (see *WotJ*, 169; and *CoH*, 36). Those stronger words would have made this a more compelling passage.

The final paragraph of the sequence also mostly comes from the *Narn* version of the story. In the first part of the paragraph, up through the brothers' arrival back in Dor-lómin, the differences from *GA* §166 are merely cosmetic, and it is unclear from Christopher's comments whether that part of the paragraph is from the *Narn* text. However, a comparison with the text of *The Children of Húrin* makes it clear that it is. But from the point where Húrin and Huor talk about where they have been, it does vary significantly from the version in *GA* §166. In contrast to the *Narn* version that was included in the published text, in the *Grey Annals* they do in fact admit that they dwelled for a while with King Turgon (see *WotJ*, 58). Christopher notes in his commentary to this section that on a carbon copy his father wrote next to this, "They did not reveal Turgon's name" (*WotJ*, 127).

However, the last part of the last sentence of the paragraph, explaining that the tale of the brothers' strange fate eventually was heard by Morgoth's servants, does come from *GA* §166. This replaces the statement from the *Narn* text that "both the oath of silence and the Eagles pointed to Turgon, men thought" (see *WotJ*, 169–70; and *CoH*, 37).

With the next paragraph ("Now when Turgon . . ."; *Silm*, 159) we turn back to QS §154, with some language added from *GA* §§151 and 152, and one insert that may be loosely based on older language. The statement that Turgon "deemed that Gondolin was strong, and the time not yet ripe for its revealing" appears to be based on the statement in the *Quenta Noldorinwa* "for they purposed at first to come forth to war, when the hour was ripe" (*SoMe*, 140).

The following paragraph comes mostly from QS §155, but with an insert from QS §135 and another insert from *GA* §170. The portion inserted from QS §135 is the statement that is omitted from paragraph 4 of this chapter saying how Morgoth misjudged the valor of the Noldor and the might of their human allies (see *Lost Road*, 281). As I said above, it is strange that Christopher felt the need to move this passage.

Chapter 18 concludes with a brief statement of Beren escaping from Dorthonion and coming alone to Doriath, the same way that the chapter ended in both the "earlier *Quenta*" and the "later *Quenta*," leading into the crucial chapter on Beren and Lúthien. Now the task will become more difficult, as little or no further work was done to the text of the "earlier *Quenta*" (which extended partway into the story of Túrin) in the following chapters, and though the *Grey Annals* extends partway into the story of Túrin, much of the following chapters are based on older materials and are substantially rewritten or invented by the editors.

Chapter 19 "Of Beren and Lúthien"

CHAPTER 19 IS THE LONGEST CHAPTER, SAVE ONE, OF THE PUBLISHED *Quenta Silmarillion,* behind only chapter 21, "Of Túrin Turambar," which is fitting because the *Lay of the Children of Húrin* is the one "song concerning the world of old" that is longer than the *Lay of Leithian* (the verse version of the story of Beren and Lúthien), as stated in the first paragraph of this chapter (*Silm,* 162). The story of Beren and Lúthien was actually told in three chapters in the "earlier *Quenta*" manuscript, which is the last time the story was told in the *Quenta* tradition.

The textual history is complex, and it obviously is not appropriate (or necessary) for me to repeat what Christopher has already described (see *Lost Road,* 292–96 for his extended discussion). In short, after creating a series of four related prose texts, there was a fifth text (referred to as "QS I" by Christopher) that Tolkien began. It was to be included in the *Quenta Silmarillion,* but was abandoned because it was getting too long. Then he started a new, somewhat more compressed text ("QS II"), which was finally completed in 1951. As Christopher states, the published text was based on the fuller form QS I, so far as it goes, and then follows the shorter, complete form, QS II, with some additions from the *Grey Annals* (*Lost Road,* 295–96).

Thus, we see here Christopher including as a large part of this long chapter the narrative that his father himself deemed to be too long and had replaced with a somewhat more compressed version. Contrast this with his repeated refusal to take up the longer narratives (but still not nearly as long or as detailed as even the more compressed version of this story) earlier in the book. There can be no better evidence that Christopher was driven more by his own sense of what should be included than by any other consideration. I certainly do not question the importance of this chapter, and I am glad that so much detail is included here. But it does highlight how unbalanced the book is in that regard (particularly when the even longer chapter about Túrin Turambar is considered). That imbalance would have been redressed to some degree if Christopher had included the more complete narratives in the earlier chapters.

Christopher does not give these texts in full; he restricts himself to describing some features and commenting on some aspects of his creation of this chapter. Nonetheless, I have traced the source material paragraph by paragraph as much as possible. This can be found in table 19, with comments about the important changes in the text (but disregarding the minor editorial changes he describes). Although this obviously entails some repetition of Christopher's work, I decided that it would be insufficient to just refer to his comments, as I did in the previous chapter on Maeglin. Unlike in that chapter, Christopher does not himself go paragraph by paragraph, and (what is perhaps more important) unlike that chapter, there is more than one source here. Moreover, Christopher does not specify the actual sections of the *Grey Annals* that are used.[1] In addition (just to further complicate things), there are actually two different compressed versions of the story in the *Grey Annals*.

After going through a list of editorial changes for the chapter (except for the beginning and end, which are treated separately, as will be seen), Christopher states (as he does in several other places) that he regrets some of the changes made to this tale (*Lost Road*, 302). Generally speaking, however, I do not find the changes that he made to this chapter as problematic as some made elsewhere.

In the first paragraph (*Silm*, 162), which is taken from the first paragraph and beginning of the second paragraph of the text that is common to both QS I and QS II, there is one omission that Christopher makes a point of saying was a mistake to leave out. At the end of the sentence stating that the tale of Beren and Lúthien is the most fair of all of the histories of the Elves, the words "for it is sad and joyous, and touches upon mysteries, and it is not ended" are omitted. Christopher says in a footnote that the words "and it is not ended" should not have been omitted. It is not entirely clear, but Christopher appears to suggest that the meaning of these words is related to the fact that through Lúthien's choice the two kindreds are joined, and her likeness continues to appear in her descendants (see *Lost Road*, 296, 304). Alternatively, these words could refer to the fact that Lúthien and Beren are "joined forever."

In this early part of the text, which is common to both QS I and QS II, the story of Gorlim (the companion of Barahir who reveals his lair to Sauron) is virtually omitted. All that is said is "Gorlim was caught by the guile of Sauron the wizard, as the lay tells, and Morgoth wrung from him knowledge of the hiding-place of Barahir" (*Lost Road*, 297). Christopher states, "When I composed the text of the opening of chapter 19 in *The Silmarillion* I did not at all foresee the possibility of the publication of the *Lay of Leithian*, and I wished to include the story of Gorlim, which is virtually excluded from QS" (ibid.) He therefore inserted a portion of the *Grey Annals* (*GA* §167), and then added in the story of Gorlim from another text, as will be seen next. It is interesting to note, however, that in the *Grey Annals* it is stated that "much is told" in the *Quenta* (as well as in the *Lay of Leithian*) about Sauron's ensnaring Gorlim and inducing his betrayal of Barahir (see *WotJ,* 59). So it appears that at least when he composed this part of the *Grey Annals,* Tolkien did intend a fuller version of Gorlim's story to be included in the *Quenta Silmarillion,* and Christopher was simply following that intention.

The next eight paragraphs ("Now among the . . ." through "There Beren buried . . ."; *Silm,* 162–64) cover the story of Gorlim. The "other source" that Christopher referred to is the final version of the text "A," which Christopher describes as "the first essay at a prose version of the tale since the original *Tale of Tinúviel*" (see *Lost Road,* 292). Christopher indicates that "years later" (presumably in the early 1950s) his father went back and revised this text (which reaches only the point where the woods of Doriath fall silent). In the original text of QS(A) the story was basically the same as in the original *Lay of Leithian,* with Gorlim's treachery being much more deliberate than in the final story. The revisions brought the QS(A) text to the same form as the final version of the rewritten *Lay,* and that is what is used here (see *Lost Road,* 297).

In the following eight paragraphs ("Thereafter for four years . . ." through "Beyond his hope . . ."; *Silm,* 164–66) Christopher says that he "interwove" some elements of QS II into QS I. The only changes worth noting are in the thirteenth paragraph ("Terrible was his southward . . ."; *Silm,* 164–65). First, "the rising of the Moon" is an error; Christopher notes that all the texts had "the raising of the Moon" (*Lost Road,* 299). More significantly, the final sentence of the paragraph, describing Beren's passing through Melian's mazes, as she foretold, because of the great doom that was laid upon him, is taken from the *Grey Annals.* It replaces a different statement from the QS texts that indicated that he could not have passed through unless Melian willed it (ibid.) Christopher explains that he made this change because of the earlier comment made by Melian that "one of Men, even of Bëor's house, shall indeed come, and the Girdle of Melian shall not restrain him, for doom greater than my power shall send him," which had been inserted into chapter 17, paragraph 16, from *GA* §130 (*Silm,* 144).

Except where noted otherwise, the text follows QS I from paragraph 19 ("But Daeron the minstrel . . ."; *Silm,* 166) through the end of paragraph 42 ("Then Felagund gave . . ."; *Silm,* 170), at which point

Table 19. Source Material by Paragraph for Chapter 19 "Of Beren and Lúthien"

Paragraph no.	Paragraph headwords	*Silm* page no.	Primary source	Secondary sources
1	"Among the tales . . ."	162	First paragraph and beginning of the second paragraph of the text that is common to both QS I and II	Second paragraph of the text common to both QS I and QS II: the first sentence
2	"It has been told . . ."	162	GA §167	
3–10	"Now among the . . ." through "There Beren buried . . ."	162–64	QS(A) (see *Lost Road*, 297)	GA §44: "Fen of Serech" GA §168: "Rivel's Well" (both in paragraph 10)
11–18	"Thereafter for four years . . ." through "Beyond his hope . . ."	164–66	Interwoven between QS I and QS II	GA §175 (version 1) and GA §187 (version 2): "And he passed through the mazes that Melian wove about the kingdom of Thingol, even as she had foretold; for a great doom lay upon him" (Paragraph 13)
19–42	"But Daeron the minstrel . . ." through "Then Felagund gave . . ."	166–70	QS I	GA §189 (version 2): first sentence of paragraph 19 GA §191 (version 2): "and he knew that the oath he had sworn was come upon him for his death, as long before he had foretold to Galadriel" (Paragraph 37, *Silm*, 169) GA §193: "Edrahil" (Paragraph 41, *Silm*, 170) *Lay of Leithian*, Canto VII, lines 2173–2205 (*The Lays of Beleriand*, 230–31): "He chanted a song of wizardry" through
43–113	"On an evening of . . ." through "This doom she chose . . ."	170–87	QS II	

"And Finrod fell before the throne" (Paragraph 44, *Silm*, 171)

GA §196: "but she sought the aid of Daeron, and he betrayed her purpose to the King" (paragraph 47, *Silm*, 172)

Editorial addition: "in Tol-in-Gaurhoth, whose great tower he himself had built" (paragraph 54, *Silm*, 174)

GA §199: "fairest and most beloved of the house of Finwë" (paragraph 54, *Silm*, 174)

Rewritten *Lay of Leithian*, Canto X, lines 20–21 (see *The Lays of Beleriand*, 358): "beneath the trees in Eldamar" (paragraph 62, *Silm*, 176)

Editorial addition based on a late note (see *PoMe*, 317–19): "In that time Celebrimbor the son of Curufin repudiated the deeds of his father, and remained in Nargothrond" (paragraph 65, *Silm*, 176)

GA §205: "There Beren slunk in wolf's form beneath his throne" (paragraph 82, *Silm*, 180)

GA §210: "and among the great in Arda" (paragraph 100, *Silm*, 184)

Note: The text for the beginning of both QS I and QS II is identical and is found in *The Lost Road*, 296–97; the editorial changes to the bulk of the chapter are discussed in *Lost Road*, 298–302; and discussion of the ending texts is given in *Lost Road*, 303–6. The two versions of the tale in the *Grey Annals* can be found in *GA* §§175–214, which are given in *WotJ*, 61–70 (see also commentary on these sections on 129–33), and an earlier insert comes from *GA* §167 (*WotJ*, 58–59).

that text ended. In the nineteenth paragraph, the first sentence, in which it is told how Daeron the minstrel loved Lúthien and betrayed her and Beren to Thingol, is a replacement sentence derived from *GA* §189 (version 2). This replaces the text from QS I (and II) where it states simply that Beren's coming became known to Thingol, with no indication of how. Christopher notes, however, that there was a penciled note on QS I: "Dairon," with a mark of insertion (see *Lost Road*, 299).

There is another insert from the *Grey Annals* in paragraph 37 ("Thus Beren came before . . ."; *Silm*, 169). In the third sentence of that paragraph, the statement that Finrod "knew that the oath he had sworn was come upon him for his death, as long before he had foretold to Galadriel" is added in from *GA* §191 (version 2) (see *WotJ*, 65).[2]

In paragraph 38 ("Then King Felagund spoke . . ."; *Silm*, 169), a statement that Celegorm's hair was "golden" is omitted (*Lost Road*, 299). Christopher says he removed this because of the reference to the dark hair of the Noldorin princes other than in "the golden house of Finarfin," but Celegorm is still referred to as "Celegorm the fair" in chapter 5, paragraph 14 (*Silm*, 60).

Except where otherwise noted, the rest of the chapter—*Silm*, 170–87, paragraph 43 ("On an evening of . . .") through paragraph 113 ("This doom she chose . . .")—comes from QS II. I will therefore note only the major changes referenced by Christopher.

The long passage from the *Lay of Leithian* included at the end of the forty-fourth paragraph ("Thus befell the contest . . ."; *Silm*, 170–71) is added by the editors.[3] Christopher states that QS II had only "Sauron had the mastery, and he stripped from them their disguise" (see *Lost Road*, 300). Presumably, "as is told in the Lay of Leithian" is added in as well as the actual verses, although Christopher does not specifically say so. Christopher points out that it was Guy Kay's suggestion that they insert a portion of the *Lay* (*Lost Road*, 302).[4] He also states (somewhat defensively) that he felt that adding the passage from the *Lay* was justified "or so [he] thought" by the passage from the *Lay* included later in the chapter (*Silm*, 178; see *Lost Road*, 300). The addition of the portion of the *Lay* was an inspired idea that greatly increases the power of this part of the story, and I am very glad that Christopher agreed to it.

The reference in paragraph 47 ("In the time when . . ."; *Silm*, 172), to Daeron's second betrayal of Lúthien, when she sought his aid, is another addition from the *Grey Annals*. There is then a puzzling omission in the fifty-fourth paragraph ("In the pits of Sauron . . ."; *Silm*, 174), which describes Finrod's death. In his dying words, after he says that the fates of the two kindreds are apart, eliminated is an additional sentence indicating that even that sadness would eventually be healed (see *Lost Road,* 300). Christopher gives no explanation for the omission of this sentence, and I am at a loss to understand why he would have deleted it.

In the last sentence of paragraph 59 ("But no wizardry nor spell . . ."; *Silm,* 175), after Lúthien tells Sauron to yield the mastery of the tower to her, the words "and reveal to me the spell that bindeth stone to stone" are omitted. Then in the first sentence of paragraph 61 ("Then Lúthien stood upon . . ."), the words "and the spell was loosed that bound stone to stone" were added in. Christopher concedes that "this rearrangement was mistaken" (see *Lost Road,* 300). This helps explain something that I have often wondered about when reading this chapter: why it is that Lúthien was willing to let Sauron go when she had him in her (and Huan's) power. I have always attributed it to her showing him mercy, and that may have been part of it, but in the text as written by Tolkien there evidently was also a practical element to it.

There is a small but interesting addition in the sixty-second paragraph ("They buried the body . . ."; *Silm,* 175–76). The statement that Finrod walks with his father "beneath the trees in Eldamar" is taken from the rewritten *Lay of Leithian,* Canto X, lines 20–21 (see *Lays of Beleriand,* 358) and replaces a longer statement in the QS II text that they walked among his people in the light of the blessed realm, and that it is not said that he ever returned to Middle-earth (see *Lost Road,* 300). There are a number of other cosmetic editorial changes in this paragraph that do not alter the substance, but it is curious that Christopher decided to make this single substitution from the rewritten *Lay.*

In the sixty-fifth paragraph ("'Let it be so!' . . ."; *Silm,* 176), the last sentence, in which it is stated that Celebrimbor repudiated his father's (Curufin's) deeds and stayed in Nargothrond is an "editorial addition based on a late note" (*Lost Road,* 300–301). It is likely that this late note is a note that Tolkien wrote on one of his copies of the second edition of *The Return of the King,* next to the statement in Appendix B that Celebrimbor was descended from Fëanor. There he indicates that Celebrimbor was the son of Curufin, was aghast at his father's behavior in Nargothrond, and would not go with him. Christopher describes this in a footnote to the text *Of Dwarves and Men* (*PoMe,* 317–19 n. 7).

Then, in the following paragraph, "and still they might hope with speed to traverse it" replaces "In the days of Siege the high road had run that way, and it was still passable with speed." Christopher indicates that he is not sure why that change was made (*Lost Road,*

301). I find this telling, given the massive number of similar changes throughout the book. It seems clear that Christopher himself cannot explain why so many minor changes in the wording were made.

In the eighty-second paragraph ("Then Beren and Lúthien . . ."; *Silm*, 180), the statement that Beren "slunk in wolf's form" beneath Morgoth's throne is inserted from *GA* §205 (see *WotJ*, 68). It should be noted that this addition is consistent with the *Lay* (see Canto XIII, lines 3939–43, in *The Lays of Beleriand*, 297), though no mention is made there of his being in "wolf's form." More significantly, removed from the statement in the next sentence that Lúthien was not daunted by Morgoth's eyes is the qualifier that she was the only one in Middle-earth about whom that was true. I find this change surprising and unfortunate, since Lúthien's uniqueness (she is described as "the greatest of the all the Eldar" in *The Shibboleth of Fëanor;* see *PoMe*, 357 n. 14) is such an important idea to Tolkien.

In the final sentence of the ninetieth paragraph ("Thus the quest of . . ."; *Silm*, 182), the description of Thorondor and his vassals soaring high above Morgoth's realm replaces a statement that Thorondor was the leader of the eagles, and specifies that his "mightiest vassals" were Lhandroval and Gwaihir. Christopher explains that this change was made to avoid confusion with the passage in *The Return of the King* describing Gwaihir and Landroval as the "mightiest of the descendants of old Thorondor, who built his eyries in the inaccessible peaks of the Encircling Mountains when Middle-earth was young" (*LOTR*, 948). He points out that at the time he did not understand that Gwaihir's name in this passage was actually changed from "Gwaewar" in 1951 in order to bring it into accord with *The Lord of the Rings* and that this change should not have been made (see *Lost Road*, 301). It is interesting to note that Gwaihir and Landroval's history actually dates back to the First Age.

In the next paragraph a passage stating that it was sung that Lúthien's tears "from on high as she passed came like silver raindrops on the plain" and resulted in the arising of "the Fountain of Tinúviel, Eithel Ninui, most healing water until it withered in the flame." Christopher acknowledges that this should not have been omitted (*Lost Road*, 301).

In paragraph 94 ("Upon Doriath evil days . . ."; *Silm*, 183) we find the first mention of Daeron that actually comes from the QS texts. This explains why the passage describing him as having played the music for Lúthien's singing and dancing before Beren's coming— and having loved her and therefore having set the thought of her in all his music—is included in this paragraph, despite being somewhat redundant since earlier passages describing him were inserted from the *Grey Annals.*

Finally, in the second sentence of paragraph 112 ("These were the choices that . . ."; *Silm,* 187), in addition to stating that Lúthien was offered the choice to be released from Mandos and live in Valinor with the Valar "Because of her labours and her sorrow," the added reason that she was Melian's daughter is removed (*Lost Road,* 302). Christopher expresses regret about this omission, and I regret it as well.

It is beyond the scope of this work to trace the evolution of the "Choice of Lúthien," but I strongly recommend Christopher's discussion of that evolution in *Lost Road,* 303–5.

That is the end of chapter 19. Christopher notes that the list of changes that he gives is not exhaustive, but I hope that everything of significance is covered.

Chapter 20 "Of the Fifth Battle"

CHRISTOPHER INDICATES THAT THIS CHAPTER 20 IS MOSTLY DERIVED from the *Grey Annals,* with elements added from the old chapter 16 in the "earlier *Quenta,*" and also from a third text that was intended as a component of the long prose story *Narn I Chîn Húrin* (*Tale of the Children of Húrin*) (the *Narn*), but which was omitted from the version of that tale included in *Unfinished Tales* (*WotJ,* 165).

This statement (taken from Christopher's introduction to his discussion about that *Narn* text in a note at the end of the *Grey Annals* in *The War of the Jewels*) pretty much sums up the sources of this chapter, except that the beginning of the chapter actually comes, in part, from the end of the old chapter 15 (the last Beren and Lúthien chapter) of the "earlier *Quenta.*" And since the full *Narn* text regarding the Battle of Unnumbered Tears is included in *The Children of Húrin,* it is now possible to trace with more certainty what portions of this chapter come from that source. It also should be noted that chapter 16 in QS is actually the continuation of the texts that were labeled by Christopher as "QS(C)" and "QS(D)" in the discussion of the chapter on Beren and Lúthien, with "QS(C)" followed through §8, and then "QS(D)" followed the rest of the way. For ease of reference I refer to the first eight paragraphs as QS16(C) §§1–8, and the rest as QS16(D) §§9–23. The source materials are traced by paragraph in table 20.

The first paragraph (*Silm,* 188) is another complicated one, blending the last paragraph of the QS chapter on Beren and Lúthien with *GA* §§214 and 215. QS16(C) §1 also covers some of this material, but the language is not taken from that text. There are a number of items of note in this paragraph.

First, omitted is a very interesting statement that the only grief that may have been greater than Melian's grief at Lúthien's impending death was the grief of Elrond and Arwen (see *WotJ,* 71). This is one of the few direct connectors of *The Silmarillion* with *The Lord of the Rings,* and I regret that it was removed. Its inclusion would have helped emphasize the continuity between the two works, much as Sam's observation in *The Lord of the Rings* that he and Frodo were in the same tale as Beren and Lúthien (*LOTR,* 712) does.

The name "Dor Firn-i-Guinar, the Land of the Dead that Live" for the land where Beren and Lúthien live after their return is most puzzling. *GA* §214 has "Gwerth-i-guinar, the land of the Dead that Live" (*WotJ*, 71), and QS has "Gyrth-i-Guinar, the country of the Dead that Live" (*Lost Road*, 305). I have not located a source for the version of the name that was used in the published text.

In the final sentence of the paragraph, a statement from the QS text that none among Men or Elves knew whether the span of Beren's second life was long or short is removed. Christopher says that he made this omission because in the *Annals of Beleriand* (the precursor to the *Grey Annals*) the final departure of Beren and Lúthien is recorded under the year 503, and the same date is found in the post—*Lord of the Rings* version of *The Tale of Years* (the *Grey Annals* do not reach that date). He points out, however, that the omission was an error, because the annal for that year also states that the date of their death is unknown and that it is only a surmise that the bringing of the Necklace of the Dwarves (with the Silmaril) to Dior signified their death (see *Lost Road*, 306).

The third paragraph comes mostly from QS16(C) §5 (skipping §§3 and 4, though pieces of those paragraphs are inserted later in the text), with an addition from *GA* §212, and another one from *GA* §225. It is the latter insert that is most of interest. This insert describes how Gwindor went to war against the will of Orodreth because of his grief for the loss of his brother Gelmir in the Dagor Bragollach. However, in the *Annals* this statement is made at a later part of the story, when battle has already commenced. Moreover, the statement regarding Gwindor's going to war against Orodreth's will contradicts QS16(C) §5, which states that only those whom Orodreth "suffered to go" went to war (see *Lost Road*, 308.)

The next paragraph comes almost directly from QS16(C) §6, with surprisingly minor changes. However, the final sentence comes from *GA* §221, except that there it was only Mablung who received Thingol's leave to go to war, not both he and Beleg, as it had been in the older story (see *WotJ*, 72; and *Lost Road*, 308). There is no explanation for why in the latest version of the story, Tolkien omitted Beleg here, and Christopher's decision to add him back in certainly makes sense.

In the fifth paragraph ("But Maedhros had . . ."; *Silm*, 189), the primary source switches to the *Grey Annals*, with several inserts from paragraphs QS16(C) §§3 and 4 from the *Quenta* text, which were skipped above. However, there is a major difference in what is said in that *Quenta* text from what appears in the published version. In

Table 20. Source Material by Paragraph for Chapter 20 "Of the Fifth Battle"

Paragraph no.	Paragraph headwords	*Silm* page no.	Primary source	Secondary sources
1	"It is said that . . ."	188	Last paragraph of the QS chapter on Beren and Lúthien	GA §214: "Those that saw them" through "in that hour," "The Eldar," "country" Unknown: "Dor Firn-i-Guinar"; GA §215: "and there was born" through "Thingol's heir"; December 1959 Elvish genealogies (see *WotJ*, 350): "Eluchíl"
2	"In those days . . ."	188	QS16(C) §2	GA §212: "and he began" through the end
3	"Yet the oath of . . ."	188–89	QS16(C) §5	GA §212: "and the Elves of Nargothrond trusted still to defend their hidden stronghold by secrecy and stealth"; GA §225: "and against the will of Orodreth he went to the northern war, because he grieved for the loss of Gelmir his brother in the Dagor Bragollach"
4	"From Doriath came . . ."	189	QS16(C) §6	GA §221: final sentence
5	"But Maedhros had . . ."	189	GA §212	QS16(C) §3: "the smithies of Nogrod and Belegost were busy in those days"; QS16(C) §4: "in the west" and "in Hithlum the Noldor and the Men of the house of Hador" (based on)
6	"But Maedhros made . . ."	189	GA §213	QS16(C) §3: "the northward regions of"
7	"At length Maedhros . . ."	190	GA §217	*Narn* text (see *WotJ*, 166–67 and *CoH*, 54): final sentence
8	"On the appointed . . ."	190	Second and third paragraphs of the *Narn* text (see *WotJ*, 165–66 and *CoH*, 52–53)	

#	Quote	Page	Source reference	Notes
9	"Then Fingon looked ..."	190	Fourth paragraph of the *Narn* text (see *WotJ*, 166 and *CoH*, 53)	*GA* §220 and/or QS16(D): final sentence
10	"But now a cry ..."	190	Fourth paragraph of the *Narn* text (see *WotJ*, 166 and *CoH*, 53)	
11	"Now Morgoth, who ..."	190–91	*GA* §222	Fifth paragraph of the *Narn* text (see *WotJ*, 166 and *CoH*, 54): "and designed by his enemies" and "and they were clad" to the end
12	"Then the hearts ..."	191	Sixth and seventh paragraphs of the *Narn* text (see *WotJ*, 166–67 and *CoH*, 54)	*GA* §220: "And though the signal of the approach of Maedhros came not, and the host grew impatient" *GA* §222: "Húrin urged them still to await it, and to let the Orcs break themselves upon the hills" (based on) *GA* §223: "swiftly"
13	"But the Captain of ..."	191	*Narn* text (see *CoH*, 54–55)	
14	"By ill chance, at ..."	191–92	*Narn* text (see *CoH*, 55–56)	
15	"Then in the plain ..."	192	*GA* §228	*Narn* text (see *CoH*, 56–57): "Nirnaeth Arnoediad," "Haldir," "on the fifth day," "came hope, when the horns of Turgon were heard as he marched up with the main host of Gondolin," "for they had been stationed southward guarding the Pass of Sirion, and Turgon restrained most of his people from the rash onslaught" and the final sentence QS16(D) §13: "song or tale" and "and" and "and with him fell most of the Men of Brethil, and came never back to their woods"
16	"Now the phalanx of ..."	192	End of *GA* §228 and *GA* §§229–30	*Narn* text (see *CoH*, 57): "Now the phalanx of the guard of the King" and "beside Fingon"

(continued)

Table 20. Continued

Paragraph no.	Paragraph headwords	*Silm* page no.	Primary source	Secondary sources
17	"Yet neither by . . ."	192–93	*GA* §231	QS16(D) §14: "then hope was renewed in the hearts of the Elves"
18	"Last of all the . . ."	193	*GA* §232	
19	"But now in the . . ."	193–94	*Narn* text (see *CoH*, 57–58)	*GA* §233: first sentence (except "and Turgon" and "them")
20	"The field was lost . . ."	194	*Narn* text (see *CoH*, 58)	
21	"But Turgon answered: . . ."	194	*Narn* text (see *CoH*, 58)	
22	"Then Huor spoke and . . ."	194	*Narn* text (see *CoH*, 58)	
23	"And Maeglin, Turgon's . . ."	194	*Narn* text (see *CoH*, 58)	*GA* §237: "but he said nothing"
24	"Then Turgon took the . . ."	194	*Narn* text (see *CoH*, 58–59)	*GA* §238: "summoning all that remained of the host of Gondolin and such of Fingon's people as could be gathered" *GA* §234: final sentence
25	"So it was that . . ."	194	*Narn* text (see *CoH*, 59)	
26	"Then all the hosts . . ."	194	*Narn* text (see *CoH*, 59)	
27	"Last of all Húrin . . ."	195	*Narn* text (see *CoH*, 59–60)	
28	"Thus ended Nirnaeth . . ."	195	*Narn* text (see *CoH*, 60)	
29	"Great was the . . ."	195	*GA* §241	*Narn* text (see *CoH*, 60): "Great was the triumph of Morgoth"
30	"The realm of Fingon . . ."	195	QS16(D) §19	Based on *Quenta Noldorinwa*, chapter 13 (see *SoMe*, 127): "In Brethil some few of the Haladin yet dwelt in the protection of their woods, and Handir son of Haldir was their lord" *GA* §242: "but to Hithlum came back never one of Fingon's host, nor any of the men

No.	Text	Pages	Reference	Notes
31	"The Orcs and the . . ."	195–96	GA §256 and the first part of GA §257	of Hador's house, nor any tidings of the battle and the fate of their lords"
				GA §252: "the Easterlings that had served him" and "denying them the rich lands of Beleriand which they coveted"
				QS16(D) §20: "The Orcs and the wolves" through "into Beleriand" and "Doriath indeed" through "purposes of his malice"
				GA §255: "even as far as" through "in field or wild"
				Editorial addition: "and among them was Ereinion Gil-galad, the son of Fingon, whom his father had sent to the Havens after the Dagor Bragollach"
				Editorial addition: final sentence
32	'And when Turgon . . .'	196	GA §257	
33	'Now the thought of . . .'	196	Narn text (see CoH, 60; see also GA §243)	
34	"Therefore Húrin was . . ."	196–97	Parts of GA §§244, 247, and 248	Narn text (see CoH, 62 and UT, 66): "for Morgoth knew that he had the friendship of the King of Gondolin" and the final two sentences
				QS16(D) §22: "There he was" through "cursed him"
				QS16(D) §23: "those who thou lovest"
35	"And even so it . . ."	197	GA §249	
36	"By the command of . . ."	197	Narn text (see CoH, 61; see also GA §250)	

Note: Chapter 15 (the last Beren and Lúthien chapter) of the "early *Quenta*" is discussed in *Lost Road*, 305–6. Then the old chapter 16 is given in *Lost Road*, 306–15 (the sections are numbered here beginning from 1). As stated in the text, I refer to the first eight paragraphs as QS16(C) 1–8, and the rest as QS16(D) §§5–23. The portion of the *Grey Annals* used for this chapter is *GA* §§212–50, which are given in *Wolf*, 69–79 (commentary on 131–35). Finally, part of the *Narn* text referred to by Christopher in the quote above (and commentary on it) is given in *Wolf*, 165–69, and the full text appears in *CoH*, 52–60.

QS16(C) §3, the Dwarves are still more ambiguous than they are presented as being in the published text. Instead of giving Maedhros help in armed force, they are portrayed as gaining great wealth from selling arms to Elves and Men, but refusing to go to war themselves, allegedly because they do not know the cause of the conflict, and therefore "favour neither side—until one hath the mastery" (see *Lost Road*, 307). Contrast this with the valorous role that they play in the *Grey Annals* version used later in the published text, in which they are the last of the "eastern force" to stand firm against Glaurung and the other dragons and therefore gain great renown (*Silm*, 193; and *WotJ*, 75).

Also omitted from this paragraph is a statement from the *Annals* that Turgon secretly prepared for a great battle (*WotJ*, 70). I think this was a wise decision, as it increases the drama of the surprising appearance of Turgon and the Gondolindrim on the battlefield later in the chapter.

The text continues from the *Annals* (but skipping several paragraphs) until the end of the seventh paragraph ("At length Maedhros . . ."; *Silm*, 190), but the final sentence of that paragraph, indicating that the signal for Fingon's forces to issue forth would be the lighting of a beacon in Dorthonion, is added from the *Narn* text, in which this statement appears later in the narrative, after the arrival of Turgon on the battlefield and Húrin's caution to wait have already been described.

The next two paragraphs come mostly from the earlier portion of the *Narn* text (before the arrival of Turgon, and his troops). However, the final sentence describing Maedhros's delay by the treachery of Uldor the Accursed is added from *GA* §220 and/or QS16(D) §9 (see *WotJ*, 72; and *Lost Road*, 309)—because, rather remarkably, the whole element of Uldor's treachery is completely expunged from the *Narn* text. It is not just omitted; a whole different story is substituted. As Christopher describes, in the new text another, larger force sets out from Angband to intercept Maedhros and prevent his union with Fingon. He indicates that the eastern battle is described as being completely separate from the western battle, and that unlike in the *Grey Annals* text included in the published *Silmarillion* "there is no suggestion here that the host of Maedros finally came up and fell upon the rear of the enemy" (*WotJ*, 167; see *CoH*, 56–57).

It is quite strange that Tolkien abandoned such a key element of the story of the fifth battle in this later text, but I am glad that Christopher decided to include it in the published *Silmarillion* nonetheless. It is interesting that he nonetheless included the alternate version in *The Children of Húrin*, so the two books contradict each other on this point.

The twelfth paragraph ("Then the hearts . . ."; *Silm*, 191) comes mostly from the *Narn* text, except that it does not take up an important change that was made to that text and follows instead what is said on this point in the *Annals*. In the *Narn* text it is Fingon, not Húrin, who speaks against assailing the foes of the Noldor on the plain. In that text it was originally stated that it was Fingon's heart that grew hot and he that wanted to assail their foes (as in *GA* §222; see *WotJ*, 72), but that was changed to the more general statements we see in the published text that the hearts of the Noldor grew hot and their captains wanted to assail their foes. However, Tolkien changed this again so that it was Fingon who spoke against this instead of Húrin. Christopher points out that the change was probably made because it was more likely that such prudence would lie with the age-old king of the Noldor than with a thirty-one-year-old Man (*WotJ*, 168). I very much agree with this observation, and have often wondered about this in reading this passage in the published text. It seems quite strange to me that Christopher elected not to take up this change, particularly since so much of this portion of the narrative comes from the *Narn* text, and he himself suggests that the version contained therein made more sense.

With the publication of *The Children of Húrin*, it can now be determined that the following paragraph follows the *Narn* text almost exactly. Only the first sentence of the first of the two paragraphs in the *Narn* text used for this paragraph, plus a couple of general comments by Christopher, are given in *The War of the Jewels*, so it was impossible to determine exactly what came from the *Narn* text, until the release of *The Children of Húrin*. Christopher states that there is a more detailed account in the *Narn* text regarding the confrontation between the two hosts, and that describes the riders of Morgoth coming to the walls of the fortress at Eithel Sirion (*WotJ*, 168). He does not, however, point out that he used that more detailed account in the published *Silmarillion*.

Another difference between the two texts in this and the next paragraph relates to the positioning of the two hosts when the Orcs kill Gelmir, Gwindor's brother. The main difference is that in the *Grey Annals* version the two hosts are facing each other across the river, whereas in the *Narn* version used in the published text (and in *The Children of Húrin*) they are not separated by the river (*Silm*, 191; *WotJ*, 73, 168; *CoH*, 55).

The fifteenth and sixteenth paragraphs ("Then in the plain . . ." and "Now the phalanx of . . ."; *Silm*, 192) come mostly from the *Annals*, but though the *Narn* text tells a significantly different story (as discussed above, with the western and eastern battles being completely separate), some of the language still appears to be taken from that source. A number of details come from QS16(D) §§13 and 14; and at one point the language taken from QS16(D) §13 is curiously split between the *Grey Annals* and *Narn* versions. The statement that no "song or tale" can contain all the grief of the Nirnaeth Arnoediad comes from QS16(D) §13, and this is particularly odd, because the more recent texts have only one or the other, with *GA* §228 having only "song" and the *Narn* text containing only "tale."

The next two paragraphs deal with the treason of the Easterlings and the bravery of the Dwarves, neither of which are present at all in the *Narn* text, so they come exclusively from the *Annals*. However, there is one noteworthy omission from the eighteenth paragraph ("Last of all the . . ."; *Silm*, 193) relating to the Dwarves' last stand. After describing how Azaghâl Lord of Belegost drove a knife into Glaurung's belly with his last stroke, it states that the Noldor would have been spared great woe in the future if Azaghâl had borne a sword rather than just a knife, which was not able to go deep enough (*WotJ*, 75). This is an interesting observation, but perhaps it was omitted by Christopher to preserve the suspense of Túrin's tale.[1]

After the first sentence of the next paragraph, the tale turns back to the *Narn* text, which gives a much more detailed description of Fingon's death than does *Annals*. However, the setup for Fingon's death is very different in the *Narn* version than what is given in the published text. After Turgon's and Húrin's glad meeting in the midst of the battle, Morgoth's forces are driven back for a while, but since in the *Narn* version Morgoth had already routed Maedhros in the East, he was able to assail Fingon and Turgon with great new forces (see *WotJ*, 167; and *CoH*, 57). This is another clear indication that Tolkien had abandoned the element of the story of Maedhros's host actually arriving and assailing the enemy from the rear. I must say, however, I prefer the version that Christopher included in the published *Silmarillion*. I am also grateful that he then turned back to the *Narn* text to include the more detailed description of Fingon's death.

The Children of Húrin reveals that the next eight paragraphs, covering the conversation of Turgon with Húrin and Huor, the escape of the remnant of the Noldor, and the last stand of the men of Hador, with Huor's death and Húrin's capture, very closely follow the *Narn* text, with just a few inserts from the *Grey Annals* (which itself does not deviate very far from the *Narn* text here, as Christopher points out; see *WotJ*, 168–69). The one small detail from the *Narn* text that is not taken up in this section is that the ax that Húrin wielded was one he had seized from an Orc captain (see *WotJ*, 169; and *CoH*, 59). This seems to be an odd detail to leave out (although not a terribly important one).

In paragraph 30 ("The realm of Fingon . . ."; *Silm*, 195, the primary source switches to the "earlier *Quenta*" text, with an addition that goes back to the *Quenta Noldorinwa* and a couple of additions from the *Annals*. The statement that the Haladin still dwelt in the protection of the woods of Brethil under the rule of Handir son of Haldir appears to be based on a similar statement in chapter 13 of the *Quenta Noldorinwa* (the chapter on Túrin) in which it is stated that a remnant of the people of Haleth dwelt in the wood as free Men, the last of the Elf-friends to linger in Beleriand unsubdued by Morgoth (see *SoMe*, 127).

The text continues to follow the "earlier *Quenta*" for the first part of the next paragraph, but then it switches back to the *Annals* as the primary source. In that paragraph, there is a misreading of the manuscript that led to "makers of fire" replacing "masters of fire" (see *WotJ*, 136). Also, the statement regarding the son of Fingon being among those of Círdan's people who escaped to the Isle of Balar is obviously an editorial addition.[2]

The thirty-second paragraph ("And when Turgon . . ."; *Silm*, 196) has a change regarding one of my favorite characters, Voronwë, the faithful Elf who later guides Tuor to Gondolin. A reference to him is deleted, but then an editorial addition regarding him is inserted. This paragraph is taken from *GA* §257, and describes the ships that Turgon unsuccessfully tried to send as messengers to the Valar. Removed is the statement that Voronwë was the captain of the last ship, the only one that returned (see *WotJ*, 80). The final sentence, in which Voronwë is named as the one survivor of that last ship, appears to be an editorial addition in its place.

Paragraph 34 ("Therefore Húrin was . . ."; *Silm*, 196–97) briefly describes the words of Húrin and Morgoth. This paragraph comes from parts of *GA* §§244, 247, and 248, with several inserts from the *Narn* text that is given in both *Unfinished Tales* and *The Children of Húrin* (the only portion of the *Narn* text about the Nirnaeth Arnoediad that is included in *Unfinished Tales*), and several inserts from QS16(D) §§22 and 23. This account is greatly reduced from the *Grey Annals* version (which is much shorter than the *Narn* version), with even important details omitted that go back to the shorter "earlier *Quenta*" version.

Christopher states, "The *Narn* text concludes with a remarkable elaboration of the confrontation of Húrin and Morgoth on the basis of *GA* §§244–8 (itself an elaboration of QS §§21–23)" (*WotJ*, 169). In fact that confrontation takes a full chapter in *The Children of Húrin*. Yet the version that Christopher includes in the published *Silmarillion* is shorter even than that original older version from the "earlier *Quenta*." I think it was a serious mistake to water down this critical confrontation so much. In fact, Shippey calls this "[p]ossibly the most important scene added to the *Narn*, and not present in *The Silmarillion*.[3]

The passage removed from *GA* §244 describes how Morgoth offered Húrin his freedom and great wealth and power if he would reveal the location of Gondolin, and Húrin's refusal (*WotJ*, 78). This important detail is in all three versions of the story (see also *Lost Road*, 312; *CoH*, 62; and *UT*, 66). There is, in my opinion, no excuse for leaving it out, since it clearly was always Tolkien's intention that it be included. Moreover, it makes a good setup for the later passage where Húrin is scorned by the men of Dor-lómin, who believe that he is in league with Morgoth, after he is finally released.

GA §§245 and 246, which are omitted in their entirety, describe how in response Morgoth threatened Húrin's wife and son, and give Húrin's reply that they did not know Turgon's secrets, and even if they did, they would not reveal them, being of the houses of Hador and Bëor (*WotJ*, 78). Again, I have to question the wisdom of leaving this out. Without getting into the extended discussion included in the *Narn* text, these short paragraphs say a lot both about how Morgoth thinks and about Húrin's pride. It also makes much more intelligible the words "Morgoth cursed Húrin and Morwen and their offspring," which do appear in the published text.

The final paragraph of this chapter is based most closely on the *Narn* text (although *GA* §250 has similar language), with one odd detail. Christopher states that in the *Narn* text the Mound of the Slain is initially named "Haudh-en-Ndengin," but then was changed to "Haudh-en-Nirnaeth" (see *WotJ*, 169). Christopher nonetheless chose to include both of those names in the published text.

And this concludes chapter 20. Overall, I think that Christopher did a good job of compiling this chapter from the different sources to give it the greatest possible power and pathos. My only major complaint is that the confrontation between Morgoth and Húrin is so condensed.

The following chapter is the longest—and perhaps the most difficult to trace—in the entire book.

Chapter 21 "Of Túrin Turambar"

Cʜᴀᴘᴛᴇʀ 21 ɪs ᴛʜᴇ ʟᴏɴɢᴇsᴛ ᴏғ ᴀʟʟ ᴛʜᴇ ᴄʜᴀᴘᴛᴇʀs ɪɴ ᴛʜᴇ *SILMARILLION*. This is fitting, since the *Narn i Chîn Húrin,* the *Tale of the Children of Húrin,* upon which is it is based, is the "longest of all the lays that speak of those days" (*Silm,* 198). In both the reference in the text of *The Silmarillion* and in *Unfinished Tales,* Christopher "improperly" changed the name of the *Narn* to *Narn i Hîn Húrin* because he was afraid that *Chîn* would cause confusion with the English word "chin" (see *Lost Road,* 322), but he did spell it correctly in *The Children of Húrin.*

While it is fitting that this is longest of the chapters in the published work, it cannot be disputed that the contrast in scope between it and the surrounding material is extremely stark. As mentioned earlier, like the story of Beren and Lúthien, this is one of the Great Tales that had particular importance to Tolkien. However, in judging the success of the creation of *The Silmarillion* as a complete work, the same standards must be applied here as to the earlier portion of the work. The argument that it was correct to leave out the expanded narrative that Tolkien intended to include in the earlier sections of the book, but also correct to include the even more expanded material here, really can not be sustained. Moreover, as we will see in a couple of chapters, Christopher greatly compressed the third of the Great Tales —the tale of the fall of Gondolin.[1]

The reason this chapter is probably the most difficult to attempt to trace is because the material from which it is derived is the one area that Christopher indicates he did not completely present in *The History of Middle-earth.* He stated in the foreword to *The War of the Jewels* that the history of his father's work on "The Silmarillion" was largely completed with the publication of that book, and then clarified that it was incomplete only in the sense that he did not enter "further into the complexities of the tale of Túrin in those parts that ⌊his⌋ father left in confusion and uncertainty, as explained in *Unfinished Tales,* 6" (*WotJ,* x).

The quote from *Unfinished Tales* that he is referring to is the following:

My father was still evolving this part when he ceased to work on it; and the shorter version for *The Silmarillion* was to wait on the final development of the Narn. In preparing the text of *The Silmarillion* for publication I derived, by necessity, much of this section of the tale of Túrin from these very materials, which are of quite extraordinary complexity in their variety and interrelations. (*UT,* 6.)

In his discussion on the "later *Quenta,*" Christopher states that in December 1937 his father abandoned the writing of the continuous *Quenta Silmarillion* at the beginning of the story of Túrin (which was then chapter 17). Christopher further points out that his father made no changes to this chapter in the last typescript of the "later *Quenta.*" He adds that his father did eventually return to that text, but that the many additions and corrections that he made, particularly in the latter half of the chapter, are "best regarded as an aspect of the vast, unfinished work on the 'Saga of Túrin' that engaged him during the 1950s, from which no brief retelling suitable in scale to the *Quenta Silmarillion* ever emerged" (*WotJ,* 244).

The *Grey Annals* does continue to the end of Túrin's story (at which point it too ends), but much of the first part of this chapter is taken from the different sources described above. Those sources also were used to generate the *Narn* account published in *Unfinished Tales* and, of course, the newly released *The Children of Húrin.*

It is not possible for me to provide a paragraph-by-paragraph listing of the source materials used through the whole chapter (which is perhaps a blessing with such a long chapter). Therefore the first part of table 21 only lists the source materials available (including the *Narn* as it is published in *Unfinished Tales* and in *The Children of Húrin,* although of course those texts were also edited by Christopher and are not really source materials but rather alternative texts compiled from the same source materials). However, from the invasion of Nargothrond by Glaurung and the Orcs (a little more than halfway through the chapter), the *Grey Annals* appears to be virtually the sole source that was used, and from that point, the table is much more complete.

Christopher claims in his introduction to chapter 17 of the "earlier *Quenta*" that other than a few phrases it is not "the antecedent of the opening of chapter 21 in *The Silmarillion*" (*Lost Road,* 315–16). However, a close analysis reveals that the first three paragraphs of the chapter do closely follow §§24 and 25 of that text (compare *Silm,* 198–99 with *Lost Road,* 316–17). The only major difference is that Túrin's first sister, Lalaith, is not mentioned in the QS text.

Small portions of the language of the next two paragraphs are taken from the *Grey Annals* (and in one place from the text of the old

Table 21. Source Material by Paragraph for Chapter 21 "Of Túrin Turambar"

Paragraph no.	Paragraph headwords	*Silm* page no.	Primary source	Secondary sources
1–3	"Rían, daughter of . . ." through "Now after the . . ."	198–99	QS (chapter 17) §§24 and 25	GA §254: first and third sentences QS (chapter 17) §27: "she named her"
4	"In the first . . ."	199	Based on *Nam* and related texts (compare with *UT*, 74–75 and *CoH*, 77–79)	GA §258: first sentence
5	"Túrin grew fair . . ."	199	Based on *Nam* and related texts (compare with *UT*, 76–77 and *CoH*, 80–86)	
6–9	'And when three . . ." and "And Beleg answered . . ."	199–200	Based on *Nam* and related texts (compare with *UT*, 79–82 and *CoH*, 86–91)	
10–24	'Then Beleg departed from . . ." through "Then Beleg departed with . . ."	200–202	Based on *Nam* and related texts (compare with *UT*, 85–96 and *CoH*, 95–120 [but see text])	
25–34	"Now when Beleg . . ." through "In the time that . . ."	202–4	Based on *Nam* and related texts (compare with *UT*, 96–104 and *CoH*, 121–38)	
35–36	"But when the year . . ." and "Thus Beleg returned . . ."	204–5	Based on *Nam* and related texts (compare with *CoH*, 138–40)	
37–42	"Who knows now . . ." through "Now Beleg was . . ."	205–6	Based on *Nam* and related texts (compare with *CoH*, 141–50)	

(*continued*)

Table 21. Continued

Paragraph no.	Paragraph headwords	*Silm* page no.	Primary source	Secondary sources
43–45	"With little hope . . ." through "And Gwindor told . . ."	206–7	Based on *Narn* and related texts (compare with *CoH*, 151–54)	
46	"When all in the . . ."	207–8	Based on *GA* §266	*Narn* (see *CoH*, 154): first sentence
47–56	"But as he stood . . ." through "And now they arose . . ."	208–9	Based on *Narn* and related texts (compare with *CoH*, 154–58)	
57–59	"At first his . . ." through "Then the heart . . ."	209–11	*GA* §§268–70	See text
60	"Then Finduilas sat . . ."	211	See *CoH*, 168	
61	"Now when Túrin . . ."	211	*GA* §271	See text
62	"But Gwindor answered . . ."	211	See *CoH*, 170	
63	"When it became . . ."	211	*GA* §272	See text
64	"In that time . . ."	211	*GA* §273	See text
65–67	"Now it came . . ." through "Orodreth was troubled . . ."	211–12	See *UT*, 159–62 and *CoH*, 171–75	
68–70	"Soon afterward Handir . . ." through "Then Gwindor said . . ."	212–13	See *WotJ*, 141–42; *CoH*, 176–77; and *GA* §§275 and 276	See text
71	"Then Túrin sped . . ."	213	*GA* §277	
72	"And even as Túrin . . ."	213	*GA* §278	
73	"And now he stood . . ."	213	*GA* §279	
74	"Then Túrin sprang . . ."	213–214	*GA* §280 and the first part of *GA* §281	

75	"And while he . . ."	214	The rest of *GA* §281	
76	"Then suddenly Glaurung . . ."	214	*GA* §282	
77	"But Túrin drawing . . ."	214	*GA* §283	
78	"Then Túrin, being . . ."	214	*GA* §284	
79	"But Túrin passed . . ."	214–15	*GA* §285	
80	"And Túrin hastened . . ."	215	*GA* §286	
81	"At last worn . . ."	215	*GA* §292 (§§287–91 were struck out and replaced; see *Wolf*, 88)	*Narn* (see *UT*, 107 and *CoH*, 187): "seizing him he drew his sword, and demanded that he be told whither Morwen had gone, and Aerin declared to him that she"
82	"Thus he came . . ."	215	*GA* §§293 and 294 (roughly)	
83	"Then Túrin strode . . ."	215–16	*GA* §§295, 296, and 297	*Narn* (see *UT*, 112 and *CoH*, 196 and 197): "which in the High-elven speech signified Master of Doom" and "and the spear"
84	"Now Túrin coming . . ."	216	*GA* §§300 and 301 (§§298–99 relate to Tuor's story)	
85	"Túrin bade them . . ."	216–17	*GA* §§302 and 303	
86	"Now new tidings . . ."	217	*GA* §304	*Narn* (see *UT*, 112 and *CoH*, 198): "And some said that all the enemy had withdrawn northwards, and others that Glaurung abode still in the halls of Felagund; and some said that the Mormegil was slain, and others that he was cast under a spell by the dragon and dwelt there yet, as one changed to stone"
87	"Then Morwen was . . ."	217	Unknown	

(*continued*)

Table 21. Continued

Paragraph no.	Paragraph headwords	*Silm* page no.	Primary source	Secondary sources
88	"They came upon . . ."	217	Unknown	GA §305: final two sentences
89	"But Glaurung was . . ."	217–18	GA §306	
90	"Seeing the onset . . ."	218	GA §307	
91	"Her will strove . . ."	218	GA §308	
92	"Now Mablung, who . . ."	218	GA §309	
93	"But they were . . ."	218	GA §§310 and 311	
94	"Then the Orcs . . ."	219	GA §312	
95	"But Nienor ran . . ."	219	GA §313	
96	"But it was a . . ."	219	GA §§314, 315, and 316	
97	"On the next day . . ."	219–20	Unknown	
98	"In that time . . ."	220	GA §318	GA §317: "In that time the woodmen were not troubled by the Orcs" and "there was peace in Brethil"
99	"But when three . . ."	220	GA §319	
100	"In the spring . . ."	220–21	GA §§320 and 321	
101	"Then Turambar asked . . ."	221	GA §322	
102	"Then Níniel being . . ."	221	GA §323	
103	"Now Turambar came . . ."	221	GA §324	
104	"This counsel he . . ."	221–22	GA §325	
105	"Then Turambar summoned . . ."	222	GA §326	*Narn* (see *UT*, 134 and *CoH*, 237): "Then he drew Gurthang, and with all the might of his arm, and of his hate"
106	"Now Gurthang had . . ."	222	GA §327	
107	"Then he wrenched . . ."	222	GA §328	
108	"The screams of . . ."	222	GA §329	
109	"Even so Brandir . . ."	222–23	GA §§330 and 331	

No.	Quote	GA	Page	Reference
110	"But even as they . . ."	GA §332	223	
111	"Thus Brandir saw . . ."	GA §333	223	*Narn* (see *UT*, 138 and *CoH*, 243): "We meet again" through the end
112	"Then Glaurung died, . . ."	GA §334	223	*Narn* (see *UT*, 138 and *CoH*, 243): "Looking down upon" through "O happy to be dead"
113	"Then Brandir came . . ."	GA §335	223–24	
114	"But Brandir made . . ."	GA §336	224	
115	"And he answered: . . ."	GA §337	224	
116	"But even as he . . ."	GA §338	224	
117	"But when the . . ."	GA §339	224	
118	"Then Brandir told . . ."	GA §340	224	
119	"Then Turambar was . . ."	GA §341	224	
120	"Then Turambar fell . . ."	GA §342	224–25	*Narn* (see *UT*, 144 and *CoH*, 254): "For in those words he heard the feet of his doom overtaking him"
121	"And even as he . . ."	GA §343	225	
122	"Then they marveled, . . ."	GA §344	225	
123	"Then Mablung was . . ."	GA §345	225	
124	"Then he fled . . ."	GA §346	225	
125	"And from the blade . . ."	GA §347	225	
126	"Then Túrin set . . ."	GA §348	225–26	
127	"Then they lifted . . ."	GA §349	226	Ballpoint addition (See *WotJ*, 103): "TÚRIN TURAMBAR" through "NIENOR NÍNIEL"
128	"But she was not . . ."	Ballpoint addition (See *WotJ*, 103)	226	

Note: The relevant *Grey Annals* sections are §§253–349 (*WotJ*, 79–103, commentary on 136–61). The *Quenta* Silmarillion chapter 17 referred to above is given in *The Lost Road*, 315–23 and is actually a continuation of the text "QS(D)" given in the previous chapter, with the sections numbered §§24–40. The *Narn* is printed in *UT*, 57–162 (including commentary and appendix showing some of the alternate versions of part of the tale) and of course the full text of *CoH*.

chapter 17), but the elements of Morwen sending the Dragon-helm to Túrin in Doriath, her messages lightening Túrin's mood, and then his going to battle after the messages stopped are not present in the *Grey Annals* and appear to be taken from the same sources from which the *Narn* texts are derived, although this material is covered more extensively in the versions in *Unfinished Tales* (see *UT*, 74–77) and *The Children of Húrin* (see *CoH*, 77–86).

Paragraphs 6 and 7 (*Silm*, 199–200) tell the story of Túrin's confrontation with Saeros, Thingol's counselor. In the *Grey Annals* Saeros was still called Orleg, and the story is only briefly told in *GA* §259, with Túrin still slaying him with the cup at the dinner table as in the "earlier *Quenta*" version, without the element of Saeros waylaying Túrin the following day. It is clear that these paragraphs come from a later source. However, they are greatly condensed compared to the other published versions of the confrontation (see *UT*, 79–82; and *CoH*, 86–91).

Thingol's pardon of Túrin and his discussion with Beleg ("But when all that . . ." and "And Beleg answered . . ."; *Silm*, 200) do not appear in the *Grey Annals* at all (although the pardon is mentioned later). One element from the *Narn* texts in this part of the story that Christopher excludes entirely is the role played by the young Elvish maiden, Nellas, who had looked after Túrin in his youth and provided the testimony that proved that he was not responsible for Saeros's death. I miss the presence of this minor but interesting character, particularly since she foreshadows Túrin's later relationship with Finduilas. An argument can be made that this is another example of Christopher's reduction of the roles played by female characters in *The Silmarillion*. It is true, however, that this chapter is already very long, and incorporating another minor character would only have made it longer still.

There is an element in the published *Silmarillion* that contradicts the version of the story told in *The Children of Húrin*, although it is not taken from the *Grey Annals*. In the published text of *The Silmarillion*, Beleg departs from Menegroth, finds Túrin among the outlaws, fails to convince him to return with him to Doriath, goes back himself, and then is given the gifts of his sword Anglachel from Thingol and the waybread *lembas* from Melian (*Silm*, 200–202). However, in the longer account in *The Children of Húrin* (95–97, 107–20) Beleg is given Anglachel before he leaves Doriath in search of Túrin the first time, and is given only the *lembas* when he returns to Doriath after locating Túrin and failing to convince him to return to Doriath. Neither the version of the *Narn* in *Unfinished Tales* nor that in the *Grey Annals* describes the giving of either gift. Christopher explains this contradiction in the second appendix to *The Children of Húrin* (entitled "The Composition of the Text"), stating it was "demonstrable" that his father had rejected the story of Beleg receiving Anglachel when he returned to Doriath and that "'what really happened' was that Thingol gave Anglachel to Beleg after the trial of Túrin, when Beleg first set off to find him" (see *CoH*, 287).

Similarly, virtually none of the material covered in the next seventeen paragraphs (*Silm*, 202–6)—which includes Túrin and the outlaws' meeting with Mîm and their abiding in Mîm's house upon Amon Rûdh (paragraphs 25–34), Beleg's appearance at Amon Rûdh (paragraphs 35 and 36), and the betrayal of Bar-en-Danwedh by Mîm and the capture of Túrin (paragraphs 37–42)—is present in the *Grey Annals* at all. There are only two paragraphs in the *Grey Annals* covering any of this material. *GA* §260 states that Túrin's band captures Beleg and that Túrin then renews his friendship with the Elf and learns of his pardon but refuses to go back to Menegroth. *GA* §265 describes the betrayal of Túrin's company by an Easterling named Blodren son of Ban, and Mîm is completely absent.

The material covered in the next fourteen paragraphs (*Silm*, 206–9)—Beleg's healing, pursuit of the Orcs, and encounter with Gwindor (paragraphs 43–45), Beleg and Gwindor's rescue of Túrin and his accidental slaying of Beleg (paragraphs 46–48), the burial of Beleg and Túrin's healing at Eithel Ivrin (paragraphs 49–51), Gwindor and Túrin's discussion (paragraphs 52–55), and their journey to Nargothrond (paragraph 56)—is much more briefly covered in *GA* §§ 266 and 267. There is also a major difference: in *GA* §266, Beleg is actually brought back to Menegroth and healed by Melian before pursuing the Orcs instead of just healing himself as in the published text. None of the language appears to come from the *Grey Annals*.

Some of this material was drafted by Christopher. He states:

> From the point in the story where Túrin and his men established themselves in the ancient dwelling of the Petty-dwarves on Amon Rûdh there is no completed narrative on the same detailed plan [as in the preceding parts], until the Narn takes up again with Túrin's journey northwards after the fall of Nargothrond: from the existing materials I formed a brief narrative in *The Silmarillion*, Chapter 21. . . . (*UT*, 150; see also *WotJ*, 313–14).

This statement appears at first to contradict statements in the preface of *The Children of Húrin* that that book was created "with a minimum of editorial presence" and "without distortion or invention" (*CoH*, 7). However, Christopher explains this seeming anomaly in a long discussion in the appendix to *The Children of Húrin* referred to above (*CoH*, 287–89), in which he states that the text for these sections of the tale in that book was created from the same materials as those used for *The Silmarillion*, but "with a better understanding of the labyrinth of drafts and notes and their sequence" (*CoH*, 288). As a result, he states, "there is no element of extraneous 'invention' of any kind, however slight, in the longer text" presented in that book (*CoH*, 289).

Christopher also reveals in this appendix that Beleg's death in the published *Silmarillion* was "derived from the *Annals of Beleriand*" (*CoH*, 289). Presumably, he is referring to the *Grey Annals* here (*GA* §266), since the earlier versions of the *Annals of Beleriand* include no comparable details at all of Beleg's death. It is surprising that Christopher states that Beleg's death is derived from that source, because while the details are basically the same, the language is quite different.

The next set of six paragraphs (*Silm*, 210–11), dealing with Túrin's arrival at Nargothrond and his relationship with Finduilas (and Gwindor's words with both of them about it), are covered in *GA* §§268–71, and some of the language does seem to come from that source. One difference is that in the *Grey Annals* he names himself "Iarwaeth" instead of "Agarwaen the son of Úmarth" and he is not referred to as "Adanedhel" (but he is called "Mormegil" and his sword is named "Gurthang," as in the published text).

In paragraph 59, the first sentence diverges from *GA* §268 in that the published text states that Túrin "did not perceive what had befallen," regarding Finduilas' love for him, whereas the *Grey Annals* text states that he loved Finduilas "but spoke not, being loyal to Gwindor." But the next sentence in the published text, describing how Finduilas became torn in heart and sorrowful, comes almost directly from *GA* §268. The rest of the paragraph, in which Gwindor reveals Túrin's identity to Finduilas in order to warn her against entering into his doom, follows *GA*, §§269 and 270 fairly closely.

Paragraph 60, which has Finduilas's response that Túrin did not love her, does not appear in the *Grey Annals*, but matches the text that appears in *The Children of Húrin*. Paragraph 61, which contains Túrin's words to Gwindor, also follows *The Children of Húrin* version, which largely matches the words in *GA* §271, except for one major difference. In the *Grey Annals* version, Túrin does love Finduilas, but is afraid to act on it because he does not want her to share in his curse (see *WotJ*, 84). I believe this version is more moving than the version that is included in the published text in which he is unaware of her love and does not return it.

Gwindor's response in paragraph 62–that Túrin's doom lies not in his name but in himself—does not appear in the *Grey Annals* but is contained in *The Children of Húrin*. That is an important statement, and I am glad that Christopher included it.

The next long paragraph ("When it became . . ."; *Silm*, 211) appears to come mostly from *GA* §272. However, another reference to Túrin's love for Finduilas is removed, and a passage describing how Gwindor spoke against Túrin's advice and therefore fell into dishonor is added. The following paragraph seems to come partly from *GA* §274, but it is likely merged with another source (or perhaps the similarities are coincidental, and it comes entirely from another source).

This is then followed by three paragraphs that briefly tell of the coming of the Elves Gelmir and Arminas to Nargothrond (*Silm*, 211–12). There is no equivalent story told in the *Grey Annals*. It is worth noting, however, that the much longer account of this incident that Christopher published in *Unfinished Tales* and *The Children of Húrin* was actually marked by Tolkien to be added to the *Grey Annals* (see *WotJ*, 141–42). Whether the short account given in the published text was a summary of this text created by Christopher or taken from an alternative text, it is impossible to say.

The next three paragraphs come partly from a continuation of the typescript of the Gelmir and Arminas text described above, which is not part of the manuscript and was not published in *Unfinished Tales*, but was published by Christopher in the commentary to the *Grey Annals* (see *WotJ*, 141–42) and included in *The Children of Húrin*, the latter part of which is taken almost word for word from *GA* §§275 and 276. These paragraphs also are taken partly from another hastily written text regarding the location of the field of Tumhalad (where the battle for Nargothrond took place). Christopher expresses regret at following this text (see *WotJ*, 139–40).

It is also important to note that Christopher disregards (both in the published *Silmarillion* and in *The Children of Húrin*) several notes to the text that indicate that it was Tolkien's intention that Túrin was wearing the Dragon-helm of Hador at the battle, not a dwarf-mask (see *WotJ*, 86, 87, and 142–44). Christopher notes that he took the story of the dwarf-mask from a statement in the "vast assemblage of the *Narn* papers" telling of how Túrin found a dwarf-mask in the armories of Nargothrond. Christopher indicates that he "extended Túrin's wearing of it to the battle of Tumhalad" (*WotJ*, 144). This is another comment that appears to contradict Christopher's statement in the preface of *The Children of Húrin* that that work was created "without distortion or invention," since Túrin's wearing of the dwarf-mask at the battle of Tumhalad is present in that book, and the clear implication of Christopher's statement that he extended the story of the dwarf-mask to the battle is that that aspect of the story was invented by him. Unfortunately, he provides no explanation for this anomaly.

I would much prefer that Christopher had incorporated the penciled notes that his father made indicating that it was the Dragon-helm of his fathers that Túrin was wearing during the battle and his confrontation with Glaurung, although this would have required some editorial additions in order show how the Dragon-helm got to Nargothrond. However, Christopher gives a glimpse as to how he feels about incorporating the Dragon-helm into the story when he describes as "extremely artificial" the first sentence of paragraph 36, where Beleg brings Túrin the Dragon-helm out of Dimbar (*WotJ*, 138).

From paragraph 71 ("Then Túrin sped . . ."; *Silm,* 213) to the end of the chapter, the text mostly follows the *Grey Annals* very closely. Interestingly, Christopher mentions in a commentary listed under "§§287 ff." that the *Grey Annals* was practically the only source used from the Battle of Tumhalad through the end of the chapter on Túrin (*WotJ,* 144). However, a close comparison reveals that the *Grey Annals* are followed beginning with §277, ten paragraphs earlier than Christopher stated. It also worth noting that Christopher points out that contrary to his original conclusion, the latter part of the *Narn* was actually written before this part of the *Grey Annals* and that the *Grey Annals* narrative was based directly on the final text of that in the *Narn;* it is consistent with it at almost all points, though reduced at some (ibid.).

The seventy-first paragraph comes directly from *GA* §277, save for a couple of omissions. Most interesting is the removal of the statement that the Orcs and Glaurung arrived at Nargothrond before Túrin "because of his succouring of Gwindor" (*WotJ,* 86). What a tragic concept! It should not have been removed.

The text continues mostly from the *Grey Annals* through the end of the eighty-sixth paragraph ("Now new tidings . . ."; *Silm,* 217). However, the description of Túrin seizing Brodda and drawing his sword in the eighty-third paragraph does not appear in the *Annals* and appears to be added in from the *Narn* text (see *UT,* 107; and *CoH,* 187). Similarly, in the eighty-fifth paragraph the definition of the name "Turambar" and the statement that he took up the spear as well as the bow when he set aside his black sword are also absent from the *Annals* and apparently come from the *Narn* text (see *UT,* 112; and *CoH,* 196, 197). In the eighty-sixth paragraph there is another insert from the *Narn* describing the different speculations that the folk of

Doriath had regarding the fate of the Mormegil (see *UT,* 112; and *CoH,* 198). In the latter paragraph, there was another penciled addition to the *Grey Annals* not incorporated into the text indicating that when Morwen heard of the Dragon-helm she knew it was true that the Mormegil was her son (see *WotJ,* 93).

The next paragraph and the first part of the one after that appear to come from some source other than either the *Grey Annals* or the text used for the *Narn* in both *Unfinished Tales* and *The Children of Húrin.* Paragraph 87 ("Then Morwen was . . .; *Silm,* 217) largely matches the first part of *GA,* §305, though the language is different enough that it seems clear that it comes from some other text (and not the *Narn* text as printed in *Unfinished Tales* or *The Children of Húrin*). The bulk of the following paragraph most likely comes from the same text. It covers the same material as *GA* §305, but with significantly greater detail. But the last two sentences of the paragraph come directly from the end of *GA* §305, with no changes.

The text then again continues to follow the *Grey Annals* closely up to paragraph 111 ("Thus Brandir saw . . ."; *Silm,* 223). This paragraph comes mostly from *GA,* §333, with only one tiny change, until it reaches the words of Glaurung to Nienor. Glaurung's speech, to the end of the paragraph, is taken word for word from the *Narn,* replacing the version contained in the *Grey Annals* (see *WotJ,* 100; *UT,* 138; and *CoH,* 243). I definitely think that Christopher included the superior version.

Similarly, in the following sentence, Nienor's farewell words to Túrin after Glaurung dies and the statement that his "veil of malice" is removed from her are added from the *Narn* (see *UT,* 138; and *CoH,* 243). This again significantly improves the text.

The next addition can be found in paragraph 120 ("Then Turambar fell . . ."; *Silm,* 224–25). This paragraph comes mostly from *GA* §342, but in the first sentence, Mablung's statement that Túrin "heard the feet of his doom overtaking him" is added in from the *Narn* text (see *UT,* 144; and *CoH,* 254). This is another excellent addition.

In the 124th paragraph ("Then he fled . . ."; *Silm,* 225), there is a small but interesting omission of the statement that it was Túrin who named the place where Nienor had leapt to her death "Cabad Naeramarth" (The Leap of Dreadful Doom) (see *WotJ,* 102). It is also worth noting that Túrin's address to his sword Gurthang in this paragraph and Gurthang's reply in the following paragraph are the sole places in this chapter where Christopher leaves the informal form in place, keeping all occurrences of the "thou" and "doth."

The manuscript of the *Grey Annals* seemingly came to an end at the words "carven in the Runes of Doriath," and the words of the inscription were written in much later (in ballpoint pen, so it must have been much later). Subsequently, Christopher discovered manuscript pages that were obviously the continuation of the *Grey Annals;* apparently they had been misplaced during his father's lifetime (see *WotJ,* 103, 251).

The last sentence, stating that Nienor was not there, and that it was not known where the waters of Teiglin had brought her, comes from the ballpoint pen addition referred to above (though along with the inscription, it was included also in the original "lost" manuscript). Omitted at the very end were the following words: "[Thus endeth the Narn i Chîn Húrin: which is the longest of all the lays of Beleriand, and was made by Men.]" (See *WotJ,* 160–61.)

And thus ends the longest chapter in the published *Silmarillion.* Much more of this chapter than I had originally thought possible was able to be traced based on Christopher's comments, since well over half of it does come from the *Grey Annals* and significant additions come directly from the *Narn* text. I think that most of the additions were well placed. My only serious complaint is the failure to incorporate the character of Nellas, another unfortunate reduction of the female presence in the story, although, as discussed above, her omission is probably to be attributed to the length of the chapter more than to any other factor.

Chapter 22 "Of the Ruin of Doriath"

THIS CHAPTER HAS BOTH THE MOST EXTENSIVE EDITORIAL INVENTION and the largest omission in the entire book, each of which Christopher expressed some regrets over. However, he was certainly faced with a difficult task, for the last completed version of the story told in this chapter goes all the way back to the *Quenta Noldorinwa* (the first complete version of the *Quenta*), which was written in 1930 and was published in *The Shaping of Middle-earth*. Indeed, one must go back to that source to trace the language of part of this chapter (and much of the last two chapters of the published *Quenta Silmarillion*, as well). However, as Christopher points out, some of the conception in this older version is clearly incompatible with the later work that forms the basis for most of the published *Silmarillion*. So a certain amount of innovation was certainly necessary.

I already alluded to the invented material in this chapter back in chapter 13, paragraph 26, when discussing the Naugrim's creation of the Nauglamîr for Finrod, As I mentioned in that chapter, at the end of Section V of *The War of the Jewels* there is a short section entitled "A note on Chapter 22 Of the Ruin of Doriath in the published Silmarillion" in which Christopher reveals that the story of the downfall of Doriath was a complete invention by him. He states that if the materials that his father wrote on the subject of the ruin of Doriath are compared with what is stated in the published text, "it is seen at once that this latter is fundamentally changed, to a form for which in certain essential features there is no authority whatever in my father's writings" (*WotJ*, 354).

Christopher goes on to state that this story "was not lightly or easily conceived" but that he felt that the existing materials were so "radically incompatible with '*The Silmarillion*' as projected" that his choice was either to alter that story or abandon the project. He concludes in hindsight that this was a mistake, and that he could have overcome the difficulties "without so far overstepping the bounds of the editorial function" (*WotJ*, 356).

This overstepping of the bounds of the editorial function was compounded by the omission of most of *The Wanderings of Húrin*, which continues the story told in the *Narn*, and is written with a level of detail comparable to the one in that work. Christopher chose to use only a small portion of the text of *The Wanderings of Húrin* and to leave the rest out, rather than to try to condense it to make it more compatible with the rest of the published work. He again expresses regret for this decision, stating that in retrospect he has concluded that it was "an excessive tampering with my father's actual thought and intention . . ." (*WotJ*, 298).

The story of Húrin in Brethil, which makes up the bulk of *The Wanderings of Húrin*, is omitted in its entirety. The failure to include any of this part of the tale is unfortunate, because the story does such a wonderful job of showing how the shadow fell on that land. It provides the kind of detail that makes *The Lord of the Rings* such a fascinating work, and is often missing in *The Silmarillion*. I do not believe that the full text of *The Wanderings of Húrin* could have been incorporated into *The Silmarillion*, but I do believe that significant portions should have been included. Christopher is correct, however, in pointing out that it is written on such a scale that it would have required significant editorial changes in order to incorporate it into *The Silmarillion*.

However, had he done so, it might have helped avoid the even more significant editorial invention that he was forced to make in this chapter. Christopher points out that *The Wanderings of Húrin* was supposed to serve as a link to the "Necklace of the Dwarves" and the "Necklace of the Woe of Thingol," but that it remained unfinished (see *WotJ*, 258, 297–98). However, had Christopher incorporated more of this text, it might have been easier for him to avoid the inventions regarding the Nauglamír, because he could have included the outlaws that Húrin recruited, which would have helped him retain the story of the gold taken from Nargothrond, rather than change it so that Húrin, being alone, was able to bring only one thing from the remnants of the hoard that Glaurung had left there.

To the extent possible, the source materials are detailed in table 22.

The first sixteen paragraphs of this chapter (*Silm*, 227–30) are all taken from the beginning and the ending of the *Wanderings of Húrin* text, with the bulk of the material in between left out. Some of the earlier material closely follows the "lost" continuation of the *Grey Annals* referred to in the previous chapter. There are a number of omissions from these paragraphs.

In the first paragraph, a statement that Túrin's tale was the worst of Morgoth's works among Men in the ancient world is removed[1] (see *WotJ*, 259). Also removed are two sentences of dialogue between Morgoth and Húrin, in which Morgoth praises Húrin for his steadfast-

Table 22. Source Material by Paragraph for Chapter 22 "Of the Ruin of Doriath"

Paragraph no.	Paragraph headwords	*Silm* page no.	Primary source	Secondary sources
1 and 2	"So ended the . . ." and "Unhappy was the . . ."	227	*WH* text (*WotJ*, 259)	
3	"Then little though . . ."	227	*WH* text (but based on the *Grey Annals* continuation, *WotJ*, 252–53)	
4	"Thus his freedom . . ."	227–28	*WH* "Gondolin" text, *WotJ*, (271–72)	*WH* text (but based on the *Grey Annals* continuation, *WotJ*, 253): "Thus his freedom did but increase the bitterness of Húrin's heart" *WH* text (*WotJ*, 260): "and he departed" through "hidden realm of Gondolin"
5–10	"But the watch . . ." through "Yet there were . . ."	228	*WH* "Gondolin" text, (*WotJ*, 272–73)	
11–14	"As darkness fell . . ." through "But Morwen said: . . ."	229	*WH* "Morwen" text (*WotJ*, 273–74)	
15	"But Húrin did not . . ."	229	*WH* "Morwen" text (*WotJ*, 273)	*WH* "Concluding" text (*WotJ*, 295–96): last sentence
16	"It is told that . . ."	230	*WH* "Concluding" text (*WotJ*, 296)	
17–21	"Now Húrin crossed . . ." through "Then Mím in great . . ."	230	Editorial	
22–26	"Now Húrin journeyed . . ." through "Then he turned . . ."	231	Editorial	*QN* (chapter 14) (*SoMe*, 132): last sentence of paragraph 22 and first sentence of paragraph 23

(continued)

Table 22. Source Material by Paragraph for Chapter 22 "Of the Ruin of Doriath"

Paragraph no.	Paragraph headwords	*Silm* page no.	Primary source	Secondary sources
				WH text (*WotJ*, 259): "he that seeth through Morgoth's eyes, willing or unwilling seeth all things crooked" (paragraph 24) *QN* (chapter 14) (*SoMe*, 132): "cast himself" to the end of paragraph 26
27–35	"But when Húrin . . ." through "Thus it was . . ."	232–34	Editorial	"Turambar and the Foalókë" (*BoLT2*, 115): "How do ye of uncouth race dare to demand aught of me, Elu Thingol, Lord of Beleriand, whose life began by the waters of Cuivienen years un-counted ere the fathers of the stunted people awoke?" and "he bade them with shameful words be gone" (paragraph 29, *Silm*, 233)
36–40	"At that time . . ." through "Now Dior Thingol's heir . . ."	234–35	Editorial	"Series of Elvish genealogies which can be dated to December 1959" (See *WotJ*, 350): "Nimloth" *The Problem of Ros* (*PoMe*, 369, 372): "the sons of Dior" through the end
37–39	"Now word went . . ." through "In that battle . . ."	235	Letter 247 to Colonel Worskett, September 20, 1963 (*Letters*, 334)	*The Tale of Years* (*WotJ*, 353): "and from that time the river was named anew, Rathlóriel, the Goldenbed" (paragraph 39) *The Nauglafring* (*BoLT2*, 238): "Then Beren gazed in wonder on the selfsame jewel of Fëanor that he had cut from Morgoth's iron crown, now shining set amid gold and gems by the cunning of the Dwarves; and he washed it clean of blood in the waters of the river" and "Little did it ease the grief of Lúthien to learn that the Lord of Nogrod was slain and many Dwarves" (paragraph 39)
40	"Now Dior Thingol's . . ."	235–36	Editorial	*QN* (chapter 14) (*SoMe*, 134): "Dior Eluchíl set himself to raise anew the glory of the kingdom of Doriath"

41	"There came a night . . ."	236	Based on *The Tale of Years*, version C, Annal 503 (changed from 505)	*The Tale of Years*, version C, Annal 503 (changed from 505): second sentence
42	'Long did Dior . . .'	236	Editorial	Editorial: "Then Dior arose, and about his neck he clasped the Nauglamír"
43	"Then Dior arose . . ."	236	QN (chapter 14) (*SoMe*, 134)	Editorial: first sentence, through "woods of Doriath" QN (chapter 14) (*SoMe*, 134): "the oath" to the end of the first sentence
44	"But now the rumour . . ."	236	See secondary sources	Annal 503 of version C of *The Tale of Years* (*WotJ*, 351): "For while Lúthien wore the Necklace of the Dwarves no Elf would dare to assail her" Annal 505 from version D2 of *The Tale of Years* (*WotJ*, 351): "But now hearing of the renewal of Doriath and of Dior's pride the seven gathered again from wandering, and they sent to him to claim their own"
45	"But Dior returned . . ."	236–37	Annal 506–507 from version D2 of *The Tale of Years* (*WotJ*, 351)	Annal 505 from version D2 of *The Tale of Years* (*WotJ*, 351): "But Dior returned no answer to the sons of Fëanor" Annal 506 from version D2 of *The Tale of Years* (*WotJ*, 351): "and Celegorm" through "winter" QN (Chapter 14) (*SoMe*, 134): "so befell the second slaying of Elf by Elf"
46	"Thus Doriath was . . ."	237	QN (chapter 14) (*SoMe*, 134)	Editorial: first sentence

Note: The portions of *The Wanderings of Húrin* ("WH text") that were used can be found in *WotJ*, 252–53, 258–60, and 271–74. The relevant chapter from the *Quenta Noldorinwa* is chapter 14, which can be found in *SoMe*, 132–35. A small amount of the language of the chapter comes from *The Tale of Years* (of which there are several different versions, labeled A, B, C, D, and D2) and related later writings, the relevant portions of which are printed in *WotJ*, 348–54. There are also several additions based on the original tales *Turambar and the Foalókë* and *The Nauglafring* from *BoLT2*.

ness, indicates that it would have been "otherwise rewarded" had it been dedicated to a better cause, and makes the false statement that he had no further use for Húrin (ibid.).

I really cannot understand why the words of Morgoth were not included here. They definitely give this more depth, without taking up much room. Moreover, the exclusion of this dialogue makes the statement that "he lied" and the reference to "the words of Morgoth" included in the next paragraph less understandable.

That next paragraph is even more significantly reduced. Omitted is a passage indicating that though Húrin was sixty years old (and had been held captive for twenty-eight years), he still had great strength, "for it suited the purpose of Morgoth that this should be so." This omitted passage also states that despite his grimness, none that knew him before could fail to recognize him. The sentence describing his return to Hithlum is greatly reduced, eliminating the sense of great wonder and dread that fell on that land when Húrin arrived, and the dismay of the Easterlings, who feared that it was a sign that Morgoth was planning to give the land back to "the Westrons" and enslave them instead (see *WotJ*, 252–53).[2]

The next paragraph is also taken from the *Wanderings of Húrin* text.[3] But omitted altogether is the rest of Húrin's history in Hithlum, in which he gathers up several outlaws and then takes leave of Lorgan, the chieftain of the Easterlings, and the capture of the outlaws by the men of Brethil after Húrin has left them to seek Gondolin (see *WotJ*, 253–54, 261–71).[4] Instead, the rest of the paragraph is taken from the later section of the *Wanderings of Húrin* text in which his attempt to find Gondolin is described (*WotJ*, 271–72). The next six paragraphs (*Silm*, 229) follow that text fairly closely.

The following four paragraphs (I count four single lines of dialogue as one paragraph) continue from the *Wanderings of Húrin* text where it turns to Húrin's encounter with Morwen. However, there are some very unfortunate reductions to this text.

The first major reduction comes where the text describes Húrin's coming to the Crossing of Teiglin. The source text describes how his scanty food was spent at the end of his four-day journey and how he was famished but "went on like the shadow of a man driven by a dark wind" (see *WotJ*, 273). Also eliminated from that paragraph are some details elaborating on the dread that the night-sentinels felt at his coming (ibid.).

The next paragraph is even more sadly reduced. First, a sentence is omitted describing Morwen as a seemingly aged homeless wanderer whose gender could only be seen by the fact that the rags the person was wearing were remnants of a woman's garb. Additional details describing her as "haggard and hungry as a long-hunted wolf" and "sharp-nosed with broken teeth, and with a lean hand [that] clawed at the cloak upon her breast" are also removed. Finally, and in my opinion most inexcusably, a sentence is omitted at the end of this paragraph in which Húrin cries out her name and she gets up and stumbles, and he catches her in his arms (ibid).

The description of Húrin's encounter with Morwen really loses a lot from the reductions made to it, particularly the omission of Húrin calling out her name and her falling into his arms. I really cannot understand why these omissions were made. The emotional power of this desperately sad and poignant scene is greatly reduced.

The dialogue between Morwen and Húrin follows the source text fairly closely, with the only reduction a removal of her acknowledgment that their children are lost, as she clutches at his cloak (*WotJ*, 274). The beginning of the following paragraph ("But Húrin did not . . ."; *Silm*, 229) continues from the text we have been discussing, with one more unfortunate omission. In the first sentence, the statement that they sat beside the stone is changed from saying that he sat beside the stone with her in his arms. It is another lost detail, and its absence reduces the poignancy of the scene. Also omitted is the description of Morwen as "the proud and fair" as well as the statement that Húrin thought that he too would sit there beside the stone until he died (ibid.).

The end of that paragraph and the following one are based loosely on the conclusion of the *Wanderings of Húrin* text, skipping the whole history of Húrin in Brethil, which is the major part of that text. I say "loosely" based on it, because it is changed significantly, presaging the even greater editorial inventions to come in this chapter.

In the *Wanderings of Húrin* text, Húrin lifts up Morwen's body but finds that he cannot bear her alone, and bids her wait a while (*WotJ*, 274). He then encounters the men of Brethil, and the whole story of his capture and the battle that ensues is told.[5] Finally, he returns to the stone with some of the people of Brethil. It is from this part that the last sentence of this paragraph comes. However, in the source text it was "they" who made her grave and carved the additional inscription on the stone, not "he" as in the published text. Also, after the inscription, there is a statement that some of the people of Brethil sang laments in the old tongue that had been in the past "for those of their people [who] had fallen on the March far beyond the Mountains" (see *WotJ*, 295–96).

The next paragraph is taken from the following paragraph in the *Wanderings of Húrin* text, but a large portion of that paragraph is omitted. The omitted portion describes how, while they sang, a gray rain fell "and all that desolate place was heavy with grief, and the roaring of the river was like the mourning of many voices." Then after saying that Húrin "went bowed on his staff," it describes how "after that day fear left that place, though sorrow remained" and tells of the women of Brethil singing at the place "of the Grey Lady who sought in vain for her son" (*WotJ*, 296).[6]

The next five paragraphs ("Now Húrin crossed . . ." through "Then Mîm in great . . ."; *Silm*, 230), which tell of Húrin's coming to Nargothrond, his slaying of Mîm the petty-dwarf, and his bearing away with him "out of all that great hoard but one thing only" are complete editorial inventions. As Christopher says, the writing of *Wanderings of Húrin* caused his father to postpone writing the story of Húrin in Nargothrond (*WotJ*, 260). The story that Christopher created varied greatly from the last version of that part of the tale that his father wrote, back in the *Quenta Noldorinwa*, where Húrin and his outlaws bore a hoard of cursed gold from Nargothrond, from which Thingol had the Dwarves fashion the Nauglamîr to house the Silmaril given to him by Beren. As Christopher himself points out, he completely removed both the outlaws and the curse of Mîm from the story he included in the published *Silmarillion,* and he substituted the Nauglamîr (which was supposed to have been made by Dwarves for Finrod Felagund and to have been the most prized by him of all the hoard of Nargothrond), for the gold that Húrin and the outlaws took from Nargothrond (*WotJ*, 355). I can find no place in these paragraphs in which the language of Tolkien was used in any way; these paragraphs appear to be complete editorial inventions.

Paragraphs 22–26 ("Now Húrin journeyed . . ." through "Then he turned . . ."; *Silm*, 231), which tell of Húrin's coming to Doriath, his delivery of the Nauglamîr to Thingol in scorn, his final release from Morgoth's spell, and his death, continue to mostly be editorial invention. But the last sentence of paragraph 22 (Húrin casting the treasure at the feet of Thingol) and the first sentence of the next paragraph (Húrin's bitter, sarcastic statement to Thingol that this was his fee for his keeping of his children and wife) are based on or taken directly from the old *Quenta Noldorinwa*. Of course, the treasure referred to is different than that in the older story (see *SoMe*, 132).

As Christopher says, in the published text "Húrin was represented as being at last freed from the delusions inspired by Morgoth in his encounter with Melian in Menegroth" (*WotJ*, 355), but nowhere did Tolkien ever describe such an encounter. However, one part of Melian's dialogue, where she states that "he that seeth through Morgoth's eyes, willing or unwilling seeth all things crooked," does come directly from the introductory text of *Wanderings of Húrin*, though there it is just narration, not words stated by any character.[7] The rest of her dialogue, however, is purely editorial invention.

Christopher correctly points out that a particular problem with the old story as told in the *Quenta Noldorinwa* is how the gold got to Doriath. In that story, each of Húrin's companions falls prey to the curse of the gold and dies, and Húrin is forced to go to Thingol and enlist the aid of the people of Doriath to bear the treasure to the Thousand Caves. As Christopher points out, the gesture is ruined if Húrin has to enlist Thingol's aid to get the gold that he then is going to use to humiliate Thingol (*WotJ*, 354–55). This is certainly true, but Christopher's solution—to eliminate the gold altogether, as well as Húrin's companions, and create a whole new history for the Nauglamîr—does indeed, as he admits, overstep the bounds of the editorial function.

The nine paragraphs that follow ("But when Húrin . . ." through "Thus it was . . ."; *Silm*, 232–34) tell of the Dwarves' remaking of the Nauglamîr with the Silmaril amidst it, Thingol's death at their hands, the killing of all but two of the craftsmen of the Dwarves of Nogrod, Melian's leaving Middle-earth, and the Dwarves of Nogrod's invasion of Menegroth and their taking of the Nauglamîr and Silmaril over Mablung's dead body. They are almost entirely editorial inventions. I can find no language that is even based on the old story contained in the *Quenta Noldorinwa,* or in the brief snippets contained in *The Tale of Years*. The only portion of these paragraphs that seems to be taken from Tolkien's texts is one passage that seems loosely based on language from the original tale *Turambar and the Foalókë*. Compare Thingol's words to the Dwarves—"'How do ye of uncouth race dare to demand aught of me, Elu Thingol, Lord of Beleriand, whose life began by the waters of Cuivienen years uncounted ere the fathers of the stunted people awoke?' And . . . he bade them with shameful words be gone" (*Silm*, 233)—with Tinwelint's words to Úrin in the original tale: "'Wherefore dost thou of the uncouth race of Men endure to upbraid a king of the Eldalie? Lo! In Palisor my life began years uncounted before the first of Men awoke. Get thee gone'" (*BoLT2*, 115).

In a brief note associated with *The Tale of Years*, Tolkien acknowledged that a problem with the old story was that Doriath should not have been able to be invaded by a hostile army, because of Melian's power. He suggested that a solution needed to be found in which Thingol was lured outside the borders and then killed by the Dwarves. Thereupon Melian would depart, and with the girdle removed Doriath could be ravaged by the Dwarves (*WotJ*, 352).

Instead, Christopher came up with a completely different solution: having the Dwarves already be in Menegroth engaged in other works.

Then after they slay Thingol, Melian leaves Middle-earth and her power is withdrawn from Neldoreth and Region, leaving Doriath unprotected (see *Silm*, 232–34; and *WotJ*, 355).

Having the Dwarves already be in Menegroth was really quite a simple—and clever—solution to the problem of a hostile army not being able to enter Doriath. It is, in my opinion, much better than Tolkien's suggestion that Thingol would need to be lured outside the Girdle, and better also than the old stories, in which "the protective magic was defeated by the device of a treacherous Elf (in the Tale) or Elves (in the Sketch and the *Quenta* [*Noldorinwa*])" (*WotJ*, 352). However, it did not require the radical change of having the Nauglamîr already exist; the Dwarves already in Menegroth could have been the ones whom Thingol tapped to create the Nauglamîr in the first place.

It is interesting to note that Tom Shippey cites "Thingol's death in the dark while he looks at the captured Light" as an example of Tolkien's genius for creating compelling images.[8] Yet, as we have seen, Thingol's death in the dark recesses of Menegroth was completely an invention of the editors. In the last version written by Tolkien, Thingol was killed by the Dwarves when they caught him by surprise on a hunt (presumably outside, not in the dark; see *SoMe*, 133). The fact that as renown a Tolkien scholar as Shippey[9] would have this kind of mistaken impression is a strong indication of the need for a work like the present one.[10]

Another point worth mentioning is that in all the versions in *The Tale of Years* (as well as in the old story in the *Quenta Noldorinwa*), the Dwarves of both Nogrod and Belegost took part in the invasion of Doriath, whereas in the version created by Christopher for the published *Silmarillion*, only the Dwarves of Nogrod were involved. Christopher points out that this is based on a suggestion in the text *Concerning Galadriel and Celeborn* that was published in *Unfinished Tales* (see *WotJ*, 352–53; and *UT*, 235).

The next five paragraphs ("At that time . . ." through "Now Dior Thingol's heir . . ."; *Silm*, 234–36), describing the defeat of the Dwarves by Beren and the Elves of Ossiriand (and other allies), continue to be mostly editorial invention, with scattered details taken from *The Tale of Years* and other related sources (including in one case a 1963 letter), and two additions based on *The Nauglafring* from *The Book of Lost Tales 2*.

In paragraph 36, the name "Nimloth" for Dior's wife was taken from a series of Elvish genealogies that were created in December 1959. One version has her as Celeborn's sister, and another as his niece. Hence the more ambiguous "kinswoman of Celeborn" that Christopher adopted (see *WotJ*, 350). The names of the sons of Dior are given in both the continuation of the *Grey Annals* and *The Tale of Years* as "Elrún" and "Eldún" (see *WotJ*, 255, 300, 348, 349, 351). However, these names morphed into "Eluréd" and "Elurín" in the late work *The Problem of Ros*, where the explanation for Elwing's name—that she was born on a night of stars whose light glittered in the spray of a waterfall—is also given (*PoMe*, 369, 372 n. 9).

In *The Tale of Years* it is Curufin and Celegorm, not Beren, Dior, and the Green-elves of Ossiriand, who ambush the Dwarves who have sacked Menegroth (see *WotJ*, 346, 348, 350). The story of Beren's ambush of the Dwarves told in paragraphs 37–39 is based loosely on a 1963 letter (Letter 247), particularly the part in paragraph 38 where it states "there came forth the Shepherds of the Trees, and they drove the Dwarves into the shadowy woods of Ered Lindon." This is based on the statement in the letter that "Beren, who had no army, received the aid of the Ents" (see *Letters*, 334). Beren's slaying of the Lord of Nogrod and his taking of the Necklace of the Dwarves with the Silmaril amidst it, told in paragraph 38, is also based on this letter (ibid.).

Paragraph 39 says that the river Ascar was renamed as "Rathlóriel" (Goldenbed), because of the gold that was "drowned" in the water as a result of the battle described above. This is taken from *The Tale of Years* and goes back to the *Quenta Noldorinwa* (see *WotJ*, 351; and *SoMe*, 134, 135 n. 11), but of course in both of those texts the gold that was drowned in the river had been taken from Nargothrond, whereas in the published text it is "treasure of Doriath." The sentence in which Beren gazes in wonder at the Silmaril that he had cut from Morgoth's crown and was now "set amid gold and gems by the cunning of the Dwarves," after washing the blood off of it in the river, is closely based on a passage from *The Tale of the Nauglafring* (*BoLT2*, 238). In addition, the statement that the knowledge that the Lord of Nogrod and many other Dwarves were slain did little to ease Lúthien's grief comes from a line on the same page of *The Tale of the Nauglafring*.

Finally (as to these five paragraphs), the last part of the last sentence of paragraph 40, in which Dior sets himself "to raise anew the glory of the kingdom of Doriath," appears to be taken from the statement in the *Quenta Noldorinwa* "For Dior went back to Doriath and for a time a part of its ancient glory was raised anew" (*SoMe*, 134).

The next three paragraphs mix editorial invention with material from both *The Tale of Years* and the *Quenta Noldorinwa*. Paragraph 41 ("There came a night . . ."), in which Dior receives the Necklace of the Dwarves with the Silmaril set in it, appears to be based on the statement in *The Tale of Years*, version C, *Annal 503* (changed from 505) (see *WotJ*, 348). But the language appears to be editorial.

The first sentence of the following paragraph, describing Dior gazing at the Silmaril, also appears to be editorial, but the second sentence, indicating that the wise claimed that the Silmaril hastened Beren and Lúthien's end because Lúthien's beauty wearing it "was too bright for mortal lands," comes from the continuation of *Annal 503* (ibid.). The beginning of paragraph 43 appears to be editorial, but the rest, describing Dior as the fairest of all the children of the world, being from the Edain, the Eldar, and the Maiar, comes from the *Quenta Noldorinwa* (see *SoMe,* 134). Except that, of course, in the *Quenta Noldorinwa* it was not Dior's wearing of the Silmaril that made him the "fairest of the children of the world."

The last three paragraphs, which tell of the second Kinslaying and the final destruction of Doriath, are a complex mix of editorial language with material from both *The Tale of Years* and the *Quenta Noldorinwa.*

The first sentence of paragraph 44 is editorial, except that the last phrase, regarding the Oath of Fëanor, comes from the second-to-last paragraph of the *Quenta Noldorinwa,* chapter 14 (*SoMe,* 134). The first part of the next sentence, stating that no Elf was willing to assail Lúthien while she wore the Necklace of the Dwarves, is based on a statement in *Annal 503* of version C of *The Tale of Years* (see *WotJ,* 348). The rest of the sentence, about the sons of Fëanor claiming their own, is based loosely on *Annal 505* from version D2 of *The Tale of Years* (see *WotJ,* 351).

Most of paragraph 45, which describes the battle in which Dior is slain after he kills Celegorm, and Curufin and Caranthir are also killed, comes from the end of *Annal 503,* and the next two annals (*Annal* 506 and *Annal* 506–7), with some of the language directly quoted and some editorial, except that "so befell the second slaying of Elf by Elf" comes directly from the second-to-last paragraph of chapter 14 of the *Quenta Noldorinwa* (see *WotJ,* 351; and *SoMe,* 134). The only substantive difference between the published text of *The Silmarillion* and *Annal 506–7* is that in the published text it states that Nimloth was killed, and in *Annal 506–7* it states that the Lady Lindis (her earlier name) escaped with Elwing.

The first sentence of paragraph 46, stating that Doriath was destroyed, is editorial, but the rest, describing Elwing's escape with the Silmaril and her coming with a remnant of the people of Doriath to the mouths of the river Sirion, comes from the last paragraph of chapter 14 of the *Quenta Noldorinwa* (*SoMe,* 134).

And that brings us, finally, to the end of chapter 22. It is fascinating to see how Christopher blended older material with newer material and outright editorial invention. Ultimately, however, this chapter does overstep the bounds of the editorial function.

Chapter 23 "Of Tuor and the Fall of Gondolin"

As MENTIONED EARLIER, THE STORY OF THE FALL OF GONDOLIN WAS the third of the "Great Tales" that Tolkien's considered the most important stories of his mythology, along with the tales of Beren and Lúthien and Túrin Turambar. However, unlike those two, an extended narrative of this story is not included in the published text. The chapter on Beren and Lúthien is 113 paragraphs and twenty-five pages long, and that dedicated to Túrin is 128 paragraphs and twenty-eight pages. In comparison, this chapter is only 21 paragraphs long and fewer than seven pages.

This is largely due to the state in which Tolkien left the material on this story. He did begin an extended narrative in 1951, but only got as far as Tuor's coming to Gondolin (see *UT,* 5, 17–56). Christopher says in the introduction to that book, "[T]he only full account that my father ever wrote of the story of Tuor's sojourn in Gondolin, his union with Idril Celebrindal, the birth of Eärendil, the treachery of Maeglin, the sack of the city, and the escape of the fugitives—a story that was a central element in his imagination of the First Age—was the narrative composed in his youth" (*UT,* 5). He is referring, of course, to text included in *The Book of Lost Tales 2* as *Tuor and the Exiles of Gondolin* (but often referred to as *The Fall of Gondolin*).

In addition to being one of the Great Tales, the fall of Gondolin is built up throughout the text of the *Silmarillion* as a climactic moment —from the point where Turgon first discovers the hidden rock, through Ulmo's revealing that it will be the longest lasting of the strongholds of the Noldor, but would eventually fall. Maeglin comes there with his dark secret, Húrin and Huor sojourn in the hidden realm, Turgon makes a surprise appearance at and then an escape from the battle of Unnumbered Tears, and Morgoth desperately searches for its location. After this buildup, the very short, truncated version included in the published text feels very anticlimactic. Despite the wide gulf in time between the writing of the abandoned new text and the original full tale, I believe that it would have been better had Christopher attempted to include a fuller version of this story—closer to the scale of that used for Beren and Lúthien and for Túrin. He could have accomplished this by combining significant portions of the new extended narrative with elements from the old tale that were never superseded by later work, while eliminating features clearly incompatible with the other material, such as the metallic dragons, and adjusting the more archaic language to match the rest of the work.

Instead, the main source for this chapter goes back to the very truncated chapter 16 of the *Quenta Noldorinwa,* and extends into the beginning of chapter 17.[1] There are two versions of parts of each of those chapters, which Christopher labeled Q1 and Q2, but which I prefer to call *QN* 1 and *QN* 2.

Actually, the earlier part of this chapter, through Tuor's coming to Gondolin (the first six paragraphs), is really an extremely brief synopsis of the tale published in *Unfinished Tales* and cannot really be said to follow the *Quenta Noldorinwa* versions; the differences are too stark. The rest of the chapter follows the *Quenta Noldorinwa* versions relatively closely, particularly considering the deep abyss of time between their writing and the writing of most of the other material used as a source for the published *Silmarillion,* though obviously much of the writing is editorial. There are some snippets regarding this part of the story in both the continuation text to the *Grey Annals* and the different versions of *The Tale of Years,* but none that seem to significantly affect either the language used or the details of the story told. The source materials are traced by paragraph in table 23.

It is ironic that the most truncated part of Tuor's tale is the part for which Tolkien wrote the most developed version: the story of Tuor's coming to Gondolin. As discussed above, the first six paragraphs of the chapter represent a brief synopsis of the story told in *Unfinished Tales* as *Of Tuor and His Coming to Gondolin.* However, the telling is so brief—the six paragraphs take up only two pages, compared to the thirty-eight pages the tale takes up in *Unfinished Tales*—that it is impossible really to trace any of the language to that source, though in all details the two versions are consistent, and it seems plain that these paragraphs come from no other source.

It will come as no surprise that I believe that this synopsis is far too brief. Including the full tale would perhaps have provided too much detail compared to the rest of the story, but there can be no question that Christopher went too far to the other extreme. He all but eliminates Voronwë the Faithful (the last of the Elves sent by Turgon to seek Valinor and petition for the assistance of the Valar, who was saved from the Sea by Ulmo to guide Tuor to Gondolin) as a character in the story. Lost as well is the sense that the longer story gives of the

Table 23. Source Material by Paragraph for Chapter 23 "Of Tuor and the Fall of Gondolin"

Paragraph no.	Paragraph headwords	*Silm* page no.	Primary source	Secondary sources
1–6	"It has been told . . ." through "And at the last . . ."	238–39	Based on *Tuor and His Coming to Gondolin* (see *UT*, 17–56)	
7	"Thus it was that . . ."	240	Based loosely on part of the third and first (in that order) paragraphs of the *QN* 2 (chapter 16)	
8	"Then Turgon pondered . . ."	240–41	Editorial	Third paragraph of *QN* 2 (chapter 16): second sentence Fourth paragraph of *QN* 2 (chapter 16): fifth sentence
9	"And Tuor remained in . . ."	241	Fifth paragraph of *QN* 2 (chapter 16)	Editorial: "But so high" to the end, except "But so high did Tuor stand in the favour of the King"
10	"Then there was . . ."	241	Fifth paragraph of *QN* 2 (chapter 16)	
11	"In the spring of . . ."	241	See secondary sources	*Annal 503* of version C of *The Tale of Years* (see *WotJ*, 348): first sentence End of *QN* 2 (chapter 16): "Of surpassing beauty" through "of the Eldar" *QN* 1 (chapter 16) (*SoMe*, 143): "and the strength" to the end

(continued)

Table 23. Source Material by Paragraph for Chapter 23 "Of Tuor and the Fall of Gondolin"

Paragraph no.	Paragraph headwords	*Silm* page no.	Primary source	Secondary sources
12	"Then the days . . ."	241	Editorial	*QN* 1 (chapter 16) (*SoMe*, 143): "the days of Gondolin were yet full of joy and peace" and "But Idril Celebrindal was wise and far-seeing, and her heart misgave her, and foreboding crept upon her spirit as a cloud" *QN* 1 (chapter 16) (*SoMe*, 144): "Therefore in that time she let prepare a secret way" and "that should lead down from the city and passing out beneath the surface of the plain issue far beyond the walls, northward of Amon Gwareth"
13	"Now on a time . . ."	242	*QN* 1 (chapter 16) (*SoMe*, 143–144)	
14	"At last, in the . . ."	242	*QN* 1 (chapter 16) (*SoMe*, 144)	
15	"Tuor sought to . . ."	242–43	*QN* 1 (Chapter 16) (*SoMe*, 144–45)	*The Fall of Gondolin* (*BoLT* 2, 178): "far out and his body as it fell smote the rocky slopes of Amon Gwareth thrice ere it pitched into the flames below"
16	"There was a . . ."	243	*QN* 1 (chapter 16) (*SoMe*, 145)	

17	"Many are the songs . . ."	243	QN1 (chapter 16) (SoMe, 145)	
18	"Thus led by Tuor . . ."	243–244	QN1 (chapter 16) (SoMe, 145)	Based on *The Tale of Years*, version C, *Annal* 511 (*Wolf*, 348): "led by Tuor son of Huor the remnant of Gondolin passed over the mountains, and came down into the Vale of Sirion; and fleeing southward" Editorial: "the Land of Willows, for the power of Ulmo yet ran in the great river and it was about them," "under the willows of Nan-tathren in the waning of the year," and the last sentence
19	"But Morgoth thought . . ."	244	QN1 (chapter 16) (SoMe, 145–46)	First paragraph of QN1 (chapter 17): last sentence Editorial: "and from Balar the mariners of Cirdan came among them"
20	"And it is said that . . ."	244	Second paragraph of QN2 (chapter 17)	
21	"In those days Tuor . . ."	244–245	Beginning of third paragraph of QN2 (chapter 17)	

*Note: QN*1, chapter 16, appears in *SoMe*, 140–46, and *QN*2, chapter 16, is printed in *SoMe*, 140–46, and *QN*2, chapter 16, is printed on pages 146–48 of that book. The relevant portion of *QN*1, chapter 17, is printed in *SoMe*, 148, and the relevant portions of the *QN*2 version are on pages 151 and 155. There is also a short expansion based on a passage from *The Fall of Gondolin*, in *BoLT*2, 178 as well as *SoMe* additions based on *The Tale of Years* printed in *Wolf*.

Voronwë leading Tuor from Vinyamar, the ancient dwelling of Turgon. By Anushka Mouriño. Courtesy of the artist.

struggle of the two companions to reach Gondolin, and of the awe that the Seven Gates of Gondolin generate in Tuor.

But most disappointing by far is the failure to include Ulmo's words to Tuor in Vinyamar regarding the "armour of fate" and the doom of the Noldor, which I believe to be among the most important passages that Tolkien ever wrote (see *UT*, 28–30). In his (mostly negative) review of *Unfinished Tales*, Guy Kay himself states that the description of this encounter "is as good as anything [Tolkien] ever wrote."[2] This is another place where it appears that Christopher avoids letting the text veer into philosophical exploration; nowhere in all of Tolkien's writings does he make more explicit his views on the relationship between fate and free will. However, that dynamic was an essential aspect of his father's work, and should not have been shied away from.

The seventh paragraph ("Thus it was that . . ."; *Silm*, 240) is based loosely on part of the third and first paragraphs (in that order) of the *QN* 2 chapter 16, liberally mixed with editorial language. One difference is in the advice that Ulmo bid Tuor to give to Turgon. Instead of just advising Turgon to abandon Gondolin and go down Sirion to the Sea as in the published text, in the *Quenta Noldorinwa* Ulmo's full advice was to leave Gondolin and prepare for war, and, if Turgon was unwilling to do that, to lead his people to Sirion "and build there his fleets and seek back to Valinor and the mercy of the Gods" (see *SoMe*,

147). I think that Christopher was wise to leave out the part in which Ulmo advised Turgon to prepare for war; that would have contrasted sharply with the advice Ulmo was reported to have sent to Nargothrond with Arminas and Gelmir in the chapter on Túrin.

The next, long, paragraph is mostly editorial.[3] However, there are a couple of sentences that closely follow the *Quenta Noldorinwa* text. The first describes Turgon's pride and his love of the beauty of Gondolin, and his people's desire to avoid the woes of the outside world after the Nirnaeth; the second describes how Maeglin's advice helped convince him to ultimately reject Ulmo's counsel (see *SoMe*, 147).

The text continues to follow *QN* 2 (with significant editorial additions) through the beginning of the eleventh paragraph ("In the spring of . . ."; *Silm*, 241). The first sentence of that paragraph, describing the birth of Eärendil 503 years after the coming of the Noldor to Middle-earth, comes directly from *Annal 503* of version C of *The Tale of Years* (this entry was specifically changed from "*505*"; see *WotJ*, 348). Then the rest of the paragraph comes from the *Quenta Noldorinwa*, partly from *QN* 2 and then continuing from *QN* 1 (see *SoMe*, 143, 148).[4]

The next paragraph is mostly editorial, with the statements regarding Gondolin being still full of joy and peace, but Idril having misgivings, taken from the continuation of the *Quenta Noldorinwa* text where it leaves off at the end of the previous paragraph (*SoMe*, 143). However, parts of the description of the "secret way" out of Gondolin that Idril arranges are taken from a long passage several paragraphs later in the *Quenta Noldorinwa* text that, as will be seen shortly, was otherwise omitted (*SoMe*, 144).

Paragraphs thirteen and fourteen are two long, critical paragraphs, describing Maeglin's capture, his subversion, and the subsequent as-sault that Morgoth unleashes on Gondolin. They follow the *Quenta Noldorinwa* text with remarkably few changes, given the antiquity of the source material (see *SoMe*, 143–44). The fifteenth paragraph ("Tuor sought to . . ."; *Silm*, 242–43) combines the next two paragraphs from *QN* 1, again following the language closely, except that a large chunk of the first of the two paragraphs describing Idril's "secret way" and the fate of those unlucky souls who fled to the old Way of Escape is omitted. Retained was that part of it regarding Idril's "secret way," which appears in paragraph 12, as described above (see *SoMe*, 144).

Also, this paragraph contains the one passage that goes back to the original tale *The Fall of Gondolin*, a passage describing how Maeglin's body thrice smote the "rocky slopes of Amon Gwareth" as he fell into the flames below (see *BoLT2*, 178). It seems very odd that Christopher was willing to include this one detail from the original story, but failed to add any of the rest of the descriptive detail contained in the only full account of this pivotal story that his father ever wrote.

The next two paragraphs, which focus on Glorfindel's duel with the Balrog and his death, again follow the *Quenta Noldorinwa* text closely, with the seventeenth paragraph having perhaps the fewest changes of any in the chapter (although, oddly, the order of two of the sentences is reversed) (compare *Silm*, 243 with *SoMe*, 145).

The eighteenth paragraph ("Thus led by Tuor . . ."; *Silm*, 243–44) mostly follows the next paragraph of the *Quenta Noldorinwa* text, but it is significantly expanded, with the portion regarding Tuor leading the remnant of the people of Gondolin over the mountains based on *The Tale of Years* (see *WotJ*, 348). And the final sentence about Gilgalad is, of course, an editorial insertion, since he did not even exist at the time the *Quenta Noldorinwa* was written.

Another aspect of this paragraph shows why it is unfortunate that Christopher so greatly reduced the beginning part of this chapter describing Tuor's coming to Gondolin. In this paragraph, we see Tuor and the folk that escaped from the sack of Gondolin come to Nan-tathren and find a measure of healing there.[5] In the text *Of Tuor and his Coming to Gondolin* published in *Unfinished Tales*, Voronwë gives a moving description of his coming to Nan-tathren during his journey to the Sea on his way to attempting to bring Turgon's message to the Valar. He tells Tuor that if ever he came there he would find it "[l]ovely to heart's enchantment," and says that there Ulmo is but the servant of Yavanna, and that "fairest of all are the willows of Nan-tathren, pale green, or silver in the wind, and the rustle of their innumerable leaves is a spell of music. . . ." (see *UT*, 34–35 for the full, very moving description).

It is such a shame that this description of Nan-tathren is not included in the published *Silmarillion*, given the role that land later plays in the healing of the survivors of Gondolin and the fact that Tuor does in fact find that it is "[l]ovely to heart's enchantment." And we can only presume, since he is virtually left out of the published text altogether, that the faithful Voronwë was present at this return to the Land of Willows.[6]

Most of the following paragraph comes from the next and last paragraph of chapter 16 of *QN* 1, but the last sentence comes from the first paragraph of chapter 17 of *QN* 1.[7] The statement that Círdan's mariners came among them is an editorial addition.

The two final paragraphs continue from the *QN* 2 version of chapter 17 (the next and final chapter continues from the middle of the

QN 2 paragraph from which the final paragraph of this chapter is taken), with a sentence omitted from each. The sentence omitted from the penultimate paragraph points out that it was from the Vanyar (then called the Quendi) that the Noldor had learned that Ulmo had called for the Valar to succor them at this time (see *SoMe*, 151). More problematic is the omission from the final paragraph. Removed is a statement (which Christopher notes had been added by Tolkien) that Tuor dwelt ever after on his ship or resting in the harbors of Tol Eressëa (see *SoMe*, 155 n. 3). This omission is unfortunate. It leaves Tuor and Idril's fate unresolved, and leaves open a question regarding whether Eärendil and Elwing were really the first to break the ban against Men setting foot on Valinor (and against the Noldor returning to Valinor). The omitted portion makes it clear that Tuor and Idril did not in fact set foot on Valinor. It should not have been left out.

This concludes chapter 23. I find it truly remarkable that so much of the language and content of this chapter comes from the *Quenta Noldorinwa*, which was written more than twenty years before the source material of most of the rest of the published *Silmarillion*. But it is nonetheless unfortunate that more of the even older material from the only full version of the story of the fall of Gondolin was not incorporated into the text, as well as a greater amount of the more recent, fuller narrative of Tuor's coming to Gondolin.

Chapter 24 "Of the Voyage of Eärendil and the War of Wrath"

CHAPTER 24 IS THE FINAL CHAPTER OF THE *QUENTA SILMARILLION*. THE first part (through the point where Eärendil and Elwing and their companions pass Tol Eressëa) continues from chapter 17 of the *Quenta Noldorinwa*, from the point where it leaves off at the end of the previous chapter. From that point the "earlier *Quenta*," which had abruptly stopped in the middle of the chapter on Túrin, suddenly picks up again in the middle of this chapter, and Tolkien rewrote the concluding passages from the *Quenta Noldorinwa*. As Christopher points out, this rewritten conclusion actually picks up in the middle of a sentence (*Lost Road*, 323). Then, after describing why he concludes that this ending portion was written at roughly the same time as the rest of the "earlier *Quenta*," he notes that he is unable to explain why his father never returned to the portions of the *Quenta* dealing with the greater part of the tale of Túrin, the destruction of Doriath, the fall of Gondolin, and the earlier part of the tale of Eärendil, and instead "jumped to the end in this way, taking up in mid-sentence" (*Lost Road*, 324).

When Tolkien was preparing the "later *Quenta*" (approximately fifteen years later) he made some emendations to this concluding chapter (despite the gap in the *Quenta* manuscript that jumps from the middle of the Túrin chapter to the middle of this concluding chapter). Christopher notes that it was remarkable that the end of "The Silmarillion" still had this form at the time when his father started writing *The Lord of the Rings*, but that it was even more remarkable—and "difficult to interpret"—that his father "was treating it as a text requiring only minor and particular revision at this much later time" (*WotJ*, 247).

In any event, Christopher followed these texts fairly closely; the editorial invention in this final chapter of the *Quenta Silmarillion* in the published text is not as extensive as one might expect. The biggest change is that the final paragraphs, relating to the Second Prophecy of Mandos, are omitted altogether. They are replaced with the postscript taken from the end of the *Valaquenta*.[1] I think that including the second prophecy would have made a better ending of the *Quenta*

Silmarillion—particularly because it would have introduced the concept of the final Healing of Arda, which was particularly important to Tolkien because of his strong Christian faith.

The source materials are traced by paragraph in table 24.

The first paragraph is taken from the remaining portion of the third paragraph of chapter 17 in *QN 2*, picking up where it left off at the end of the previous chapter, with remarkably few changes. This is another example of Christopher moving the place where his father designated a chapter break, which we saw in several places earlier with the chapters taken from what had been subchapters in the second-phase work on the "later *Quenta*."[2] This is a small example of Christopher's willingness to rearrange the structure of the work, rather than following his father's intentions.

The next paragraph continues from the *Quenta Noldorinwa* text, but a significant portion at the beginning is most likely an editorial invention, and an equally significant portion is omitted toward the end of the paragraph. The first sentence and the beginning of the second sentence, regarding Eärendil's friendship with Círdan and the aid that the old Elf gave him in building his ship *Vingilot,* is the portion that appears to be an editorial addition. Then, toward the end of the paragraph a sentence is omitted describing how Eärendil slew Ungoliant (it is worth noting that that spelling was used originally here, before it was changed to "Ungoliantë") "and her darkness was destroyed, and light came to many regions which had yet long been hid" (see *SoMe,* 152). This omission was made necessary by the inclusion of the statement from the second-phase work on the "later *Quenta*" speculating that Ungoliant's ultimate fate was to devour herself in her uttermost famine.[3] This is one occasion where I would have preferred that Christopher kept the older story rather than the newer one. Having Eärendil slay Ungoliant bolsters his stature, which is helpful, since he is ultimately the main hero of the story.

Most of the next four paragraphs continue from the *Quenta Noldorinwa* text. There are only two points in these paragraphs where the text significantly diverges from the *Quenta Noldorinwa* text. The first sentence of the fourth paragraph ("Now when the . . ."; *Silm,* 246–47), describing how Maedhros initially restrained himself and his brothers from attacking the community that dwelt by the mouths of Sirion, is based on version D2 of *The Tale of Years,* in *Annal 512* (see *WotJ,* 352). Then, in the following paragraph, the statement that the ships of Círdan and "Gil-galad the High King" came too late to save the folk living by Sirion appears to be an editorial addition.

The first part of the eighth paragraph ("Yet Eärendil saw . . ."; *Silm,* 247–48) continues from the *Quenta Noldorinwa* text, with one small

Table 24. Source Material by Paragraph for Chapter 24 "Of the Voyage of Eärendil and the War of Wrath"

Paragraph no.	Paragraph headwords	*Silm* page no.	Primary source	Secondary sources
1	"Bright Eärendil was . . ."	246	QN 2 (chapter 17) (*SoMe*, 151–52)	
2	"Now Eärendil became . . ."	246	QN 2 (chapter 17) (*SoMe*, 152)	Editorial: "Now Eärendil" through "aid of Círdan"
3	"Eärendil found not . . ."	246	QN 2 (chapter 17) (*SoMe*, 152)	
4	"Now when the . . ."	246–47	QN 2 (chapter 17) (*SoMe*, 152)	Version D2 of *The Tale of Years*, Annal 512 (*WotJ*, 351): "Now when first the tidings came to Maedhros that Elwing yet lived, and dwelt in possession of the Silmaril by the mouths of Sirion, he repenting of the deeds in Doriath withheld his hand"
5	"For the sons of . . ."	247	QN 2 (chapter 17) (*SoMe*, 152–53)	Editorial: "Too late the ships of Círdan and Gil-galad the High King came hasting to the aid of the Elves of Sirion; and Elwing was gone, and her sons"
6	"Thus Maedhros . . ."	247	QN 2 (chapter 17) (*SoMe*, 153)	
7	"Great was the . . ."	247	QN 2 (chapter 17) (*SoMe*, 153)	
8	"Yet Eärendil saw . . ."	247–248	QN 2 (chapter 17) (*SoMe*, 153)	QS(Conc)§1: "and they looked upon" to the end
9	"But Elwing answered . . ."	248	QS(Conc) §2	
10	"Then Eärendil said . . ."	248	QS(Conc) §3	
11	"But some there were . . ."	248	QS(Conc) §4	

12	"Hail Eärendil, of . . ."	248–49	QS(Conc) §4	QS(Conc) §8: "Then the Valar took counsel together, and they summoned Ulmo from the deeps of the sea"
13	"That voice was the . . ."	249	LQ/QS(Conc) §5	
14	"It is told among . . ."	249	QS(Conc) §8	Editorial: "It is told among the Elves that after Eärendil departed, seeking Elwing his wife"
15	"But when all was . . ."	249	QS(Conc) §9	
16	"Now when Eärendil . . ."	249	QS(Conc) §7	
17	"Then Eärendil said . . ."	249–50	QS(Conc) §10 and the first part of LQ/QS(Conc) §11	QS(Conc) §10: last sentence
18	"Now fair and . . ."	250	The rest of QS(Conc) §11	
19	"On those journeys . . ."	250	LQ/QS(Conc) §12	
20	"Now when first . . ."	250	LQ/QS(Conc) §13	
21	"And Maglor . . ."	250	QS(Conc) §13	
22	"Yet it is said . . ."	250–51	LQ/QS(Cont) §6	
23	"Of the march of . . ."	251	LQ/QS(Conc) §15 (but see text)	QS(Conc) §14: beginning through "beyond reckoning"
24	"The meeting of . . ."	251	QS(Conc) §16	
25	"But it availed . . ."	251	LQ/QS(Conc) §16	
26	"Then, seeing . . ."	252	LQ/QS(Conc) §17	
27	"But Eärendil . . ."	252	LQ/QS(Conc) §18	
28	"Thus an end was . . ."	252	QS(Conc) §19	
29	"Then Eönwë as . . ."	252–53	LQ/QS(Conc) §20	
30	"But Eönwë answered . . ."	253	QS(Conc) §21 and the first sentence of QS(Conc) §22	
31	"But Maedhros answered . . ."	253	QS(Conc) §22	

(continued)

Table 24. Continued

Paragraph no.	Paragraph headwords	*Silm* page no.	Primary source	Secondary sources
32	"Yet Maglor still . . ."	253	QS(Conc) §22	
33	"And Maedhros answered: . . ."	253	QS(Conc) §22	
34	"'If none can . . ."	253	QS(Conc) §22	
35	"Yet he yielded . . ."	253	QS(Conc) §22 and QS(Conc) §23	
36	"But the jewel . . ."	253–54	QS(Conc) §24	
37	"And it is told . . ."	254	QS(Conc) §25	Editorial: "named only after Daeron of Doriath"
38	"In those days . . ."	254	LQ/QS(Conc) §26	
39	"And when they . . ."	254	QS(Conc) §27	
40	"Yet not all the . . ."	254	QS(Conc) §28	Editorial: "those were Cirdan the Ship-wright, and Celeborn of Doriath, with Galadriel his wife, who alone remained of those who led the Noldor to exile in Beleriand. In Middle-earth dwelt also Gil-galad the High King"
41	"But Morgoth himself . . ."	254–55	Last sentence of QS(Conc) §29 and the first sentence of LQ/QS(Conc) §30	
42	"Here ends the . . ."	255	*Valaquenta* (*MR*, 203)	

Note: The relevant portion of chapter 17 of *QN 2* can be found in *SoMe*, 151–55. The revised concluding chapter is printed in *Lost Road*, 323–38 and is numbered from §1 to §33. I will refer to those sections as "QS(Conc) §x." The revisions made to that concluding chapter can be found in *WotJ*, 246–47. Following the convention that I adopted earlier, I will refer to those sections where changes in the "later *Quenta*" are described as "LQ/QS(Conc) §x." There is also at least one detail that be traced to *The Tale of Years*, version D2 (*WotJ*, 351).

but interesting change. The statement that Eärendil saw no hope in the lands of Middle-earth is significantly broadened from the source text, where it states only that he saw no hope in the lands of Sirion (*SoMe*, 153).

Almost exactly halfway through this paragraph, in the middle of the sentence where it describes Eärendil, Elwing, and their companions passing Tol Eressëa, the text picks up from the concluding chapter that Tolkien revised in both the "earlier *Quenta*" and "later *Quenta*," as discussed above. There is one small but important omission from that part of the paragraph. Where Eärendil states that only he shall set foot on the immortal shores and risk the wrath of the Valar, in the source text he also states that they would risk "the doom of death" and that it is forbidden (*Lost Road*, 325). This minor edit is unfortunate. As discussed above, the distinction between the mortality of Men and the immortality of the Elves is one of the most important themes of Tolkien's mythology, and once again, Christopher has de-emphasized it.[4]

The text then continues to follow the concluding chapter of the *Quenta* with only minor changes through the next three paragraphs. The only change of any significance is that in the source material after Eärendil was spotted and the watchers went in great haste to Valmar "all the bells in Valmar pealed" (see *Lost Road*, 325). But in the twelfth paragraph ("'Hail Eärendil, of mariners . . .'"; *Silm*, 248–49) the words of Eönwë greeting Eärendil are significantly emended. The description of him as "of mariners most renowned" is changed from "radiant star, messenger most fair!" Among the other changes is that "slayer of the dark!" is omitted, since Eärendil's slaying of Ungoliant had been removed (see *Lost Road*, 325).

The next paragraph continues to follow the concluding chapter (incorporating some changes made in the "later *Quenta*" revisions), but the statement regarding the Valar taking counsel and summoning Ulmo from the Sea is inserted from QS(Conc) §8, several paragraphs later. Then paragraph 14 ("It is told among . . ."; *Silm*, 249) is mostly taken from that section, skipping for now §§6 and 7 (see *Lost Road*, 326).

There are significant changes in the following paragraph, including in the order in which the sentences appear. The most interesting change is the omission of an unequivocal statement that all those who have any amount of the blood of mortal Men are mortal "unless other doom be granted to them" (*Lost Road*, 326). It should also be noted that there was a change made by Tolkien in the "later *Quenta*" in which the words "the Elder King" were added after "Manwë," words that were *not* taken up in the published text (see *WotJ*, 246).

The next paragraph mostly is taken from QS(Conc) §7, which had been skipped previously. The text continues from LQ/QS(Conc) §§10–13 with only minor edits until paragraph 22 ("Yet it is said . . ."; *Silm*, 250–51, which combines QS(Conc) §14 with the heretofore unused LQ/QS(Conc) §6, in that order.

The following paragraph has some fairly significant changes in the language at places, primarily in reducing the role that Eönwë plays as the primary leader of the forces opposing Morgoth. Christopher points out in commentary about the *Akallabêth* that this was the result of the elimination of the conception of "the Children of the Valar" and the resulting change of Eönwë's status from being Manwë's son to being his herald. Christopher states that in hindsight he considered his editorial reduction of Eönwë's role to be a "mistaken treatment of the original text" (*PoMe*, 143).[5] Also in this paragraph, most curiously, the phrase "for the host of the Valar were arrayed in forms young and fair and terrible" mixes the language used in the "later *Quenta*," "The host of the Gods were arrayed in forms of Valinor," with the language that it replaces from the "earlier *Quenta*," "the sons of the Gods were young and fair and terrible" (see *WotJ*, 246; and *Lost Road*, 328).

The next paragraph ("But it availed . . ."; *Silm*, 251) has an omission worth noting. In the source text, after the statement that those who were left of the houses of the Edain fought for the Valar, there was an explicit reminder that the old prophecy that Ulmo had made to Turgon had been fulfilled, since help was brought to the Elves by Eärendil son of Tuor, and they were strengthened in their battles "by the swords of Men" (see *Lost Road*, 328–29).[6]

The next twelve paragraphs ("Then, seeing that . . ." through "In those days . . ."; *Silm*, 252–54) continue with remarkably small changes, given how old and how critical most of the material is. The most substantive changes are the elimination of the idea (surviving from the original Lost Tales) that the winged dragons' wings were made of steel (see *Lost Road*, 329) and a change from the statement that Maglor was the "mightiest of the singers of old" (*Lost Road*, 331) to match the earlier statement in that Daeron is named as a singer even before Maglor.[7]

However, in the last of those twelve paragraphs there is a seemingly very small change that does prove to be quite significant. The statement that the joy in the victory over Morgoth was tempered by the knowledge that they returned without the Silmarils from Morgoth's crown and that those jewels "would not be found or brought together again unless" the world was broken and remade is changed from saying until the world was broken and remade (see *Lost Road*, 331). This seemingly small change presages the elimination of the Second Prophecy of Mandos at the end of this chapter. Its importance lies in the fact that it reduces the promise of the Healing of Arda from a certain event sometime in the future to an uncertain event that may never happen.

The next paragraph ("And when they . . ."; *Silm*, 254) also has an interesting change. The statement that the Elves of Middle-earth "might come even to Valinor" replaces the more explicit statement that some did return to Valinor, and that all were free to do so who so wished (see *Lost Road*, 332). This leaves many readers with the somewhat misleading impression that the exiles were forbidden to dwell in Valinor, from whence they came.

The following paragraph also has some fairly significant editorial changes. There are one substantial addition and one equally substantial omission. The naming of Círdan, Celeborn, Galadriel, and Gil-galad among those who chose to remain in Middle-earth is added (though based, of course, on their later presence in Middle-earth as told in *The Lord of the Rings*), and in the statement "with him was Elrond Half-Elven" the meaning of "him" is changed from Maglor to Gil-galad (see *Lost Road*, 332). This has the effect of reducing the connection between Elrond and Maglor as his foster father, and is particularly noteworthy, given Maglor's role in stealing the remaining Silmarils. At the end of this paragraph, a sentence is omitted describing how the Elf-folk faded as the ages drew on, and set sail from the western shores, until few lingered "of their lonely companies" (ibid.). I cannot imagine why this was omitted. It seems to complement the story of *The Lord of the Rings* very well, since the theme of the fading of the Elves is so prevalent in that book.

The final paragraph of the text (disregarding the postscript that ends the *Quenta Silmarillion*) contains major omissions. This paragraph combines the last sentence of QS(Conc) §29 with the first sentence of LQ/QS(Conc) §30, with very minor changes. But the bulk of both of those paragraphs is omitted entirely.

The portion of LQ/QS(Conc) §29 omitted from the published text describes how the Valar declared (through Eönwë) that henceforth the lands of Middle-earth would be for Mankind, but that the road into the West would only be open to the Elves, who would slowly fade if they remained in the land of Men. It goes on to state that the sundering of the fates of the two kindreds was the most grievous result of Morgoth's actions, because all of the other evils that he devised or nurtured would eventually perish (see *Lost Road*, 332). This is the third occasion in which Christopher removed an explicit statement regarding one of Morgoth's actions being the "worst" of his actions, or words to that effect.[8] The passage that was omitted from LQ/QS(Conc) §30 indicates that although some claim that Morgoth himself at times crept back into the World, others say that this was Sauron, who "fled from the Great Battle and escaped, and he dwelt in dark places and perverted Men to his dreadful allegiance and his foul worship" (see *Lost Road,* 332–33; and *WotJ,* 247).

Other than the statement that the sundering of Men and Elves was Morgoth's most grievous action, I am at a loss as to why most of both of these passages were omitted. They contain important aspects of Tolkien's mythology and provide a strong bridge to both the *Akallabêth* and *The Lord of the Rings.*

Finally, as has already been mentioned, the final postscript of the *Quenta Silmarillion* in the published work is taken from the end of the *Valaquenta,* with "Here ends the *SILMARILLION*" replacing "Here ends the *Valaquenta.*" This postscript replaces the last three paragraphs of LQ/QS(Conc). The first two of those paragraphs contain "the Second Prophecy of Mandos" and the last one provides the conclusion of the story of Ælfwine's bringing these tales back from Tol Eressëa (see *Lost Road,* 333–34; and *WotJ,* 247). The removal of the final paragraph is understandable, since Tolkien himself moved away from the idea of the *Quenta* being told to Ælfwine. However, the removal of the other two paragraphs is more controversial.

Christopher states in his discussion of the *Valaquenta* that the text used for this paragraph shows that "The Second Prophecy of Mandos had now therefore definitively disappeared" (*MR,* 204). He is referring to the statement that if Manwë, Varda, or Mandos has any knowledge of the Marring of Arda being amended, he or she has not revealed it (*Silm,* 255).

However, it is (not surprisingly) not as simple as that. I believe that Christopher gave too much weight to these words, in light of the other available evidence, including Tolkien's other writings from the same time period and soon after, and that it was ultimately misleading to move these words from the end of the *Valaquenta* and use them to replace the Second Prophecy at the end of the *Quenta.* Tolkien himself never indicated any intention to remove the Second Prophecy; quite the contrary, actually. His actions strongly indicate that it was his intention to retain it.

There are two main components of the Second Prophecy. The first part of the prophecy deals with the final battle, in which Túrin is described as dealing Morgoth his final deathblow. The second part relates how the Earth will be broken and remade, with the Silmarils recovered and delivered by Fëanor to Yavanna, who uses them to rekindle the Two Trees. The latter then give Light to all the world, rather than just to Valinor. There was also a statement included that indicates that Túrin was the only Man named in the prophecy, and that he was to be given a place among the sons of the Valar. However, that portion of the text was marked by Tolkien with a large X in the "later *Quenta*" revisions (see *Lost Road*, 333; and *WotJ*, 247). The fact that Tolkien made this one specific edit to the text including the Second Prophecy in his latest work on the *Silmarillion*, but made no effort at all to remove the part of the prophecy in which Túrin returns from the Doom of Men to deal Morgoth his deathblow, or the portion regarding the Earth being remade, is a strong indication that it was his intention to retain them.

The continued viability of the Second Prophecy is tied up with the complicated question of which tradition the *Silmarillion* and related works came from: Elvish or Mannish, and to what extent the mythology is meant to be considered the true story of what was or (in this case) what will be. In note 7 to the commentary of the *Athrabeth*, which was written around 1959—most likely later than the *Valaquenta*—Tolkien states: "It is noteworthy that the Elves had no myths or legends dealing with the end of the world. The myth that appears at the end of the *Silmarillion* is of Númenórean origin; it is clearly made by Men, though Men acquainted with Elvish tradition. All Elvish traditions are presented as 'histories,' or as accounts of what once was" (*MR*, 342; see also *PoMe*, 374–75 n. 17, in which a version of part of the Second Prophecy is attributed to Andreth the Wise-woman, and Christopher also offers a good summary of the history of the Second Prophecy). Had Christopher followed his father's express stated wishes about the *Athrabeth*,[9] it would have been much easier for him to have left the conclusion of the *Valaquenta* with the *Valaquenta*, and include the "myth that appears at the end of the *Silmarillion*," since its inclusion would have been explained.

The idea of at least some of the material regarding the Elder Days being filtered through Mannish eyes is consistent with what Tolkien stated elsewhere. For instance, in one of the two versions of the preamble to the *Annals of Aman* he specifically states the *Annals* were written in Númenor before its fall, and held in memory by the Exiles (see *MR*, 47, 64–65). This idea became even more firmly fixed in Tolkien's mind in his later years. In a very interesting passage in one of the "Myths Transformed" texts (Text VII, entitled "Notes on motives in the Silmarillion"), he explicitly states that the mythology is based on Elvish lore that is passed on to us through Númenórean traditions, "supplemented by anthropocentric histories and tales" (*MR*, 401–2). This idea was expressed several more times in his last writings, including a note to *The Shibboleth of Fëanor* in which he states that *The Sil-*

marillion is a Mannish work, a compilation probably made in Númenor (see *PoMe,* 357 n. 17 and 390 n. 17; and *MR,* 373).

The portion of the Second Prophecy in which Túrin strikes down Morgoth is valuable, because it provides some resolution to the unrelenting darkness of the story of the children of Húrin. But it is not necessarily meant to be taken as truth, as what really happens (or rather, what really will happen). It is not "Elvish history"; it is "Mannish mythology" as stated in the *Athrabeth* commentary. But I see no reason why the two cannot exist side by side with each other. This is the type of anthropomorphic tale supplementing the Elvish histories that Tolkien referred to in the text cited above. It makes sense that the Númenóreans would devise such a hopeful resolution of their ancestor's story. It ties into the Númenórean obsession with immortality; if Túrin can "return from the Doom of Men" (see *WotJ,* 247), then so can they.

However, I would suggest that the portion dealing with Túrin's vanquishing of Morgoth is a comparatively minor component of the Second Prophecy. The really important part of the Second Prophecy is what I think can properly be referred to as "Arda Healed"—one of the most important concepts in all of Tolkien's work. Unlike the part of the prophecy describing Túrin vanquishing Morgoth, this part of the prophecy clearly is meant to reflect "what really will happen." It is consistent with the long discussion of the Valar in the essay *Laws and Customs among the Eldar* (which was written contemporaneously with the *Athrabeth* and the commentaries to it, and thus was also written after the *Valaquenta*), in which Manwë himself states that "Arda Healed" will be "greater and more fair than the first, because of the Marring" and that the "Hope that sustaineth" comes "from trust in Eru the Lord everlasting, that he is good, and that his works shall all end in good" (*MR,* 245). It is also consistent with comments made in the entry on the root PHAN in the late linguistic essay referred to earlier, in which he again references the importance of the idea of Arda Healed.[10] As discussed earlier, it is likely that this document was written around 1963 or 1964, again well after the *Valaquenta*.

It is the lack of any sense of the inevitability of the Healing of Arda, of the concept that all of Eru's works will eventually end in good, that I miss most as a result of the removal of the Second Prophecy from the published *Silmarillion*. As Verlyn Flieger states, "Tolkien wrote that the legendarium 'ends with a vision of the end of the world, its breaking and remaking, and the recovery of the Silmarilli and the "light before the sun."' . . . It would be strange if he had not envisioned such an end, for the mythologies on which he draws most heavily, Judeo-Christian and Norse, both included remaking and renewal in surprisingly similar terms."[11] The passage from which she quotes is taken from the preface that Christopher added to the second edition of *The Silmarillion,* which contains large portions of Tolkien's 1951 letter to Milton Waldman of Collins Publishers, describing his mythology. It is quite ironic that Christopher included those quoted words in the preface, and yet did not include the passage that they refer to in the published text.

The concept of the Healing of Arda is consistent with statements made in *The Lord of the Rings* by both Galadriel and Tom Bombadil. Galadriel tells Treebeard that they will not meet again "until the lands that lie under the wave are lifted up again" (*LOTR,* 981). And Bombadil's song that drives away the Barrow-wight includes the words "till the world is mended" (142). To the extent that Christopher's goal was to achieve consistency with the already published works in creating the published *Silmarillion,* this concept should have been included. More importantly, I believe that his failure to do so constitutes a failure to properly reflect an important part of his father's vision (and I think that Flieger's words cited above support that belief).

This brings us to the end of the *Quenta Silmarillion* portion of the published *Silmarillion.* Among the numerous omissions from the source material that I have detailed, few if any are more egregious than this one at the very end.

III

The *Akallabêth, Of the Rings of Power and the Third Age,* and Appendices to the *Silmarillion*

Akallabêth (The Downfall of Númenor)

THE *AKALLABÊTH* IS THE FIRST OF THE TWO SEPARATE WORKS THAT FOL-
low the *Quenta Silmarillion* in the published *Silmarillion*. The *Akallabêth*
was the final version of the story of the downfall of Númenor, which
had already gone through several previous iterations and had great
meaning to Tolkien. In several letters he describes the dream of
the "ineluctable Wave" that often troubled his sleep, and which
he "bequeathed" to Faramir in *The Lord of the Rings* (see *Letters*, 213,
232, and 347). This dream was the genesis of the story of the fall of
Númenor.

The final history of the *Akallabêth* is given in *PoMe*, 140–65. However, none of the texts of the drafts of the work are given. Instead, as
with the *Valaquenta* and the material on Maeglin, Christopher uses
the version in the published work as his base, and traces the changes
that were made through the previous versions, including describing
the editorial changes that he made. He notes that much of the language of the older work *The Drowning of Anadûnê* was preserved in the
final version of the *Akallabêth*, but that large portions of the final work
were expanded from the other older work, *The Fall of Númenor* (see
Sauron Defeated, 375–87; and *PoMe*, 142). This combining of different
texts to devise a final form may have provided something of a precedent for Christopher's own combining of the *Annals* and the *Quenta*.

It is also interesting to note that *The Drowning of Anadûnê*, while pro-
viding much of the language for the final version of the *Akallabêth*,
differed fundamentally in that it was in a "round-world" version of the
story, written perhaps in conjunction with the "round world" version
C* of the *Ainulindalë* (see discussion in *MR*, 5–6).[1] However, as with
the *Ainulindalë*, the final version of the story of the fall of Númenor
is a flat-world version. I am particularly thankful that this aspect was
preserved in this tale, because it is here that we see the actual bend-
ing of the world and the removal of the Undying Lands from the circles of the world (although, as we will see, that is made somewhat less
explicit by Christopher's edits to the text). This is an utterly critical
element of Tolkien's mythology, and one of the most powerfully sym-
bolic as well.

Since the *Akallabêth* was itself a completed work, there is no need for a table tracing the source material used by Christopher. He notes that he made some editorial changes, mostly "for coherence and consistency with other writings," but says that in hindsight that quest was "somewhat excessively pursued" (*PoMe*, 142). I discuss only the most significant of the edits that he describes.

In the beginning of the first sentence (*Silm*, 259), the words "It is said by the Eldar that Men" replace "Of Men, Ælfwine, it is said by the Eldar." Christopher notes that the *Akallabêth* was conceived as a tale told by Pengoloð to Ælfwine in Tol Eressëa, and that he removed that element (*PoMe*, 142–43). As discussed in reference to the *Ainulindalë* and elsewhere, the question of the context of the various different works was left in a confusing state: the *Ainulindalë* and the *Akallabêth* continued to be conceived as told by Pengoloð to Ælfwine in Tol Eressëa, whereas the *Quenta* and other related texts had moved toward the conception of being myths preserved by the Númenóreans. As discussed earlier, Christopher evidently concluded that the best solution to this confusion was to eliminate any reference to the context of all the works—though he later expressed some regret for that decision.

In the third paragraph, a reference to Eönwë, the herald of Manwë, overcoming Morgoth is removed. It is here that Christopher makes the comment cited in the last chapter of the *Quenta Silmarillion* expressing regret regarding his decision to reduce Eönwë's role (*PoMe*, 143).[2]

In the following paragraph, after stating that the Men of the faithful houses of the Edain were given "wisdom and power and life" greater than those of other Men, a more specific statement that their lives were three times those of the men of Middle-earth (and even longer for Hador's descendants) is removed. Christopher says this omission was made because of divergent statements on the subject, but describes the edit as "scarcely necessary" (see *PoMe*, 144, and *UT*, 224 n. 1).

There are a number of other changes and omissions in the following paragraphs (see *PoMe*, 144–49) but none of much significance until the thirteenth paragraph ("Thus it was that . . ."; *Silm*, 263). In that paragraph, a sentence is omitted describing how the Númenóreans taught the Men of Middle-earth about language, because other than in the lands where the Edain had lived, they "were fallen into brutishness, and they cried like harsh birds, or snarled like savage beasts" (*PoMe*, 149). Christopher gives no reason for this omission, and it seems odd, since this statement connects so well to the passage in *The Lord of the Rings* in which Gamling recognizes the tongue of the

Dunlendings, while to Éomer "they are only the screams of birds and the bellowing of beasts" (*LOTR*, 536–37).

In paragraph 21 ("To which they . . ."; *Silm*, 264–65), "you" is changed from "thou" in several places. Christopher notes that there was a complex interplay here between "thou" and "you" reflecting whether the messengers were addressing the king or the people as a whole, but that in the published text, only "you" was used (*PoMe*, 150).

At the end of the twenty-eighth paragraph ("In all this . . ."; *Silm*, 267), Christopher removed a statement that the only one of the strongholds of Men of which the Eldar knew was Pelargir, because it was the haven of the Elf-friends. Christopher attributes this change to his removal of Pengoloð as the teller of the tale, a change he characterizes as due to "an excess of vigilance" (*PoMe*, 152–53).

There are several incorrect changes to the numbers of the kings of Númenor in the thirty-first and thirty-eighth paragraphs ("In those days . . ." and "The mightiest and proudest . . ."; *Silm*, 267–68, 270). Christopher explains the reason for these changes in note 11 to "The Line of Elros" in *Unfinished Tales,* where he points out that Tar-Ardamin was omitted in error from the list of rulers in appendix A to *The Lord of the Rings* (see *PoMe*, 154; and *UT*, 226–27 n. 11).

Also worth mentioning are two notes regarding the lords of Andúnië (from whom Elendil and the kings of Gondor and Arnor were descended) that were omitted from paragraph 33 ("Highest in honour . . ."; *Silm*, 268). The first indicates that this was the only house save that of the kings to take names in Quenya. The second is a fairly long note stating that if the later law holding that the oldest child would be heir to the throne regardless of gender—which was adopted when Tar-Ankalimë became the first ruling queen—had been in place earlier, the lords of Andúnië would have held the scepter, since they were descended from Silmarien, the oldest child of Tar-Elendil (see *PoMe*, 154–155; see also *UT*, 201).

There are several changes of note in paragraph 41 ("And men saw his sails . . ."; *Silm*, 270). Christopher notes that the sails of Ar-Pharazôn's ships should have been described as gleaming with "red gold," not "red and gold," since that was a phrase that went all the way back to *The Drowning of Anadûnê* (*PoMe*, 155). More significantly, he says that he made two changes in this paragraph based on the statement in the entry for Second Age 2280 in appendix B of *The Lord of the Rings* indicating that Umbar was made into a fortress of Númenor more than a thousand years before Ar-Pharazôn's coming. The first change is understandable; it was simply to add the words "of the Númenóreans" to the description of Umbar being a mighty haven that no hand had wrought (*PoMe*, 155–56). The second change makes less sense. Christopher indicates that the words "were all the lands about when the King of the Sea marched upon Middle-earth" replaced "under the sickle moon was the land when the King of the Sea set foot upon the shore" for the same reason (*PoMe*, 156). It is unclear why the fact that Umbar had long since been a Númenórean haven would dictate this change.

There is a small but significant change in paragraph 57 ("'The days are dark . . .'"; *Silm*, 275). Where Elendil's father Amandil tells him that "there is no hope for Men," the "for Men" is changed from "in Men." Christopher notes that this apparently was a "mere error," since he could think of no reason for the change (*PoMe*, 156). However, this seemingly small error really changes the tenor of Amandil's comments, from a cynical distrust of his own kind to a mere hopeless acceptance of their fate. It is an unfortunate mistake.

The next change noted by Christopher is not until the seventy-fifth paragraph ("But the fleets of . . ."; *Silm*, 278). Omitted from the beginning of this paragraph is a long prefatory statement by Pengoloð in which he tells Ælfwine that while none among Men can tell the tale of the fate of the ships of Ar-Pharazôn, the wisest among the Eldar know that "neither ship nor man or all that host returned ever to the lands of the living; and the world was changed in that time" (*PoMe*, 156–57). In addition to contributing to removing the context of this tale, this omission also removes an explicit reference to the changing of the world, another indication that the Second Prophecy should not have been removed.

Similarly, in the seventy-seventh paragraph ("But the land of Aman . . ."; *Silm*, 279) two references to the Undying Lands being removed from the "circles of the world" are omitted. This also makes it less explicit how the world was changed. Christopher provides no explanation for why he made these changes.

Another short reference to Ælfwine is removed from paragraph 81 ("Elendil and his sons . . ."; *Silm*, 280). The first part of paragraph 84 ("Among the Exiles . . ."; *Silm*, 281) is significantly rewritten. Removed is not only Pengoloð explaining to Ælfwine that the reason he (Ælfwine) desires to venture upon the Sea is that he is "of the seed of Eärendil," but also an explicit reference to the Exiles believing that the summit of the Meneltarma would someday rise out of the Sea, to be a "a lonely island lost in the great waters, unless haply a mariner should come upon it" (see *PoMe*, 158). This would have better explained the statement in the following paragraph that the great mariners among the Dúnedain would search for the "Isle of the Meneltarma."

Finally, at the end of the text, the following statement by Pengoloð is removed: "And whether all these tales be feigned, or whether some at least be true, and by them the Valar still keep alight among Men a memory beyond the darkness of Middle-earth, thou knowest now, Ælfwine, in thyself. Yet haply none shall believe thee" (see *PoMe*, 158–59).

This statement demonstrates why it was a shame that Christopher removed the context that his father had set for this tale. The sense of mingled myth and history keeping alive the spiritual truths of an earlier time reflected in this statement is exactly the tone that I think *The Silmarillion* is meant to capture.

And that brings us to end of the *Akallabêth*.

Of the Rings of Power and the Third Age

OF THE RINGS OF POWER AND THE THIRD AGE, THE FINAL WORK IN THE published *Silmarillion,* brings the history up to the time of the War of the Rings, the period covered in *The Lord of the Rings.* There is only a small amount that can be said about this text. We know that it was probably in existence by 1948, because in a letter to a Mrs. Katherine Farrer most likely dated June 15 of that year Tolkien says he was unable to find it (see *Letters,* 130; see also *MR,* 5–6, in which a draft of that letter is quoted). In *The Treason of Isengard,* Christopher quotes a passage that was originally written for the Council of Elrond chapter in *The Lord of the Rings,* and then states:

> It will be found that in this passage are the bones of a part of the narra-
> tive of the separate work *Of the Rings of Power and the Third Age,* which was
> published in *The Silmarillion* (see pp. 290–93). In the later development
> of "The Council of Elrond" the chapter became the vehicle of a far fuller
> account of the early Númenórean kingdoms in Middle-earth, and much
> of this is now found not in *The Lord of the Rings* but in *Of the Rings of Power
> and the Third Age. (Treason of Isengard,* 143–45)

Later, discussing a passage in the chapter "Galadriel," Christopher states, "Ultimately, this passage foreshadows that in *Of the Rings of Power* in *The Silmarillion;* my father at this stage probably intended it for 'The Council of Elrond'" (*The Treason of Isengard,* 260).

In addition, Christopher points out that the note regarding Cele-brimbor in the footnote regarding *Of Dwarves and Men* referred to in the discussion about Chapter 19 was also "introduced editorially" in *Of the Rings of Power* (*PoMe,* 318). Also, there is a mention in the note on "the parentage of Gil-galad" that the statement in *Of the Rings of Power* that Gil-galad was the son of Fingon is an editorial change from "Felagund" (*PoMe,* 349.)

I have located no other source material for this work.

Appendices to *The Silmarillion*

IMMEDIATELY FOLLOWING THE TEXT OF *OF THE RINGS OF POWER AND the Third Age* there are some genealogical tables of the Eldar and the Edain. Versions of the tables of the Edain are published in *WotJ*, 231, 234, and 237. The versions in the published *Silmarillion* differ significantly from these versions, but I do not believe that it would be productive to try to describe all of the differences. However, one change worth noting is that, on the genealogical table of the House of Bëor, the placement of Bregolas's sons Belegund and Baragund is reversed, making it seem that the latter is the elder, which conflicts with the text. Moreover, their elder sister, Beleth, is left off the table altogether (as discussed earlier, another reduction of the female presence).[1] There are references in the text to the genealogies of the Eldar, but no tables are published in *The War of the Jewels*. This was perhaps an oversight.

There is then a note on pronunciation. This is simply a summary of that provided in appendix E of *The Lord of the Rings*. Finally, after the index of names, there is—labeled as "Appendix"—a text called "Elements in Quenya and Sindarin Names." This may be based in part on the long linguistic work "The Etymologies," which is published in *Lost Road*, 341–400 or it may be based on a completely separate text not published in *HoMe*.

More interesting is the question of what additional appended material might have been included to supplement the main text. Noad suggests that in addition to appendices, there would be a section where the Great Tales would be included in full.[2] He actually includes an unwritten fourth Great Tale, called "Eärendil the Wanderer," based on a reference in a letter to Milton Waldman (*Letters*, 150) and a brief reference in a note to the *Shibboleth of Fëanor* to "the four great tales or lays of the heroes of the Atani" (*PoMe*, 357 n. 7). Noad does not state what evidence he bases this suggestion upon, but Tolkien did mention the possibility of whether the long Númenórean versions of the Great Tales (*Beren and Lúthien, The Children of Húrin, The Fall of Gondolin* and *The Rising of the Star*, suggesting that he did want to include Eärendil's story) should be given as appendices to the *Silmarillion* (*MR*, 373). However, this was posed as a question, not a definitive statement of intent, and I am not convinced that such an action would have been practical, particularly given the length of the versions of two of the Great Tales in the published text. The publication of *The Children of Húrin* as a separate, stand-alone work certainly supports that concern. To have included that work with the *Quenta* would have resulted in far too much duplicated material in one work. And the same is true of the tale of Beren and Lúthien. It would also be true of the tale *The Fall of Gondolin*, if it had been included in the published text at anywhere near the same scale as the other two.

Noad also suggests that the following texts would have been included by Tolkien as appendices: *The Tale of Years; Dangweth Pengoloð;*[3] *Of the Laws and Customs among the Eldar; Athrabeth Finrod ah Andreth;* and *Quendi and Eldar".*[4] However, he again gives no evidence to support why he believes these texts would have been included, but that other texts (such as, for instance *The Shibboleth of Fëanor, The Problem of Ros,* or *Of Dwarves and Men*) would not have been included.

I have already suggested that Tolkien would have wanted to include *Of Laws and Customs among the Eldar* as an appendix, given the importance of that work, particularly if the full tale of Finwë and Míriel had been included. However, no explicit statement regarding such an intention is quoted in *Morgoth's Ring* (where it is published) or elsewhere. Nor do there appear to be any such explicit statements regarding *The Tale of Years, Dangweth Pengoloð,* or *Quendi and Eldar;* the suggestion of their inclusion appears to be pure speculation. In a 1965 letter to Dick Plotz, Tolkien suggests that two works published in *Unfinished Tales, Concerning Galadriel and Celeborn* and *The Mariner's Wife* (that is, *Aldarion and Erendis*) might possibly have been included (*Letters*, 359–60).[5] However, no such speculation is needed regarding the *Athrabeth,* because Tolkien did make quite clear his intention that that work be included. Christopher notes that the newspapers in which the *Athrabeth* and its commentary were preserved bore the inscription "Addit. *Silmarillion*." He adds, "On one of these wrappers my father added: 'Should be last item in an appendix' (i.e., to *The Silmarillion*)" (*MR*, 329).

I consider Christopher's failure to follow his father's expressly stated desire regarding this highly critical work to be among the most unfortunate decisions that he made in the "difficult and doubtful task of preparing the text of the book" (*Silm*, ix). The *Athrabeth* is one of Tolkien's most moving and powerful texts. In addition to including some of his most profound spiritual and philosophical reflections, it contains some of the best dialogue that Tolkien ever wrote. It reveals the depth of character of both Finrod and Andreth (the

Wise woman of the Edain who was befriended by Finrod, and who hopelessly loved his brother Aegnor), as well as the depth of the relationships that they share with each other and with Aegnor.

It is possible that Christopher was reluctant to include the *Athrabeth* because it contains the most explicitly Christian symbolism in all of Tolkien's work, with its discussion of Eru "entering into Arda." However, as David Bratman states in his essay "The Literary Value of *The History of Middle-earth*," Tolkien is careful "to keep anything specifically Christian out of his mythology, leading him to make Andreth evasive on this point. Thus some of the greatest unexplained mysteries of the mythology have nothing to do with the Elves or the Valar, who have been explained thoroughly, but are among the matters that the reader knows best. This paradoxical reversal is one of Tolkien's most virtuosic literary achievements."[6] Verlyn Flieger says the *Athrabeth* is "one of the most thoughtful and thought-provoking pieces he ever wrote . . . the one work written to directly address the mystery and deliberately avoid explaining or solving it. Despite the absence of a definitive pronouncement, the *Athrabeth* is the closest Tolkien comes to examining the consequences of both death and deathlessness in his world."[7] I fully concur with Bratman and Flieger. While it is gratifying that this literary achievement has been made available in *Morgoth's Ring*, it would have reached a far wider audience had it been included as appendix to *The Silmarillion*, as Tolkien specifically intended.

Andreth and Aegnor. By Anushka Mouriño. Courtesy of the artist.

Conclusion: Arda Reconstructed

CHRISTOPHER'S "RECONSTRUCTION" OF HIS FATHER'S VISION FOR "THE Silmarillion" was perhaps inevitable, given the state in which Tolkien left the work. However, there are number of areas in which he may be said to have "overstepped the bounds of the editorial function." I have identified five major types of changes to *The Silmarillion* that result from the edits made by Christopher in the process of preparing the work for publication. In addition, there are a plethora of minor editorial changes that, when take together, also affect the tone of the work. Finally, Christopher attempted to standardize the spelling of names of people and places. Table 25 gives a list of names, showing the final forms and the forms from which they were changed.

The first type of major change, as I have stated several times already, is the reduction of the importance of female characters in the story. There are at least eight female characters whose role or character could be said to be reduced to a greater or lesser extent by the editorial decisions made: Uinen, Galadriel, Míriel, Nerdanel, Indis, Ungoliant, Arien, and Nellas (in addition to the removal of the two or three daughters of Finwë and Indis, of Baragund and Belegund's older sister, Beleth and of Andreth from the *Athrabeth*). Some of these changes can be explained in other ways, such as Nellas being left out of the text because of the length of the chapter on Túrin (although some, like the elimination of the reference to Galadriel as the "most valiant" of the house of Finwë, really do seem inexplicable). However, the net result is a significant reduction in the female presence in the book. Although it is true, as Scull and Hammond point out, that *The Silmarillion* does not have nearly the paucity of women as does *The Lord of the Rings* or (most particularly) *The Hobbit*,[1] these changes still serve to feed that impression, and (more importantly) they make *The Silmarillion* a lesser work.

The second type of major change caused by the editorial decisions made in the process of constructing the work is the elimination of much of the philosophical speculation that it contained. This is most evident in the removal of most references to the fading of the Elves and discussions of their mortality. It is particularly stark in the elimi-

nation of most of the extended tale of Finwë and Míriel (and the associated essay *Laws and Customs among the Eldar*) and the failure to incorporate an important work, the *Athrabeth Finrod Ah Andreth,* as an
appendix, despite Tolkien's explicit direction to do so. It is also seen
in the removal of the Second Prophecy of Mandos at the end of the
Quenta. Another example is the failure to include Ulmo's words to
Tuor regarding "the armour of fate." In my opinion, these are some
of the most important aspects of Tolkien's work. While I am gratified
that they were eventually made available in *The History of Middle-earth*
and *Unfinished Tales,* I strongly believe that they should have been
included in *The Silmarillion* itself.

The third type of major change is the condensing (or in certain
cases virtual elimination) of important parts of the tale. In addition
to the condensing of the stories of Míriel and Ungoliant, we see this
in the removal of Maedhros's reporting of the death of Finwë and the
rape of the Silmarils, the elimination of the entire story of Húrin in
Brethil, and the condensing of his confrontation with Morgoth. This
trend reaches its culmination, however, in the extreme compression
of the story of Tuor and the fall of Gondolin. This is particularly disturbing because *The Fall of Gondolin* was the third of the Great Tales
that served as the underpinnings of the whole mythology, and it is
built up as a climactic event throughout much of the book. Yet it is
told in significantly lesser detail than the other two Great Tales, and
ends up feeling somewhat anticlimactic. That is unfortunate.

The fourth major change is the virtual re-creation of the story of
the ruin of Doriath, with the invention of the preexisting Nauglamîr.
This is the single major editorial invention in the book, and although
Christopher could perhaps have avoided overstepping the bounds of
the editorial function quite so flagrantly, he was faced with a difficult
task in this instance. Still, it would have been preferable if he had
been able to overcome the difficulties in this chapter without ven-
turing so far from his father's intention.

The final major type of change involves removing the contexts in
which these stories were placed. This is an area of some confusion,
and Christopher elected to address that confusion by simply removing the context altogether. However, it seems clear (at least in retrospect) that Tolkien intended *The Silmarillion* to be a compilation from
different sources, with the *Ainulindalë* and *Akallabêth* conceived as
tales told by Pengoloð to Ælfwine in Tol Eressëa, and the *Quenta* itself
considered to be a mix of Elvish history and Mannish myths preserved by the Númenóreans. I believe that including these different
contexts would have enhanced the work, giving it more of a sense of

Table 25. Names Changed in the Published Text of *The Silmarillion* from Forms Used in the Source Material

Page number of first appearance in published text	Name in published text	Name in source material	Comments
25	Lórien	Lorien, Lorin, Lorion, Lorinen, Lórïen	Lórien was the original name for this Vala, before it was changed to Lórien in the "earlier *Quenta*" (*MR*, 56 n. 2). It went through a number of different forms in the chapter in the "later *Quenta*" that would become the *Valaquenta*, with Lórïen being the final form (*MR*, 148, 201). In the essay *Laws and Customs of the Eldar* and the second and third versions of the tale of Finwë and Míriel it was "Lorien," whereas in the fourth version of that tale, it was originally written with the accent, which was then removed.
25	Nienna	Niënna	The name of this Vala is written with the diaeresis over the *e* in almost all instances, throughout most of the *Annals of Aman*, the *Valaquenta*, and (with one exception) both phases of the "later *Quenta*" and the essay *Laws and Customs of the Eldar*. The only exceptions are in the *Ainulindalë*, version C, §25, the alternative portion of the *Annals of Aman* (designated "AAm*" by Christopher) and one reference in the chapter "Of the Sun and the Moon" in the "later *Quenta*," LQ §74.
25	Vána	Vana	This Vala's name was spelled without the accent throughout the *Annals of Aman*, but in one place in "AAm*" the text is marked to add the accent. It is included in the first chapter of the "later *Quenta*," even before it gets broken off to become the *Valaquenta*.
38	Corollairë	Korlairë, Korolairë, Corolairë, Korollairë	The form "Korlairë" for the green mound where the Two Trees grew appears in *AAm* §122, which was then amended to "Korolairë." It finds the form "Corolairë" in LQ §58d. In the essay *Quendi and Eldar* it is spelled "Korollairë" (*Wolf*, 401).
38	Culúrien	Kulúrien	This name for Laurelin appears in LQ §16; apparently the first letter was changed to *C* to match other names.
48	Menelmacar	Menelmakar	This name for the constellation Orion appears in LQ §19, and the *K* was again changed to *C* to match other spellings, and to match the spelling in appendix E of *The Lord of the Rings*.

48	Valacirca	Valakirka	This name for the constellation of the Great Bear appears with two *K*s in both AAm §36 and LQ §19 as well as one of the "Myths Transformed" texts (*MR*, 378) but with two *G*s in another "Myths Transformed" text (*MR*, 388).
48	Cuiviénen	Kuiviénen	The spelling with a *K* for the Water of Awakening where the Elves first arose appears in LQ §20. It appears that Cuiviénen was first spelled with the *C* later in LQ, in the second phase version of chapter 6, §52a (see *MR*, 277).
48	Elentári	Elentárië	This name for Varda from AAm §37 is changed to match the spelling in the previous paragraph, where it came from LQ §19.
49	Helcar	Helkar	This is the Inland Sea where the lamp Illuin once stood and of which Cuiviénen was a bay. This spelling (with the *K*) appears in the *Ainulindalë* (for the lamp itself) and AAm §§38, 41, and 58. It appears to be another name in which the *K* was changed to a *C* by the editors to match the other names.
49	Orocarni	Orokarni	This means "The Red Mountains," another name from AAm §41 in which the editors changed the *K* to a *C*.
50	Orcs	Orkor	The older spelling for the plural of "Orc" first appears in AAm §45 and is changed throughout to "Orcs" (as is "Ork" to "Orc").
53	Calaquendi	Kalaquendi, Calapendi	The name for the Elves of the Light was spelled with the *K* in LQ §§29 and 85, GA §48, and the essay *Quendi and Eldar* (*WotJ*, 361), but the essay also lists the Telerin, form "Calapendi" (*WotJ*, 362, 375).
54	Lenwë	Dán, Nano	See discussion regarding chapter 3, paragraph 33.
54	Ered Luin	Eryd Luin, Eredluin, Eredlindon	This name for the Blue Mountains was written with a *y* throughout the *Grey Annals*, but in a footnote to LQ §108 and a penciled addition to LQ §120 it was written "Eredluin." However, in *Quendi and Eldar* it was once again spelled "Eryd Luin." It was also changed from "Eredlindon" on some occasions (although the name "Ered Lindon" for the Blue Mountains also appears in the published text; see below).
58	Círdan	Cirdan	The accent is missing in AAm §70 and GA §§ 14, 18, 22, 37, 40, 44, 85, 100, 172, 243, 256, and 257. But it is present in LQ §119 and in *Quendi and Eldar* (*WotJ*, 379, 380 and 384). And of course it is present in *The Lord of the Rings*.
59	Calacirya	Kalakiryan	See discussion regarding chapter 5, paragraph 8.

(continued)

Table 25. Continued

Page number of first appearance in published text	Name in published text	Name in source material	Comments
59	Tirion, Túna	Tûn, Kôr	The older forms of the city of the Elves and hill where the city was built are of course still present in the QN material used in the later chapters.
60	Finarfin (and Fingolfin)	Finarphin (and Fingolphin), Finrod	See text. In the chapters that are taken from the pre-*Lord of the Rings* material, "Finarfin" replaces "Finrod."
60	Maedhros, Celegorm, Caranthir, Amrod, and Amras	Maidros, Celegorm, Cranthir, Damrod, and Díriel (Diriol)	The names of these sons of Fëanor were amended in the text of LQ §41 (Maglor and Curufin were already so spelled). They are changed to match those names thereafter.
60	Aredhel Ar-Feiniel	Írith, Isfin	See discussion regarding chapter 5, paragraph 15.
61	Finrod, Aegnor	Inglor, Egnor	In the chapters that are taken from the earlier material, "Finrod" and "Aegnor" replace "Ingrod" and "Egnor," respectively.
61	Galadriel	Galaðriel	Galadriel's name is spelled this way throughout much of the *Grey Annals*.
63	Curufinwë	Kurufinwë	Fëanor's "real" name was spelled with a K in FM 4 §2, but with a C in a rejected addition to AAm §61, in *Laws and Customs of the Eldar* (MR, 217, 236), in FM 2 (MR, 263), and LQ §52d.
72	Araman	Eraman	Where the name for the barren wasteland on the coast of Aman is taken from the "earlier *Quenta*" (e.g., QS §73), it is replaced with the newer name.
73	Ungoliant	Ungoliantë	Her name is written "Ungoliantë" throughout the *Annals of Aman*, the first phase of the "later *Quenta*," and even the second-phase work on chapter 6 of the "later *Quenta*," but it switches to Ungoliant in the second-phase work on chapter 7 of the "later *Quenta*."
73	Avathar	Arvalin	"Arvalin," which appears in AAm §106, was the former name of "Avathar" (the forsaken land where Melkor meets Ungoliant), which makes its first appearance in the second-phase work on chapter 6 of the "later *Quenta*."

81	Ered Gorgoroth	Eryd Gorgoroth, Ered Orgonoth, Eryd Orgonoth, Ered-orgoroth, Ered'orgoroth	The name for the Mountains of Terror was originally written as "Ered Orgoroth" in *AAm* §126, but the typescript was later emended. In LQ (Later Chap. 7) §20 it is written as "Eryd Gorgoroth." It also appears as "Eryd Orgonoth" (see e.g., *GA* §34.) It appears in the last two forms in the QS I and QS II versions of the tale of Beren and Lúthien.
89	Endor	Endar	See discussion regarding chapter 9, paragraph 45.
89	Dor-lómin	Dor-Lómen, Dorlómen	This name for a region in the south of Hithlum ruled first by Fingon, and then by the House of Hador, was spelled in most cases as in the published text, but written as "Dor-Lómen" on the map, and as "Dorlómen" in LQ §129.
91	Hadhodrond	Nornhabar	This Sindarin name for Moria comes from *Quendi and Eldar* and replaces the name from LQ (CtD) §7 (see *Wölf*, 389, 414).
92	Maeglin	Meglin, Glindûr	This name was still spelled with no *a* in LQ (CtD) §7, which is the text from which its first appearance is taken. However, the later name appears in edits to the *Grey Annals*, replacing the intermediate name "Glindûr," and of course in the final version of the text *Maeglin*, which provides the source of chapter 16 in the published text.
92	Sarn Athrad	Sarn-athrad	This name for the Ford of Stones was written with the hyphen in LQ CMW §2, and *The Tale of Years*. The final form appears to be taken from the map itself.
95	Daeron	Dairon	The spelling with the *e* comes from a rider added to the *Grey Annals* following *GA* §31.
99	Hildor	Hildi	The change of "Hildor" for "Hildi" (the form that existed in *GA* §57 and LQ §83) for the Elvish name for Men appears to first have been made in a footnote to CMW §14.
99	Vása	Naira, Anar	See discussion regarding chapter 11, paragraph 6.
103	Atanatári	Atanatarni, Atanatardi	This name for the Fathers of Men is taken from *GA* §87, replacing the names in different versions of LQ §83.
105	Eärendil	Eärendel	The older name is used in the *QN* text, of course.
106	Ered Lómin	Eryd Lómin, Eredlómin, Eryd Lammad, Erydlómin	Throughout the *Grey Annals* the name for the Echoing Mountains is written "Eryd Lómin," whereas in one typescript of the "later *Quenta*" the "earlier *Quenta*" form "Eredlómin" was changed to "Erydlómin" in LQ §105 and on another it was changed to "Eryd Lammad" in LQ §106. The actual name used in the published text does not seem to appear in any source text.

(continued)

Table 25. Continued

Page number of first appearance in published text	Name in published text	Name in source material	Comments
106	Ard-galen	Ardgalen	The name for the grass plain outside Dorthonion was written with no hyphe b throughout the *Grey Annals*, but in all instances in the "later *Quenta*" in which it replaces the old name "Bladorion" the hyphen is present.
106	Ered Wethrin	Eryd-wethrin, Eredwethrin, Ered-wethrin, Erydwethrin, Erydwethion	All of the different permutations of the name for the Mountains of Shadow appear in the *Grey Annals* (except for the form used in the published text). In the "later *Quenta*" "Eryd Wethion" is changed to "Eryd Wethrin" and "Eredwethion" is changed to "Eredwethrin." Again the final published form never appears.
107	Dor Daedeloth	Dor-Daedeloth, Dor-na-Daerachas	The name for "The Land of Great Dread" was written in both the *Grey Annals* and the "later *Quenta*" with the hyphen. The name "Dor-na-Daerachas" was added by Tolkien to the map in 1971, but not adopted in the published text.
109	Ered Engrin	Ered-engrin, Eryd Engrin	It is curious that "Ered Engrin" replaces "Eryd Engrin " for the Iron Mountains, because in LQ §105 Tolkien had changed it from "Ered-engrin."
110	Thorondor	Sorontar	Sorontar was used for the King of the Eagles in the *Wanderings of Húrin* text used in chapter 22.
114	Nevrast	Nivrost	Nevrase, the later form for the land where Turgon dwelled before leaving for Gondolin, first appeared in LQ §100.
114	Aelin-uial	Aelinuial	The form of this Noldorin name for the Twilight Meres with the hyphen is actually taken from a footnote to QS §111 that was removed in the "later *Quenta*" and replaced with the form with no hyphen.
115	Tumladen	Tum-laden, Tumladin	The name for the Wide Valley, in which Gondolin stood, was written with a hyphen in "Of Turgon and the Building of Gondolin" and with the *i* instead of the *e* on one occasion in GA §149.
115	Echoriath	Echoriad	Christopher notes that the name for the Encircling Mountains was taken from the later "Tale of Tuor," but that Echoriad was a later form (*Wolf*, 302.)
120	Minas Tirith	Minnastirith,	The Tower of Watch built by Finrod was spelled "Minnas-tirith" in GA §§85

Page			Note
		Minnas-tirith	and 153 and "Minnastirith" in LQ/QS §117. It was apparently changed to match the spelling of the later name of Minas Anor in the Kingdom of Gondor.
120	Teiglin	Taiglin, Taeglin, Taeglind	Christopher adopted the older form of the name of this river; but he indicates that he should have used "Taeglin" (*Wolf*, 309–10.)
121	Crissaegrim	Crisaegrim	The spelling of this name for the mountain peaks south of Gondolin comes from a rider to LQ §110, but it was also originally spelled that way in the original text of the QS versions of the tale of Beren and Lúthien before it was emended to remove one *s*.
122	Taur-en-Faroth	Taur-na-Faroth	The earlier form of the name for the highlands west of the river Narog was present in the QS versions of the tale of Beren and Lúthien.
122	Ramdal	Rhamdal	The *h* is included on the map in this name for Wall's End. Both forms appear in the "earlier *Quenta*."
123	Ered Lindon	Eryd Lindon, Eredlindon, Ered-lindon	This alternative name for the Blue Mountains appears in *GA* §128 and in *Quendi and Eldar* in the form "Eryd Lindon," but on the map and in the "later *Quenta*" as "Eredlindon" (except for one occurrence in CMW §1, where it is written "Ered-lindon."
126	Amon Gwareth	Amon Gwared	Christopher indicates that "Amon Gwared" replaced "Amon Gwareth" for the name of the hill upon which Gondolin was built in "Of Turgon and the Building of Gondolin," yet the latter form is used in the published text.
147	Taleth Dirnen	Daleth Dirnen	The earlier form of the name for the Guarded Plain north of Nargothrond was present in the QS versions of the tale of Beren and Lúthien.
148	Galdor	Galion	The earlier form of the name of Húrin and Huor's father appears in much of the *Grey Annals*.
151, 153	Anfauglith, Dor-nu-Fauglith	Dor-nu-Fauglith, Anfauglith	See discussion regarding chapter 18, paragraph 9.
155	Taur-nu-Fuin	Taur-na-Fuin	The earlier form of the name for Dorthonion was present in the QS I version of the tale of Beren and Lúthien used as the source for chapter 19.
164	Dungortheb	Dungorthin	This alternative name for Nan Dungortheb, the Valley of Death, replaces the older name used in the QS versions of the tale of Beren and Lúthien.

(*continued*)

Table 25. Continued

Page number of first appearance in published text	Name in published text	Name in source material	Comments
156	Tol-in-Gaurhoth	Tol-na-Gaurhoth	The earlier form of the name for the Isle of Werewolves was present in the QS I version of the tale of Beren and Lúthien.
170	Edrahil	Enedrion	The name of this Elf of Nargothrond is taken from *GA* §193, replacing the name from QS I.
184	Camlost	Gamlost	The *C* and *G* in Beren's name for Empty-handed both appear in different places in the QS versions of the tale of Beren and Lúthien. The spelling with *C* appears in the *Grey Annals*, but the spelling with *G* is used in the genealogical tables that Tolkien created.
188	Dor Firn-i-Guinar	Gwerth-i-guinar, Gyrth-i-Guinar	See discussion regarding chapter 20, paragraph 1.
198	Narn i Hîn Húrin	Narn i Chîn Húrin	See discussion regarding introduction to chapter 21
199	Saeros	Orleg	Túrin's nemesis was still called "Orleg" in the *Grey Annals*.
210	Agarwaen the son of Úmarth	Iarwaeth	In the *Grey Annals* Túrin names himself "Iarwaeth" instead of "Agarwaen the son of Úmarth" when he arrives at Nargothrond.
216	Haudh-en-Elleth	Hauð-en-Ellas	The name of the mound where Finduilas was buried comes from a penciled note in the margin of *GA* §314.
221	Hunthor	Gwerin, Torbarth	Gwerin was the name of Brandir's kinsman in *GA* §322, replacing Torbarth. In *GA* §325, it was Torbarth.
234	Eluréd, Elurín	Elrún, Eldún	See discussion of chapter 22, paragraph 36.
243	Cirith Thoronath	Kirith-Thoronath	This change from the form for the Eagles Cleft used in the *QN* text appears to be editorial, since the story was never rewritten.
246	Vingilot	Vingelot, Eälotë	The name of Eärendil's ship was changed on only one occasion—in the conclusion of the "later *Quenta*"—and left intact in all other instances. "Eälotë" was used in the final version of the *Akallabêth*.

reflecting an older tradition that Tolkien was simply reporting, not creating. It also would have been appropriate, because *The Silmarillion* is, in fact, a compilation of various sources.

In the foreword to the first volume of *The Book of Lost Tales* Christopher indicates that he agrees with the speculation of Robert Foster in *The Complete Guide to Middle-earth* that the *Quenta Silmarillion* was "one of Bilbo's *Translations from the Elvish*" and that "The Silmarillion' was in fact the "books of lore" that Bilbo gave to Frodo at the end of *The Lord of the Rings*. He adds that there is to his knowledge no explicit statement to that effect made by his father (*BoLT1*, 7), but Scull and Hammond cite a report by Dick Plotz of a November 1966 visit he had with Tolkien that does indicate that it was his intention.[2] In any event, regardless of whether this device was adopted, I believe that the sense of *The Silmarillion* being a compendium of different sources—and particularly that it was a mix of Elvish history and Mannish myths preserved by the Númenóreans—should and could have been preserved. As Verlyn Flieger states (speaking specifically about the *Athrabeth,* but referring also to Tolkien's overall mythology as well), "the question of whose myth it is would appear to have its answer; it belongs to whoever is speaking whenever they are speaking."[3] I wish that Christopher had retained this simple device.

As for the minor edits, a few stylistic patterns emerge. With a few small exceptions, Christopher eliminates all reference to the Valar as "gods," although that terminology remained common in the later versions of both the *Quenta* and the *Annals*. He undoubtedly did this in order to preserve the distinction between the Valar and the gods of different traditions of ancient mythology. Tolkien repeatedly wrote in his letters that the Valar occupy the imaginative place of "gods" but that they are really more akin to "angels" that could be accepted "by a mind that believes in the Blessed Trinity" (*Letters,* 146; see also 193, 198, 205, 235, 259, 284, 368). He also makes some attempt to modernize the language, eliminating many of the instances where "Behold!" opens a sentence, and changing words such as "hath" to "has." In a similar vein, he removes most of the instances where a distinction was made between the formal ("you") and informal ("thou") forms of address. He also seems to have a particular dislike for the word "folk" and changes it in dozens of instances to "people" or some related form (although, ironically, there is one instance in which he actually changes "people" to "folk") (compare *Silm,* 141 with *WotJ,* 217). There are many instances of changes in capitalization, particularly of references to directions. However, the vast majority of the editorial changes involve small adjustments in the wording of sentences (with no real change in the meaning) or rearrangement of the structure of the sentences, with changes in the placement and use of punctuation, and the omission of small phrases.

These types of minor editorial changes are endemic throughout the book. It is the sheer volume of them that is most surprising, and something of concern. Hardly a sentence goes by without at least one small change, or several. Of course, no one was more qualified to edit Tolkien's work than his son Christopher, who was after all given the authority to use his discretion in publishing his father's work. But it seems like it would have been more appropriate to use a lighter editorial hand, particularly since Tolkien was so careful in his use of language. Some of the changes were dictated by the extensive cutting and pasting from different sources, as has been described, but many of them appear to be almost arbitrary substitutions of judgment. The net result is a work with language that is significantly different than that used by the author.

Notes

INTRODUCTION

1. *The Children of Húrin* has, of course, now been published as a stand-alone volume.
2. Carpenter, 172.
3. Fisher, "From Mythopoeia to Mythography," 130.
4. Agøy, "Viewpoints, Audiences, and Lost Texts in *The Silmarillion*," 141.
5. Shippey, 226.
6. See Scull and Hammond, *Reader's Guide*, 1116–23 for a brief discussion of some of that criticism.
7. See ibid., 910.
8. Noad, "On the Construction," 66–67.
9. In a report on a talk given by Guy Kay, Noad indicates that Kay stated that Christopher originally intended to take a more scholarly approach and that it was Kay who first suggested constructing a text from different sources (Noad, "A Tower in Beleriand," 4).
10. Noad, "On the Construction," 66.
11. Ibid., 65.

AINULINDALË

1. We will see in the discussion of Tolkien's chapter 7 (paragraph six) that he appears to have refined his conception of the creation of the two kindreds of the Children of Ilúvatar in later writings, but that change did not get reflected in the published text.
2. See "Myths Transformed" in *MR*, 369–90, discussing this and related subjects.
3. See the discussion of Chapter 11: "Of the Sun and Moon and the Hiding of Valinor."
4. See the discussion regarding the *Akallabêth*.
5. See, for example, the two alternative opening passages to *The Annals of Aman*, in *MR*, 48, 64–65, and the opening of *The Grey Annals*, in *WotJ*, 5.
6. For a discussion of the difficulties regarding Tolkien's conception of the World in his later work, see *MR*, 27–29.

VALAQUENTA

1. See the discussion of Tolkien's chapters 22–24 in the present book.
2. See below, Tolkien's chapter 24, paragraph 42.

CHAPTER 1. "BEGINNING OF DAYS"

1. Flieger, *Splintered Light*, 28.

CHAPTER 2. "OF AULË AND YAVANNA"

1. We will see later in the discussion regarding chapter 22 of *The Silmarillion* that the only other mention of the Ents in the book was actually based on this letter

CHAPTER 3. "COMING OF THE ELVES"

1. See discussion of paragraphs 14 and 16 of Tolkien's chapter 3.
2. See also the discussion of Tolkien's chapter 9, paragraph 19.
3. See the discussion regarding the Orcs in the "Myths Transformed" section of *MR*, 408–24.
4. According to Noad's report of Kay's talk, this was the first chapter that he and Christopher attempted to edit different sources to form a continuous narrative (Noad, "A Tower in Beleriand," 4).

CHAPTER 6. "OF FËANOR"

1. Mahtan is described as a great smith and one of those most dear to Aulë (see *MR*, 272; and *Silm*, 64).
2. This part of the text is closely related to the portion of the *Laws and Customs* text related to Finwë and Míriel's story (see *MR*, 233–50).
3. Thomas Mann's *The Magic Mountain* immediately comes to mind.
4. In a later text, Tolkien appears to have dropped Finvain and changed Faniel's name to either "Írimë" or "Írien" (see *PoMe*, 343, 359 nn. 26 and 28).

CHAPTER 7. "OF THE SILMARILS"

1. Christopher says this word means "vagabond" (*MR*, 102 n. 12), but it has a much more negative connotation than that.

CHAPTER 8. "DARKENING OF VALINOR"

1. Manwë's great mountain.
2. The place referred to is Formenos, where the Silmarils were kept by Fëanor.

CHAPTER 9. "FLIGHT OF THE NOLDOR"

1. We will see later that the inclusion of the speculation in this paragraph that Ungoliant's ultimate fate was to devour herself in her uttermost famine required the omission of part of Eärendil's story in the final chapter of the *Quenta Silmarillion*.

2. This section was included in the published text, as we have seen, at chapter 3, paragraph 16.

3. This provides further proof that the version of Fëanor's oath in the *Annals of Aman* was the later written version.

CHAPTER 10. "OF THE SINDAR"

1. Shippey, *Road to Middle-earth,* 110–13.
2. Flieger, *Interrupted Music,* 142.
3. See Gilson, "Gnomish Is Sindarin," 95–104.
4. A very small piece of this (regarding the name "Green-elves") is used later in the chapter (paragraph 17). The description of the seven rivers appears later, in Chapter 14, "Of Beleriand and Its Realms," paragraph 14.
5. See paragraph 12, above.

CHAPTER 11. "OF THE SUN AND THE MOON"

1. Strangely, he never seems to have considered abandoning the concept of the Two Trees themselves, though it is hard to see how that concept is any less absurd.
2. As Hammond states in discussing this proposed change and Tolkien's essay *On Fairy-Stories,* "Reality must not intrude too strongly, and myth can be more powerful than fact" (Hammond, "A Continuing and Evolving Creation," 28).
3. See the discussion of the *Ainulindalë,* above.
4. We will see below that Tolkien was actually mistaken in saying that it was at the rising of the Moon.
5. However, we will see later in the discussions of Tolkien's chapters 22 and 24 that Christopher also removed similar statements regarding Morgoth's dealings with Túrin and his estrangement of Men and Elves.
6. See discussion at the end of Tolkien's chapter 24.
7. See the chapter on the appendices to *The Silmarillion.*

CHAPTER 12. "OF MEN"

1. Flieger, *Interrupted Music,* 45–46.

CHAPTER 13. "RETURN OF THE NOLDOR"

1. See chapter 9, *Silm,* 80–81.
2. What would become chapter 9 in the published *Silmarillion.*
3. It is in this paragraph that we finally see Fingolfin unfurl his banners at the rising of the Sun.
4. It may be recalled that portions of *GA* §§ 53, 54, and 55 were already used in chapter 11, paragraphs 8 and 9, and *GA* §56 was used in chapter 12, paragraph 2.
5. See discussion at chapter 22, below.
6. I will comment further about this text (including discussing Christopher's expression of regret for making such a radical change) when I get to chapter 22.

7. It appears in chapter 15 (see *Silm*, 130).

8. The material from §§79 and 80 is not used until chapter 17.

9. These omitted sentences form the basis for material used in chapter 18, as will be seen.

10. As will be seen, much of §§83—114 is used in the next two chapters.

CHAPTER 14. "OF BELERIAND"

1. However, some material from LQ §108 was used later in this chapter, as will be seen.

2. It also could be taken from the map, which clearly shows the river Nenning reaching the sea at Eglarest (see *WotJ*, 182, 184).

3. Part of this section from the *Grey Annals* was used previously in chapter 10, paragraph 17.

4. See the discussions of chapter 3, paragraph 16, and chapter 9, paragraph 19.

CHAPTER 15. "OF THE NOLDOR"

1. This statement is repeated again in chapter 23 when Turgon is recalling Ulmo's words.

2. Flieger, *Interrupted Music*, 142.

CHAPTER 17. "OF THE COMING OF MEN"

1. As described earlier, around this same time a new legend of the origin of the Dwarves was also written in association with the "Dwarves" part of this chapter, which form the basis of the first part of chapter 2. Portions of the new chapter called "Concerning the Dwarves" that was also created at around this same time are used in chapter 10.

CHAPTER 18. "RUIN OF BELERIAND"

1. See paragraph 26, below.

2. See paragraph 15, below.

3. See the third paragraph ("There came a time . . ."; *Silm*, 150–51), and compare with QS/LQ §134 (*Lost Road*, 280; and *WotJ*, 239–40).

4. This text actually had a date on it: August 1965 (see *PoMe*, 350).

5. See the introductory comments on Tolkien's chapter 21, below.

CHAPTER 19. "BEREN AND LÚTHIEN"

1. This would of course have been impossible to do, since at the time *The Lost Road* was published, the *Grey Annals* had not yet been published.

2. This is added in, of course, because of the statement made by Finrod to Galadriel in chapter 15, paragraph 24 (taken from *GA*, §108): "'An oath I too shall swear, and must be free to fulfill it, and go into darkness'" (*Silm*, 130).

3. See Canto VII, lines 2173—2205, in *The Lays of Beleriand,* 230–31 and compare with *Silm,* 171.

4. This is the only place in all of *HoMe* where Christopher points out a specific contribution by Guy Kay.

CHAPTER 20. "OF THE FIFTH BATTLE"

1. Túrin, of course, eventually kills Glaurung by driving his sword Gurthang deep into the dragon's belly.

2. See the discussion on Ereinion Gil-galad in chapter 18, paragraph 14, above.

3. Shippey, *Road to Middle-earth,* 262.

CHAPTER 21. "OF TÚRIN TURAMBAR"

1. See discussion of Tolkien's chapter 23.

CHAPTER 22. "RUIN OF DORIATH"

1. It will be recalled that a similar statement regarding Melkor's dealings with Fëanor was also removed from Chapter 11, and we will see that a similar statement regarding Morgoth's role in estranging Men and Elves is also omitted from chapter 24.

2. This portion of the *Wanderings of Húrin* text follows the *Grey Annals* continuation "almost without alteration" (see *WotJ,* 260).

3. The beginning of the first sentence of this paragraph continues from the text that closely follows the *Grey Annals* continuation. However, the rest of that sentence and all of the following sentence—regarding Húrin's desire to return to Gondolin—is taken from the text of *The Wanderings of Húrin* that diverges from the *Grey Annals* continuation (see *WotJ,* 260).

4. The outlaws do not appear at all in the published *Silmarillion,* despite the fact that they were always an integral part of the story of the ruin of Doriath, as written by Tolkien.

5. This is the bulk of the *Wanderings of Húrin* text, but is not relevant here, since it is not included at all in *The Silmarillion.*

6. The final paragraphs of *The Wanderings of Húrin* relate the death of Manthor, the chieftain of the Haladin who had befriended Húrin. However, that is of course not included in the published *Silmarillion,* since it is related so closely to the omitted story of Húrin's imprisonment in Brethil.

7. This was the passage that was omitted from paragraph 2, as discussed above.

8. Shippey, *Road to Middle-earth,* 268.

9. Shippey is considered by many to be a preeminent Tolkien scholar (if not *the* preeminent Tolkien scholar) writing today. Like Tolkien, he has taught Old English at both Oxford and Leeds University, which gives him a unique perspective about Tolkien's work.

10. Both Jason Fisher and Nils Ivar Agøy mention the need for this type of study. Fisher, in particular, discusses the value of such an analysis (see Agøy, "Viewpoints, Audiences and Lost Texts," 131–2; Fisher, "From Mythopoeia to Mythography," 141).

CHAPTER 23. "FALL OF GONDOLIN"

1. Chapter 15 of the *Quenta Noldorinwa* also deals with Gondolin (specifically the founding of Gondolin) but is not used at all; at that point in the development of the legendarium, Gondolin was not founded until after the Nirnaeth Arnoediad!

2. Scull and Hammond, *Reader's Guide*, 1047.

3. It is in this paragraph that Ulmo's statement to love not too well "the work of thy hands and the devices of thy heart," discussed in chapter 15, paragraph 2, is repeated as part of the editorial invention.

4. *QN* 2 (chapter 16) ends in the middle of this paragraph, whereas *QN* 1 continues to the end of the chapter.

5. This is taken from the *Quenta Noldorinwa* (though somewhat expanded by the editors), and goes back to the original tale (see *SoMe*, 145 and *BoLT2*, 196).

6. Although Voronwë is not mentioned in the brief telling of the story in the *Quenta Noldorinwa*, he is present in the original tale (see *BoLT2*, 195–96).

7. This paragraph only varies in one small detail from the *QN* 2 version (see *SoMe*, 148, 151).

CHAPTER 24. "THE VOYAGE OF EÄRENDIL"

1. See the discussion of the *Valaquenta*, above.

2. See, for example, chapters 7, 8, and 9.

3. See discussion of chapter 9, paragraph 18 (*Silm*, 80–81).

4. See the discussion regarding Chapter 10, "Of Men."

5. In a number of places Tolkien had neglected to emend the text to eliminate references to the children of the Valar, but Christopher correctly removed them.

6. The reference is to Ulmo's statement that hope would be born for the two kindreds "beyond ruin and fire" from one who came from Nevrast, wearing the gear that he bid Turgon leave there (see chapter 15, paragraph 3, *Silm*, 126).

7. See chapter 19, paragraph 94 (*Silm*, 183).

8. Recall the previous omissions in chapters 11 and 22, regarding Morgoth's marring of Fëanor being his "most wicked" action and his conduct toward Túrin being the worst of his works.

9. See the discussion about the appendices, below.

10. Tolkien, "Words, Phrases and Passages," 178.

11. Flieger, *Splintered Light*, 160–61.

THE AKALLABÊTH

1. See also the discussion regarding the *Ainulindalë*, above.

2. See the discussion of chapter 24.

APPENDICES TO THE *SILMARILLION*

1. See discussion regarding chapter 6.

2. Noad, "On the Construction," 67.

3. This is a short example of the instruction of Ælfwine by Pengoloð, printed in *PoMe*, 395–401.

4. Noad, "On the Construction," 66–67.

5. See also Scull and Hammond, *Reader's Guide*, 900.

6. Bratman, "Literary Value," 77–78.

7. Flieger, *Interrupted Music*, 48.

CONCLUSION

1. Scull and Hammond, *Readers Guide*, 1120–21.

2. Ibid., 901.

3. Flieger, *Interrupted Music*, 49.

Index

271